Second Edition

T0309291

The Virtual Training Guidebook

How to Design, Deliver, and Implement Live Online Learning

CINDY HUGGETT

atd
PRESS
Alexandria, VA

ATD Press is an internationally renowned source of insightful and practical information on talent development, training, and professional development.

ATD Press
1640 King Street
Alexandria, VA 22314 USA

Ordering information: Books published by ATD Press can be purchased by visiting ATD's website at td.org/books or by calling 800.628.2783 or 703.683.8100.

Library of Congress Control Number: 2024935396

ISBN-10: 1-957157-74-7
ISBN-13: 978-1-957157-74-0
e-ISBN: 978-1-957157-75-7

ATD Press Editorial Staff
Director: Sarah Halgas
Manager: Melissa Jones
Content Manager, Learning Technologies: Alexandria Clapp
Developmental Editor: Shelley Sperry
Production Editor: Katy Wiley Stewts
Text Designer: Shirley E.M. Raybuck
Cover Designer: Rose Richey

Text Layout: PerfecType, Nashville, TN

Printed by BR Printers, San Jose, CA

Contents

Author's Note

When the original *Virtual Training Guidebook* was released a decade ago, I told friends and colleagues it was my complete manifesto on virtual training. I poured into it everything I had learned over the years about how to design, deliver, and implement live online learning. Naively, I thought that would be the last book I'd ever write—until readers like you changed my mind. I heard your success stories of moving to the virtual classroom and how that book's resources helped in that transition. Many of you used it as a blueprint to guide your organization's virtual training initiatives. And you kept asking for more. So, I kept researching, writing, and sharing resources through conferences, articles, and teaching. Virtual training continued to evolve with countless new methods, tools, and techniques, so my work never grew stale.

Looking back, it's hard to remember what the workplace was like without virtual meetings. Online communication may now dominate our working relationships, but it was still a novelty in the not-so-recent past. When I wrote the first edition in 2014, the Association for Talent Development's *2014 State of the Industry* report said only about 9 percent of organizational learning programs occurred in an instructor-led online classroom. Virtual training wasn't new, but most organizations hadn't yet widely adopted it and certainly weren't relying on it as a first choice for their employees.

The tide soon started to turn, and in 2019, the global research organization Towards Maturity reported that 93 percent of organizations were planning to use virtual training for at least some of their offerings. And then the onset of the COVID-19 pandemic in early 2020 quickly swept nearly all learning programs online. This sudden pivot to virtual classrooms caught many organizations off guard and moved their timelines for engaging with new technology forward. Virtual training became the delivery method of choice for most.

Remote work has gone from being an unexpected necessity in 2020 to something more common and accepted, and it's becoming clear this is not a temporary change.

In 2023, 98 percent of US workers surveyed said they wanted to work remotely at least some of the time (Corbo 2023). And an estimated 22 percent of the American workforce will be entirely remote by 2025 (Ozimek 2023). And with this change, organizational learning strategies have had to shift in response. Virtual training, which came roaring into the workplace in 2020, is now here to stay.

But the training landscape is still changing. Hybrid working arrangements have added a unique and untested element to virtual training methods. Organizations that reluctantly adopted virtual training out of necessity in 2020 are now returning some programs to traditional classrooms. And those that quickly and eagerly moved their in-person classes online are now discovering they need to allot time and resources to go back and properly redesign those programs. These aren't easy tasks, but they're essential for moving virtual training forward and ensuring that it serves the needs of all learners and organizations.

Naturally, big questions followed on the heels of all this rapid change, and those questions moved me to write this book. In my annual survey of global training professionals, as well as the hundreds of conversations I have each year with clients, conference attendees, workshop participants, and others in the workplace learning industry, I hear two kinds of questions most often. The first is about the challenge of engaging remote participants. Despite the emphasis on this topic among experts who offer a variety of solutions, engagement continues to be the foremost challenge in everyone's minds.

The second is, "What's next?" People seem to believe we've mastered virtual training thanks to the sheer volume of sessions delivered during the pandemic—so now they're looking for the next big thing. They want to know about new tools and how new technologies like artificial intelligence (AI) and immersive technologies will affect the virtual classroom.

I've updated this book to address these essential challenges and more. This second edition of *The Virtual Training Guidebook* is a comprehensive guide to the modern virtual classroom that will equip you with the techniques and strategies you need to be successful in navigating the needs of today's learners and to prepare you to make use of tomorrow's technologies. If you're new to virtual training, this book provides step-by-step guidance to ensure you've got a solid foundation. If you're more experienced, you'll find answers to your unresolved questions and gain new ideas for achieving the results you and your organization are looking for.

My hope is that this book can help anyone involved with virtual training at this critical moment—from instructional designers to facilitators to administrative coordinators and learning leaders—because everyone who makes decisions about virtual training should understand what it takes to design, deliver, and implement it well.

The Best of Technology With the Benefits of Community

It's an understatement to say that a lot has changed in workplace learning over the past 10 years. Since the first edition of this book came out in 2014, virtual training has transformed thanks to technology advances, software updates, better internet connections, more video—and more recently, the arrival of generative AI and other powerful tools to expand accessibility and inclusion. But the hallmark of virtual training—bringing people together for a facilitated learning event—has remained the same. It's a unique learning solution that combines the best of technology with the benefits of community.

This new edition of *The Virtual Training Guidebook* is for everyone, including the people I meet and talk with regularly at conferences, seminars, and on-site visits to small and large organizations. It's also for the designers, facilitators, and managers who are new to the world of live online learning and need an accessible, comprehensive guide that answers their questions, helps them craft a business case for virtual training, and shares plenty of case studies, tools, and tips to improve their effectiveness. But I also wrote this book for seasoned trainers—my friends and colleagues—those veteran learning professionals who want additional guidance navigating the modern virtual classroom that's become a confusing array of new approaches to creating, designing, facilitating, and evaluating. They want more information about new tools, techniques, and methods to engage remote and hybrid participants. They need practical, proven advice from an expert who knows the virtual classroom inside and out and can help them reach the next level.

And of course, we all want to be able to look into a crystal ball to see what changes are on the horizon in the training world and how they will affect our work. So, in the last chapter of this book, we'll look toward the future of virtual training and discuss the challenges and rewards of expanding to reach a global audience, as well as the impact of AI, immersive experiences, and mobile devices.

Before we get there, however, let's address two critical, frequently asked questions:

- What's working in the virtual training and learning space right now?
- What's not working, and how can we fix it?

Spoiler alert: I wrote this book to answer those questions too.

What's Working

Even though virtual training has now permeated just about every business, government, and nonprofit organization around the world, many are still skeptical about its effectiveness. Some tell me it can't replace in-person training under any circumstance. Other critics think the technology isn't reliable enough for online interactions to be meaningful. Maybe you share these opinions thanks to a personal experience with poorly delivered online sessions. In 2012, one expert reported that "only one in five people considered their company to be very effective at virtual training" (Mina 2012). In a more recent survey, 56 percent said they thought virtual training was an engaging experience, but even that number still leaves a lot to be desired (TalentLMS 2024). Passive webinars, which are still the norm for many virtual events, are notorious for encouraging participants to multitask—checking their email or eating lunch while half-listening to the presenter. But it doesn't have to be this way.

"The number one reason we use virtual training is that it enables me to provide equality of access to training for our international staff in a cost-effective way. The second reason is that it allows for collaboration across dispersed geographies."

—Lorna Matty, former Learning and Development Manager, Crown Agents

---

Research has consistently demonstrated that virtual training is a valuable method of learning and behavior change for businesses—if it's done well (Paul and Jefferson 2016; Stack 2015, and Brady et al., 2018). We also know that live online training can be highly rewarding for organizations and learners for a variety of reasons, including:

- **Cost savings.** Virtual training lowers travel costs for both participants and facilitators. While it's not free, virtual training can result in an overall reduction in dollars spent.

- **Time savings.** Virtual training is typically delivered in shorter chunks of learning time than in-person training. This means less time away from work, which often leads to increased productivity.
- **Ending dependence on one location.** Virtual training can be delivered to almost anyone, almost anywhere. As long as someone has a computer or mobile device and a reliable internet connection, they can actively participate in a live online learning event.
- **A wider group of participants.** Virtual training can expand the reach of learning to those who might not receive training otherwise. By making participation easier for those who are unable to travel to a physical location, as well as those who are neurodiverse or have sight, hearing, or mobility impairments, virtual training has the ability to connect people who might not normally get to collaborate.

That last point—the expansive reach of live online learning to train a more diverse group of people than ever before and connect talented new collaborators and contributors with corporations, small businesses, and nonprofits—is one of the reasons I still care so much about this topic and want to share its benefits with others. However, it's still important to note that no one, including me, advocates for replacing every in-person learning experience with a virtual one. This book will help you make wise decisions about when to use virtual training, and when not to.

What Needs Fixing

Many books, resources, and references about virtual training tout engaging delivery as the key to success. And I agree that quality facilitation is important. But there are dozens of other indicators that also determine whether a virtual learning experience will be successful, including:

- Putting an intentional training plan in place
- Deploying the right technology stack for virtual learning success
- Designing interactive sessions and engaging activities
- Preparing facilitators and producers for virtual delivery
- Preparing participants for remote learning and application of their new knowledge
- Paying attention to administrative details
- Measuring results accurately

We are wasting an important opportunity if we don't take a *holistic view* of virtual training. This book will help you take a comprehensive look at all the components necessary for designing, delivering, and implementing excellent virtual training. And you can rest assured that the information and techniques outlined here and in the second edition of the companion book, *Virtual Training Tools and Templates,* are time tested, current, and forward looking.

Format

This book addresses each of the requisite factors for successful virtual training—from conception to delivery to evaluation. Here's what you'll find in each chapter:

- **Chapter 1, Get Ready,** helps you consider the role of virtual training in your organization's learning strategy. We'll look at different definitions of virtual training (including hybrid learning), decide who should be involved in a virtual training initiative, and discuss how to build a business case for virtual training resources.
- **Chapter 2, Select Technology,** outlines the types of technology needed for successful virtual training. We will consider hardware and software and discuss how to work with your IT department to select the right technology. We'll also look at the tech resources everyone needs, and how to partner with technology vendors.
- **Chapter 3, Design Content,** presents a three-step design process for virtual programs, along with tips for migrating traditional courses to online classrooms. We'll also explore five essential principles for designing an engaging virtual course.
- **Chapter 4, Develop Activities,** includes creative activity ideas for various virtual platform tools, along with techniques for ensuring your courses are accessible and inclusive. We'll also look at how to develop facilitator and participant materials.
- **Chapter 5, Prepare Facilitators,** takes a deep dive into the facilitator role. We will examine selection criteria and how to prepare facilitators to deliver online. We'll also cover the art of online facilitation and delivery, including tips and suggestions for creating an engaging, accessible, and inclusive learning environment.
- **Chapter 6, Support Producers,** defines three types of producers and how they should prepare for their role. We'll look closely at the tools and techniques they

use to support facilitators and participants. We'll also review troubleshooting tips for common virtual challenges.

- **Chapter 7, Prepare Participants,** covers an often-overlooked component in virtual training success—the preparation and commitment of your participants. We will look at tips for helping participants engage in the virtual classroom and explore three techniques you can use to set everyone up for success.

- **Chapter 8, Build Success Through Logistics,** is all about the details. We will go over the administrative support and coordination you need to make virtual training a success. We'll also examine the pre-event logistics you should consider, day-of-event preparation, and post-event logistics such as assignments, surveys, and evaluations.

- **Chapter 9, Measure Results,** reviews how to measure the success of your virtual training. We will distinguish between learning transfer and evaluation, review common evaluation models, and help you determine what kind of evaluation plan you need.

- **Chapter 10, Prepare for the Future,** wraps up our discussion of virtual training by examining ways to anticipate and prepare for current and future trends, including global virtual training, immersive learning, AI, and new mobile devices that will surely influence virtual training in the years to come.

Throughout this book, you'll learn about the experiences of and lessons learned by trainers, designers, and organizations who've been down this road already. And of course, I'll share my own experience as well. At the end of each chapter, I've listed suggested action steps you can take based upon the content, and you'll also find ready-to-use checklists and worksheets to help apply what you learn. For even more resources, check out *Virtual Training Tools and Templates*, which I've also updated and expanded. It offers 185 tools, templates, worksheets, and questionnaires designed to help you put everything you learn in *The Virtual Training Guidebook* into practice.

Now, let's begin!

CHAPTER 1

Get Ready

 In this chapter, you will learn four essential keys to a successful virtual training strategy:

- Determine your ultimate virtual training goals.
- Define virtual training for your organization.
- Ensure the right people are involved.
- Build a strategic plan.

In 2014, when the first edition was published, many organizations were just discovering virtual training as a viable learning method. It made sense to review—step by step—how to determine if virtual training was the right solution for each learning program in an organization. It was also important to demonstrate how to build business cases, get the right people on board, and create detailed implementation plans. Many global organizations followed my advice and used my recommendations to move a substantial number of programs to virtual classrooms successfully.

Fast forward to 2020, when many organizations were thrust into virtual training out of necessity. Nearly all had to pivot from in-person to online training without much time to plan or strategize. Some training departments were already well equipped for this pivot because of the foundations they'd laid in previous years, but others were caught off guard and did what they could to adapt as quickly as possible.

Today, most organizations fall into one of three categories:

1. They are continuing down the path of virtual training for most or all learning solutions.

2. They are evaluating their programs to decide which ones make sense as virtual training and which should return to in-person training.

3. They are returning as many programs as possible to in-person or hybrid classrooms.

Regardless of which category your organization is in right now, this chapter will help you make solid business decisions around virtual training, including where it fits into your learning strategy, who needs to be involved with those decisions, and what resources you need to make sure it's effective.

Determine Your Ultimate Goals

As author Stephen Covey (1983) famously wrote, "Begin with the end in mind." In other words, begin by thinking about your destination, and work backward from there. This advice applies to many things, including your organization's virtual training strategy. Whether you have extensive virtual training curriculums that require months of planning or simple one-and-done online sessions, a strategic plan will help clarify your goals. You'll have a destination in mind and a road map to help you get there.

The planning journey starts by asking questions such as:

- What's the goal for virtual learning in the organization?
- What are we trying to accomplish?
- What do we want to be different as a result of our virtual training?
- What do we need learners to be more knowledgeable about?
- What skills and capabilities do they need?
- How will the organization change or improve because of this training?
- How do these training goals support organizational initiatives?
- What's the best way to achieve these goals?
- How specifically would *virtual* training (as opposed to in-person training) help achieve these outcomes?

The answers to these questions will help you start defining your vision of virtual training success. You will determine the purpose of your learning initiatives and articulate your desired results. By intentionally setting goals, you can increase your likelihood of achieving them.

These questions can also help you determine when virtual training is the appropriate solution for your organization. Remember, virtual training is not always the answer, despite its current popularity. Your training solutions should have a positive influence on your organization because the applied knowledge and skills lead to improved business results. If your current or planned virtual training programs aren't furthering organizational goals, they might not be the best option.

It may surprise you that I'm suggesting virtual training may not be the right solution for every organization's needs. However, it's not uncommon for organizations to implement virtual training just because they think it's a cheaper alternative to traditional training, or because their employees are working remotely, or because a competitor is doing it. Those are not necessarily the right reasons, even though they may be contributing factors to the desire to establish virtual training as part of the organization's learning portfolio. The best reason to implement virtual training is that it is the right solution to meet a learning need.

When done well, virtual training can:

- Transfer knowledge.
- Increase productivity.
- Help you gain competitive advantage.
- Positively affect business results.
- Help you reach remote audiences and hybrid workers.
- Reduce travel costs in training budgets.
- Create opportunities for dispersed learners to interact with one another and a facilitator.
- Help provide training to participants who may otherwise not have access to facilitated learning.

The point is that you should be as clear as possible about your reasons for using virtual training. That's why I suggested asking those questions as the first step in your planning journey. By beginning with the end in mind, you can define what success will look like for your organization and measure how well you've achieved it.

> *"Be really intentional about choosing [virtual training] as a modality. We've never promised that virtual training is the same learning experience as face-to-face training, but with a team located in cities around the world, it's the most efficient way to deliver a consistent learning experience."*
>
> —Dan Gallagher, former Vice President of Learning and Development, Comcast, and co-author of *The Self-Aware Leader*

Let's say your organization quickly moved all training programs to the virtual classroom during the COVID-19 pandemic, and now you're evaluating which ones should stay virtual, and which should return to the traditional classroom. Your path forward may be to audit each program against a decision matrix. You would consider the priority of learning outcomes compared to business needs, along with the location of your learners and the available technology resources. You could also evaluate if the virtual training programs are getting sufficient results or if they are suffering from poor design decisions or lack of support. You could talk with facilitators and other stakeholders to get their input. This process of carefully reviewing and questioning can help you understand what's working and what's not, leading to an overall assessment and recommendation of learning goals.

In another possible scenario, imagine your organization has a new initiative, and you think virtual learning may be part of the solution. The executive team is looking to increase productivity and, as a result, plans to implement a new online expense reporting system. End users need to learn how to use this new system to make sure the cost savings are realized. After looking at travel costs, participant locations, and trainer time, you determine that live online sessions will be the best way to demonstrate and answer questions about the new features. You realize that virtual training will help you reach your geographically dispersed audience, and you think the software skills content is suited to a virtual method. You might define the goals for this initiative by factoring in the organization's aim to increase productivity and determining what end users specifically need to know and do with the new system features. These two goals will help you define the learning outcomes. But more importantly, they will help you design and deliver the appropriate type of virtual training for this initiative.

Define Virtual Training

At the core of a successful virtual learning strategy is your organization's specific definition of *virtual training*. If you look at how we use the term *virtual* in everyday life, a similar pattern emerges. We talk about *virtual reality (VR), virtual teams, virtual wallets, virtual meetings,* and *virtual presentations,* just to name a few. A cursory web search of the word *virtual* turns up more than 1.2 billion hits, and the same is true for *virtual training.*

Over the years, I've asked thousands of people what they think of when they hear those words, and I've heard about a hundred different answers. We'll discuss my definition in a moment, but first, let's talk about what else virtual training could be.

To some, virtual training is any type of training delivered online, which includes self-directed e-learning and synchronous online classes. In this case, *virtual training* is synonymous with *online learning*. In other words, if the learning happens on the web, either alone or with another person, it fits this definition.

To others, virtual training encompasses any type of knowledge transfer that happens in a live online environment, such as webcasts, webinars, or online presentations. Under this broad umbrella, any type of information shared using a web conferencing platform might be considered virtual training.

Some organizations may refer to VR when talking about virtual training. With a VR learning experience, participants put on a VR headset, join an immersive scenario, interact with others, and complete activities to learn new skills. This all takes place in a digital environment and therefore can be referred to as virtual training.

As you can see, there are as many definitions of virtual training as there are types of learning experiences—which is why you need to establish upfront what you and your organization mean when you say, "virtual training."

So, what is virtual training? Here's the definition I have used for more than two decades:

> Virtual training is a highly interactive, synchronous online facilitated training class, with defined learning objectives and participants who are individually connected from dispersed locations, using a web-based classroom platform.

Virtual Training or Virtual Learning?

There's much debate in our industry over the distinction between *training* and *learning*. Most will agree that training relates to formal instruction or teaching while learning is the process of experiencing or absorbing new information. I agree with this overall sentiment and believe that there is a clear difference between the two. For the purposes of this book, *virtual training* is the common vernacular used for a facilitated live online event and the term I'll use the most. However, from the participant's viewpoint, virtual training is an online learning experience. An engaged participant learns through collaboration and interaction, using the virtual classroom's tools. So, I'll also use the words *learning* and *learning experience* to describe the participant's perspective.

You might decide to incorporate more than one type of virtual training in your organization's training portfolio. In fact, you probably will. But for each online program, you should define exactly what your goal is, and what method or type of virtual training you will use to get there.

I can't stress this enough: Set appropriate expectations with everyone involved. Be intentional about the goals for each virtual program and ensure that everyone is aware of your intentions. The success of your virtual training implementation will depend upon it.

"It's really important to call things by the right name and set those expectations. What you call something influences the design and sets the stakeholders' expectations."
—Peggy Page, former Design Group Manager, TD Bank

Let's return to dissecting my definition of virtual training, which I introduced in my first book, *Virtual Training Basics*. Virtual training has:

- **High levels of interactivity.** Participants engage frequently—typically every few minutes—with the facilitator, other participants, the learning content, and the virtual classroom tools.
- **Synchronous learning.** Participants meet together at the same time. This is sometimes referred to as *live*, or in the case of virtual training, *live online*.
- **Facilitation.** The program is led by a professional trainer or facilitator.
- **Clear learning objectives.** Explicitly stated performance expectations tell the learners what they will be able to achieve by actively participating in the session.
- **Dispersed participants.** Learners are separated and apart from one another. Crucially, each participant joins from their own device and has their own audio connection.
- **A web-based classroom platform.** The virtual training software program allows for online screen and file sharing, and provides robust participant interaction tools such as polling, chatting, breakout sessions, and whiteboards.

A typical virtual training class might meet at 10 a.m. on Wednesday, last 90 minutes, and include 18 participants from various locations across the country. The group would meet online using a synchronous platform, such as Adobe Connect, Microsoft Teams, Butter, Engageli, or Zoom. The facilitator would lead the program activities, and participants would learn new skills that could be applied to their jobs immediately.

Of course, that might not be exactly what your virtual training looks like. Perhaps you have an alternate set of standards for timing, a different number of participants, or other learning outcomes. What's most important is that you define what your organization means by virtual training and that everyone involved is on the same page.

What Does a Virtual Training Class Look Like?

In case you are unfamiliar with the type of virtual training we've been talking about, here is an illustration, adapted from *Virtual Training Basics*:

> Michelle is a trainer for a large telecommunications company. She's located in Cincinnati, Ohio, and will be facilitating a 60-minute virtual class on Thursday at 11 a.m. ET. About a week before the program date, she sends a personalized email to her participants, introducing herself and setting expectations for the upcoming program. Thirty minutes before the start time, she sits at her home office desk, logs into the virtual classroom software, and gets ready to facilitate. She uploads slides, opens the first polling question, and prepares the virtual whiteboard. She also chats with her technical producer while they double-check the program settings before anyone else arrives.

> Around 10:55 a.m., the participants start entering the virtual classroom. They do this by clicking on the link from Michelle's email message while sitting at their own desks from the comfort of their own offices.

> One participant—Moira—is in Dallas, Texas. She clicks on the link and the software app opens on her laptop. She uses the initial screen to test her audio and video connections. Then, upon entering the virtual classroom, Moira sees Michelle on video and says hello. The other participants follow the same steps to join the class.

> The participants can see what Michelle has prepared for them on their screens. They also see the other attendees, the slides, a chat window, a whiteboard, and the first polling question. They can communicate with one another verbally and online by coming off mute and speaking, typing in the chat window, responding to polls, and writing on the whiteboard. At one point, Michelle assigns the participants to virtual breakout groups to practice one of the new skills they've learned before returning to the large group for a debrief discussion.

> By noon, class finishes, and Michelle asks everyone to complete a follow-up assignment to apply what they've just learned.

Other Types of Live Online Events

Because so many of the tips found in this book can also be applied to various types of synchronous online events, let's discuss and expand upon the definitions to distinguish them from one another.

Webcasts

A webcast primarily disseminates information from a speaker to a large audience. The speaker often uses slides to present and share information. Sometimes there are multiple speakers or a panel of experts. Webcasts typically have a large audience—anywhere from a few dozen to a few thousand attendees.

A webcast is solely one-way communication from a presenter to attendees. It's similar to a traditional television newscast with a news anchor reading from a script, using visual aids to illustrate stories, and interacting with other news presenters. There's little to no interaction with the audience.

Imagine your organization pulled together a large audience for a scripted town hall meeting with presentations on the company strategy and only a short time for Q&A at the end. This type of meeting—if held online—could be called a *webcast*.

---

*"The worst mistake I have seen is treating a virtual
webinar or training just like a meeting."*

—Jill Kennedy, Team Lead, Ally Financial

Webinars

According to its traditional definition, a *webinar* is an online seminar. Like a webcast, a webinar is primarily one-way communication from a presenter to attendees. The difference is that webinars often employ interactive techniques such as polling, chatting, and using reactions.

If you think about how television newscasts have evolved, many modern news programs incorporate audience interaction through social media and other techniques. For example, a reporter might respond to viewers' on-air questions or invite listeners to vote online and then report on the collected results. It's the same with a webinar. The information is presented via slides, and communication is mostly one-way from the speaker to the audience. However, the speaker will periodically involve attendees through polls and other brief interactions. While some webinars can be highly interactive, most are not.

You also might compare a webinar to a class at a university. The expert professor stands behind a podium while lecturing to hundreds of students sitting in the auditorium. The class likely includes some interactivity through questions and answers, assignments, and quizzes, but the large class size will limit the type and frequency of interaction possible.

Imagine your organization's human resources department holds informational sessions about a new company travel portal. If it was held online and presenters offered opportunities for discussion and dialogue, it could be called a webinar.

Attend a Free Webinar!

One popular trend is a specialized kind of online session: the marketing webinar. Organizations use these marketing events to share information about their products and services with hundreds or even thousands of people. An expert is brought in to speak on a subject aligned with the product or service, and everyone in their target market is invited to attend this free event.

Because attendees have to register for the webinar to hear from the expert speaker, organizations can use their registration data to capture interest in the topic and follow up with participants. At some point during the session, the sponsor's commercial is usually shared with attendees. The webinar recording is also posted for future viewing, which allows the sponsor to continue collecting data from interested attendees.

The positive trade-off is obvious: Attendees learn something for free, while organizations capture valuable marketing data and sponsors generate advertising.

The term *webinar* is so popular that many people believe it is synonymous with virtual training. In fact, it's increasingly common for organizations to call their virtual training sessions webinars. Some popular speakers, authors, and trainers even use the word *webinar* interchangeably with *virtual training*. I've done it myself.

The intent behind calling virtual training a webinar is good, but the effects can be challenging. First, participants who have attended passive webinars may expect the same minimal interaction if a virtual training class is called a webinar. Second, presenters may assume the session should be lecture-based and design and deliver it accordingly. Third, administrators may unknowingly set up the event using a meeting platform instead of a training platform, which can limit the available features.

When expectations are mismatched—your intent is an interactive virtual training class, but the result is a passive presentation—you'll have a higher risk of failure.

Participants expect to multitask throughout, or worse just assume they can skip it in lieu of other priorities and watch the recording afterward. They are less likely to learn or be able to apply new knowledge and skills. If you still choose to call your sessions webinars, as many organizations do, be prepared to climb the extra communication hurdles required for success.

Hybrid Learning

You may be wondering how hybrid learning relates to virtual training. Much like virtual training, there's no standard definition for hybrid learning, so confusion abounds. In the higher education or university setting, *hybrid* typically refers to a learning program that combines synchronous and asynchronous components. But in the business world, we call that *blended learning*. In the workplace, *hybrid learning* is defined as a synchronous, facilitated event that includes a mixture of participant locations—some participants are together on-site while others are remote. That's the definition we'll use for the remainder of this book. It's similar to virtual training because it's synchronous and uses a virtual classroom platform. It differs, however, because some participants are gathered together instead of dispersed.

Hybrid learning events could be in any one of the following formats:

- **Traditional hybrid.** Most participants are together in the same physical space. A few participants in remote locations join via the virtual classroom platform.
- **Remote-centric hybrid.** Most participants are individually connected to a virtual classroom from various remote locations. A few participants may meet in the same physical location and share a single connection to the virtual classroom.
- **Multipart hybrid.** Groups of participants join from various locations and are connected as a whole group via video conference or the virtual classroom platform. In other words, one group may be in a conference room in Albany, New York, another group is in Atlanta, Georgia, and a third in Boise, Idaho. The three groups connect via a video conference.
- **Facilitator hybrid.** Participants are co-located but the facilitator joins from a remote location via the virtual classroom platform.

The key to making hybrid classes work well is creating a shared experience between the in-person and remote attendees. You must equalize the experience so everyone—regardless of location—feels fully included in the learning experience and can contribute, interact, and learn.

Two specific factors contribute to a successful hybrid class: the tech setup and the skill of the facilitator. In many ways, these two factors are intertwined and both are equally important.

A technology-enabled hybrid classroom setup can overcome deficiencies in facilitation techniques, and a highly skilled facilitator can make any learning environment work. That said, "make it work" training isn't ideal. Successful hybrid learning shouldn't be difficult for anyone involved. The more barriers participants must overcome, the less likely they will be engaged and learning. To create a good hybrid learning experience, a skilled facilitator needs to be supported by proper resources. We'll explore these topics later in the book.

Blended Learning

When multiple delivery methods, including virtual events, are thoughtfully combined in a training curriculum, the result is *blended learning*. A classic definition from Allison Rossett and Rebecca Vaughan Frazee (2006) explains it this way:

> Blended learning integrates seemingly opposite approaches, such as formal and informal learning, face-to-face and online experiences, directed paths and reliance on self-direction, and digital references and collegial connections, in order to achieve individual and organizational goals.

It's typical to find a combination of asynchronous self-paced activities and synchronous live facilitated events in a blended learning journey. For example, a learner in a blended curriculum might receive instructions to complete a self-paced assignment and then attend two live virtual training classes with another self-paced assignment in-between. Each component in the blended learning program is an important step for achieving the overall learning outcome. Learners need to complete every component to realize the full results.

Blended learning has a place in this book because live online virtual training classes are often significant components in blended learning journeys. According to my annual survey respondents, 43 percent of all virtual classes are part of a series or blended program (Huggett 2024).

Stringing together multiple virtual events in a series as part of a blended learning program allows for more flexible learning implementations and better results. For example, instead of a single six-hour training session, the journey could include four

60-minute sessions spread out over two weeks, with application activities in between. It's also an opportunity for participants to learn something on their own and then meet with the facilitator and other learners to practice their skills.

Here's another example using a blended communication skills training program I created for one of my clients. The participants began by attending a virtual kickoff session to meet one another and learn what to expect in the curriculum. They also received a short, self-directed assignment to prepare for the learning topics. Two weeks later, they met for an in-person workshop to learn and practice fundamental skills, again receiving an assignment at the end. Over the next four weeks, the participants met for two virtual training classes and were given application assignments to complete between each one. The entire blended learning journey added up to approximately 24 hours of training time (including the assignments), and each component contributed to the learning outcomes.

As we dive into all aspects of virtual training throughout this book, remember that many virtual classes take place in the context of a blended journey.

My Definition of Virtual Training

From this point forward, we will use my definition of virtual training, which includes the components we've already discussed:

- A highly interactive synchronous online facilitated learning experience
- Defined learning objectives
- Participants who are individually connected from dispersed locations using a web-based classroom platform

However, regardless of what your organization implements—virtual training, webcasts, webinars, or hybrid or blended learning—the general principles outlined in this book will help you have more successful online initiatives.

Get the Right People Involved

Once you have set forth your goals and defined what you mean by virtual training, the next step is to ensure that the right people are involved with the online learning programs. Successful virtual training depends on many parts of an organization working well together, and getting all stakeholders onboard with your plans will increase your chances of success.

There are at least three reasons it pays to get the right people involved in your virtual training initiative: to gain their support, to gain their input, and to make use of their available resources—both tangible (hardware, technology, and funding) and intangible (wisdom, knowledge, and experience).

How do you know who to include as a stakeholder? In smaller organizations, the answer will probably be obvious, but in larger organizations, you'll have to do your homework to find out who the key stakeholders are for each part of your virtual training initiative. In general, it's better to invite more input than you think you need than to risk missing a key player.

> *"My advice? Involve everyone in the organization up front. Different teams have different roles to play in the virtual training initiative."*
>
> —Danielle Buscher, former Director of Global
> Learning, Marriott International

The typical roles involved in a successful virtual training program may not be job titles, per se, but are job functions with responsibilities that affect the success of any virtual training program. In some organizations, one person may play more than one role; for example, the facilitator who delivers a virtual training may also be the person who designed it, or the facilitator and the administrator might be the same person. The smaller the organization, the more likely that one person will span multiple roles. On the flip side, there may be more than one person for each function in a large organization, such as an IT representative for each location. Here are some of the key players:

- **Content owner.** Sometimes referred to as a subject matter expert (SME), this person has deep knowledge of the training content. They might be an employee in the field or a manager with responsibility for the subject matter. They can help design the training and ensure topic relevancy.
- **Designer.** An instructional designer creates the training program. This role might include graphic designers as well as workplace learning professionals who specialize in adult learning methodologies and instructional technology.
- **Facilitator.** Sometimes also called a trainer or instructor, this is the person who delivers the virtual training sessions and enables participant learning and application. Note that the preferred name is facilitator to indicate their primary responsibility of facilitating learning instead of lecturing or simply presenting content.
- **Producer.** This is the technical expert who assists the facilitator during a live online session. Some producers specialize in technology-only

assistance (working with participants who need help connecting), while others co-facilitate sessions. In some cases, a producer may be called a host or moderator.

- **Coordinator.** As the person who handles the logistical details of virtual training events, this person might administer the organization's LMS (learning management system) or LXP (learning experience platform) and communicate with participants before and after an event.
- **Tech expert.** Usually a point of contact in IT (information technology) or IS (information services), this role owns the tech stack—both hardware and software—needed for virtual training success.
- **Participant.** Also known as the learner or program attendee, this person is considered the customer or end user of the virtual training initiative. It's a good idea to include a representative sample of participants on your stakeholder list.
- **Manager.** The manager of each participant needs to support the full engagement of their employee in the program. Manager buy-in is critical to success because they will allow participants time to attend training sessions and reinforce the skills learned.
- **Resource owner.** This stakeholder controls the resources needed for creating, designing, delivering, and implementing a virtual training program. The role could be filled by those in management specializing in directing the organization's training function and ancillary roles or general managers who control the budget and other resources.
- **Executive sponsor.** This role is filled by a senior executive or learning leader who can support and champion virtual training initiatives at the highest levels of the organization.

We will explore many of these roles in more detail elsewhere in this book. For now, it's most important to realize that each person can contribute to the success of your virtual training programs. Involve them in the earliest planning stages and throughout the process.

"Our project team included human resources, IT, training design and development, and all the subject matter experts for each part of the curriculum."

—Erin Laughlin, former Senior Director of Global
Learning Delivery, Marriott International

After inviting the right people to the table for discussion, engage in an open dialogue with each one about what they think it takes to achieve a virtual training success story. This dialogue could include one-on-one conversations or a cross-functional project team discussion. The communication format is not as important as having open communication with key players.

> ### What Comes First?
>
> Should you start preparing by determining your goals and defining what you mean by virtual training and then getting the right people involved? Or should you get the right people involved first so they can help you establish goals and define virtual training? The answer is . . . it depends. There's no right or wrong answer to this chicken-or-egg question. What's most important is that you actually do all three.

When communicating with the stakeholders, start by sharing your answers to these essential questions:

- What are the strategic goals of the organization's virtual learning initiatives?
- How do these strategic goals align with business needs?
- How are you defining virtual training?

Depending on the timing of these conversations and your organization's situation, you may also ask your stakeholders for their thoughts on those questions.

After sharing the overarching goals, select the appropriate discussion questions for each stakeholder from this list:

- What suggestions or recommendations do you have?
- What questions or concerns do you have?
- From your viewpoint, what will it take for the virtual training to be successful?
- What resources do you need for your part of the initiative? What resources can you contribute?
- Who else should be involved with virtual training?
- Will I have your support?

If you form a cross-functional team, follow standard project management processes for implementation. Hold a kickoff meeting, create a project charter, and clearly define each person's role in the project.

Create a Strategic Plan

Once you have determined your goals, clarified your definition of virtual training, and identified and communicated with all relevant stakeholders, it's time to solidify your organization's virtual learning strategy. Even if your organization is already fully invested in several established virtual training programs, taking a step back to review and evaluate them can only add value to your overall plan.

In your process, you may discover that in the quick pivot to virtual learning in 2020, several training programs were not effectively redesigned for the virtual classroom and therefore aren't getting the desired results. In this case, your strategy may include creating instructional design standards for virtual training and then adapting your programs to them. Or you may discover that your virtual training results are suffering from a lack of resources. Perhaps your facilitators have not been properly upskilled in online delivery techniques or your remote learners don't have proper headsets for clear audio. In this case, your strategy could include securing the needed resources by building a business case.

Building a Business Case

If you still need stakeholder support, you may have to build and present a business case. A business case starts by defining your ultimate goal. Articulate who will benefit from the project and exactly how they will benefit. Spell out the anticipated positive impact on the organization. Identify the costs and the potential return on investment.

A typical business case includes:

- An overview of the problem to solve
- A recommended solution to the problem
- A statement explaining the benefits of the recommended solution
- A list of resources needed, including costs and other financial details
- The expected results

You should present the business case for your virtual training to the person who controls, and has the ability to share, the resources you need. All or some of the business case might also be presented to selected key stakeholders to help them see the benefits of your request.

Let's say your assessment alerts you to a virtual learning program that was moved quickly online from the traditional classroom and isn't getting the same results. You believe it would benefit from a full redesign, but that takes time and money. You will likely need to build a business case to justify the expense, and you can use the suggested components outlined in this chapter to present your case to stakeholders who can grant the resources you need.

Wendy Gates Corbett, a former global training director, shares an example from her past experience. She created a business case to establish virtual training as a method to help her company's global customer base learn about software products. Her proposal to the executive team included facts about the potential for virtual training, suggested solutions for realizing that potential, and an accounting of the resources she would need. She established the benefits and outlined the expected return on their investment. Spelling out those details gave her the momentum and approval she needed to launch the plan for virtual training.

One Organization's Story
Crafting a Business Case at the World Bank Group

To build the business case for virtual training at the World Bank Group, Senior Knowledge and Learning Officer Darlene Christopher connected virtual training to an important corporate initiative. At the time, her organization was looking to reduce its carbon footprint to create a more sustainable environment. Darlene calculated the carbon emissions savings that would be realized by conducting virtual training instead of in-person training. She then converted those savings into tangible results.

"By hosting one virtual session, we will avoid 44 tons of carbon emissions, which is equivalent to recycling 13.8 tons of waste or growing 1,024 trees for 10 years," she explained. Her well-crafted message, which was tied to helping the organization achieve its goals, resulted in growing excitement over the potential for virtual training.

Darlene's advice to others is to start small. Find a willing stakeholder or two within your organization who will support a simple virtual training initiative. Get an early win, and then think about what story you can tell from that experience. By starting small, you can get others interested and excited about the initiative and build traction. Think about what corporate initiatives you could tie your training into for support and how virtual training can help your organization achieve its big goals.

Calculating the Costs of Virtual Training

Some organizations use virtual training to lower costs. Travel budgets in many organizations have been slashed, for example, so flying somewhere to deliver or attend in-person training sessions is no longer allowed.

In this situation, it's probably not necessary to develop a traditional business case because key leaders have already given instructions to reduce training funding as opposed to granting it. Instead, you'll need to create a business case that explicitly outlines the true costs of effective virtual training. This may include the cost of more virtual classroom software licenses; better hardware for facilitators, producers, and participants; upskilling for anyone new to online learning; and improved internet bandwidth. Because the expectation will be to reduce or even eliminate funding, you will need a solid business case to illustrate clearly why any investments are needed. Virtual training is often perceived as being less expensive than traditional in-person training, but that perception does not always align with reality.

Virtual training may reduce travel expenses when learners can stay at their desks instead of hopping on a plane or driving to a training location; however, it includes other costs that do not exist for in-person training. In addition to what we've already mentioned, other investments might include noise-canceling headsets for all participants, webcams for facilitators and participants, additional design time, and the cost of providing two facilitators (or a facilitator and a producer) for each virtual event.

One Organization's Story
Converting to an All-Virtual Curriculum

Way of Life Coaching, based in Raleigh, North Carolina, offers a three-month group coaching course called "Promised Land Living." Founder Cheryl Scanlan's vision has always been to expand the program's reach beyond the local community. She wanted to make the curriculum available to anyone regardless of their geographic location. After careful consideration of various options, Cheryl decided to convert to an all-virtual curriculum. Together with her team, she:

- Worked for months planning out the implementation strategy
- Budgeted resources for the new delivery methodology
- Redesigned the content for virtual delivery
- Involved subject matter experts and stakeholders for advice and input
- Researched and selected a virtual training platform
- Created a marketing plan to communicate the new program format to potential participants
- Worked with participants and facilitators to get comfortable with virtual training

Cheryl's advice to other organizations that are considering the move to virtual is clear and practical: "Get familiar with the virtual training platform and how often the vendor makes updates to it. Be sure you test drive the platform after upgrades to make sure there are no surprises. I would also highly recommend having a producer for every virtual class so you can be focused on delivering your material. That made all the difference for us and our clients!"

Table 1-1 looks at how virtual training costs compare with the costs for in-person programs.

Table 1-1. The Costs of Virtual Training Compared With Traditional Classroom Training

Costs	Increase or Decrease
Virtual classroom software platform licenses	Increase
Integrated telephone or conference call subscriptions and per-event costs, if not using Voice over Internet Protocol (VoIP)	Increase
Computer hardware, such as noise-canceling headsets for participants	Increase
Printing classroom materials	Decrease
Printing costs for learners, who may be asked to print their own materials	Increase
Two facilitators, or a facilitator and a producer, for each virtual event	Increase
A second laptop for facilitators, who log in to the platform twice—once as a presenter and once as a participant	Increase
Training for designers and facilitators who need to learn the new virtual classroom software platform and how to design and deliver virtual training	Increase
Design and development time for the training program*	Decrease
Travel fees for participants and facilitators	Decrease
Classroom materials that no longer need to be purchased, such as chart paper and markers	Decrease
Productivity for participants who do not have to leave their desks to attend training in another location	Increase

*According to research by Robin Defelice, it takes on average 67 hours of development time to create instructor-led training, and it takes approximately 55 hours of development time to create interactive virtual training. (For more information, visit td.org/insights/how-long-does-it-take-to-develop-training-new-question-new-answers.)

"We took a two-day performance management course and converted it into a blended learning program. The new converted program included six virtual sessions along with self-paced assignments. This new solution created efficiency for learners; however, it increased the administrative work required for the trainer and the program manager. Don't assume that because you're saving on airfare that virtual training will be less expensive. While you save on learner expenses, you often increase your design, delivery, and administrative costs."

—Dan Gallagher, former Vice President of Learning and Development, Comcast, and co-author of *The Self-Aware Leader* (ATD 2012)

By fully considering the true costs of virtual training in your organization, you can request appropriate funding in your business case and set your programs up for success.

In Summary: Key Points From Chapter 1

- Determine if virtual training is the right solution for your organization.
- Define what you mean by virtual training and ensure everyone in your organization uses that definition.
- Get the right people involved as close to the project's start time as possible.
- If needed, create a business case to ensure you have the right resources for your virtual training programs.

Take Action

✓ Carefully consider your definition of virtual training; survey your peers to discover if their definitions match yours. In what ways do your approaches vary? What would you need to change to bring your views into agreement?

✓ Take inventory of all the resources your organization has available for virtual training. What's working well and ready to mobilize? What's missing?

Tool 1-1. A Thought-Starter: Is Virtual Training the Right Solution?

To help determine if virtual training is the correct solution to use for your organization, consider the questions in the tool below.

☐ **Are the participants centrally located or dispersed?** If your organization is not going to save on travel expenses because everyone is in the same location, then consider sticking with in-person training. It may be just as fast for people to walk down the hallway to the training room as it would be for them to log in to a virtual classroom.

☐ **What technology barriers affect success?** All participants need to have the appropriate technology. What they need will vary depending on the virtual software program you use; however, a typical setup requires a high-speed internet connection, a headset or external microphone, an HD webcam, and administrative privileges to install the software. Chapter 2 addresses technology in more detail.

☐ **Do you have qualified people to facilitate the virtual training program?** Traditional classroom facilitators need a different skill set to effectively deliver virtual training. They need to be comfortable with technology, able to multitask well, and know how to engage remote participants for learning and application. These skills come with training and practice. Facilitator preparation time should be factored into your decision to use virtual training. The facilitator's role is discussed in detail in chapter 5.

☐ **Will you be able to invest in producer support?** The best virtual programs benefit from producer support because good producers mean fewer technology problems. The producer assists the facilitator with technology, troubleshooting, and running the virtual event. They also help create a seamless experience for participants. We will consider producer qualifications in chapter 6.

☐ **Will every participant have an appropriate learning environment?** Each participant needs to have their own individual computer connection and telephone line to attend the virtual event. They should be in a quiet area conducive to learning. If they are in a noisy space, they will need headphones, and to show up well on video, they will benefit from a quality webcam. Chapter 7 provides a comprehensive look at how to set up participants for effective online learning environments.

☐ **Who will administer the logistical details for the training program?**
The online environment creates a long list of logistics that must be
executed to ensure a successful training experience. This includes
creating the virtual classroom event within the software's administrative
tools, getting links and passwords to everyone who needs them,
distributing handouts and other class materials to participants,
and helping participants troubleshoot technical problems before
class. Chapter 8 covers all the important administrative details for
your initiative.

☐ **Will your virtual training be inclusive and accessible for all who
need it?** While many virtual classroom platforms now have accessibility
features like closed-captioning, transcription, and video avatars, your
learners may have other needs that virtual training programs won't meet.
Some learners may be able to use screen reader tools to participate
fully in the learning experience, but others may need additional training
modalities. For example, if a neurodiverse participant struggles in the
required breakout room practice activities, they will need another way to
achieve the learning outcomes and master the new skills, such as a self-
directed immersive simulation. Virtual training can be an excellent way
to engage with international audiences as long as language barriers do
not get in the way. If your virtual classroom platform includes language
translation, this may not be an issue. If not, you may need to get creative
and provide other solutions in consultation with your participants. Always
consider the needs of your diverse audience when determining if virtual
training is the right fit for your topic and its learning requirements. Virtual
training is a fantastic learning method for many situations, but it's not
always the best method available.

Tool 1-2. A Goal-Planning Worksheet

Begin with a clear idea of the results you want to achieve when setting goals for your virtual training initiatives. Goal planning is important whether you have a single virtual program or an extensive series of virtual classes. To help you set effective goals, consider the questions on this worksheet.

1. What's the primary goal for your virtual training program or initiative? What specifically do you hope to accomplish?

2. What should participants be able to do as a result of this training program?
   - ☐ Be more knowledgeable about the topic.
   - ☐ Behave differently.
   - ☐ Take action on something.
   - ☐ Other:

3. How will the organization change or improve because of the training?

4. What's the best way to achieve the goals?

5. How specifically will virtual training help achieve these outcomes?

CHAPTER 2

Select Technology

Successful virtual training depends on having the right tech stack available to meet participants' learning needs. In this chapter, you will learn how to select technology for your virtual training programs, making sure to:

- Consider four categories—hardware, software, audio and video, and bandwidth.
- Partner with IT to select the right technology.
- Carefully choose technology vendors.

Technology is supposed to make our lives easier. It automates tasks, speeds things up, and helps us get things done. Unfortunately, there are times when it doesn't work as planned, and we get frustrated. Something that's supposed to make life easier ends up making it more complicated.

For example, if you need to write a blog post, you might use an AI program to create the first draft. It saves you time and effort because some of the research, writing, and editing processes are automated, and it's much easier than when you used stacks of library books, a typewriter, and correction tape. You can also save the post as an online draft and return to it later. However, things can also go unexpectedly wrong. If the AI program doesn't understand your prompt, you'll need to do several revisions, which may make the writing process longer than if you had just put pen to paper. Or, if a glitch occurs when you try to save the post, the information may be corrupted or even lost. And it's not unusual for AI to include factual errors, plagiarism, and hyperbole when generating content, so you'll have to edit the content and check the quality. The technology that was supposed to be so helpful can end up creating more challenges than it's worth.

Or maybe you rely on your smartphone's GPS app to guide you to a destination. You listen to its voice commands as it directs you from one turn to the next. You expect it to lead you through the most efficient path, but if the app has outdated information or goes offline, it could lead you astray. Then, you'll have to backtrack or find an alternate route.

The same potential pitfalls apply to the technology you use for virtual training. You want the tech to make your training program easier, save time, and guide you to your learning destination. You don't want it to interfere or get in the way—you just want it to seamlessly do its job. You also want to ensure that you have the right technology to get the learning results you need for a successful program.

You have probably experienced tech challenges during a virtual meeting. Perhaps it started late or you experienced disruptions—it's so common that many people associate all virtual training with tech problems. But it doesn't have to be that way. You can have successful virtual training classes that run flawlessly and with ease. With thoughtful planning, selection, and implementation, the tech can go unnoticed—just providing the means to the learning end.

Even though technology is the vehicle for virtual training, it should never be the center of attention. It's not the star of the show. The star is the learning content—which should lead to the participant's new skills or behavior change and subsequent on-the-job application.

So, what kind of tech do you need behind the scenes for successful virtual training? And how do you ensure it runs seamlessly and smoothly for everyone? This chapter will answer those questions.

Run, Don't Walk

If you're reading this during working hours, message your contact in the IT department and ask if you can go through this chapter together. Take the opportunity to discuss what technology you already have, the new technology you need, and how to close the gap between the two.

Effective virtual training requires tech in four different categories:

- Proper hardware
- Collaborative software

- Quality media (audio and video)
- Sufficient internet bandwidth

Let's review the details of each.

Proper Hardware

A device with a stable internet connection is the main piece of equipment everyone needs for virtual training success. It can be a laptop or desktop computer of any make, model, or brand as long as it meets the requirements of the software platform you choose. You could also use a tablet or other mobile device, as long as your software has an app that has the same functionality as its laptop or desktop app.

Most virtual classroom platform providers specify the tech requirements for their programs; for example, you'll need X amount of memory, a minimum internet connection speed of Y, and Z hardware space for any necessary software downloads.

Sample Virtual Training Platform Hardware Specs

- A processor that's quad-core 4Ghz or higher
- 8GB RAM
- A supported, up-to-date web browser (such as, Chrome, Edge, Safari, or Firefox)
- A high-speed internet connection; broadband wired or wireless (minimum 4G LTE)
- Speakers and a microphone (built-in, USB plug-in, or wireless Bluetooth)
- A webcam or HD webcam (built-in, USB plug-in, or virtual camera software for use with broadcasting software)

Every person attending a virtual training session should have their own connection to the virtual classroom. Remember, this book's definition of virtual training does not encompass video conferencing, which includes a group of people gathered around a boardroom table passively watching a presentation onscreen. In virtual training, each participant connects individually to the virtual classroom. Even in a hybrid learning environment, in-person attendees should each use their own device to access the virtual classroom tools.

In today's digitally saturated environment, the suggestion that everyone should have an internet-connected device may seem like a no-brainer; we usually assume everyone has one. However, plenty of industries and organizations—including some retail employers, construction companies, and manufacturing businesses—don't supply devices to most of their workforce. In this case, you must ask yourself if virtual learning will still work effectively. Can participants to go to a learning lab to attend a class? Is there a library of laptops available for check out? Could participants use their personal devices? Solutions exist; you'll just need to think through them intentionally.

Review the following questions as you make decisions about equipping training participants with devices:

- What other business needs could be met by providing individual devices to your workforce? Is now the right time for this to happen? Would the individuals and the organization benefit as a result? If so, could you build a business case for supplying participants with devices for learning and frame it as an investment in your workforce?
- Could participants borrow a laptop from your organization's lending library? Should you establish a lending library for this purpose?
- Is there a shared space you could set up for virtual learning? Could you establish a hotel-style office space that includes an individual learning lab?
- Are mobile devices robust enough for your learning solution? If so, could the organization supply those to participants? (We will explore the use of mobile devices for virtual training in the next section.)
- Is virtual training right for your organization? It may not be. Remember, while there are many reasons to use virtual training, it is not always the best learning solution. If your participants won't benefit from virtual training—or can't take full advantage of it because of their physical locations or lack of equipment—you may want to explore a better option for their learning needs.

The Facilitator's Hardware Needs

As the primary session leader, facilitators usually need a more robust hardware setup than the participants. Therefore, carefully consider the specific equipment required for high-quality virtual facilitation. Facilitators need a powerful laptop with a solid internet connection; they will also benefit from an external monitor, an external webcam, and a noise-canceling microphone. If you are planning to incorporate immersive technologies in your virtual classes, the facilitator may also need a VR headset.

In addition, it's ideal for facilitators to be able to use two devices when delivering virtual training. This setup is beneficial because:

- The facilitator may need a backup device in case of a technology failure or another unexpected glitch. This is especially important if the facilitator is flying solo, without a co-presenter or producer. (We'll discuss the importance of these roles in chapters 5 and 6.)

- The facilitator can simultaneously look at the participants' view and the presenter's view, enabling them to see exactly what the participants have on their screens and the subtleties of the software unique to that view.

If your organization has a standard issue one-device-per-person rule, it may be time to make an exception for virtual trainers. A seasoned online facilitator can usually find a way to access multiple computers per session—by using their personal laptop and their company laptop, by using a mobile device as their second connection, or by borrowing a laptop from someone else during the training session timeframe.

If it's not possible to provide each trainer in your organization with a second laptop, then perhaps you could use a shared laptop. Or you could create a designated virtual training room with computers that are already set up, similar to a hotel-style office or learning lab for participants.

We'll dive deep into the facilitator role in chapter 5 and talk more about what they do with these items during the training program. In addition, note that the producer will have nearly identical hardware needs as the facilitator. (Chapter 6 goes into more detail on the producer's role.)

Cost Considerations

If the cost of providing a second laptop for facilitators is a budget issue in your organization, think of it this way: Eliminating the cost of just one or two airplane tickets for a traveling trainer would easily cover the cost of a basic backup laptop.

Mobile devices like smartphones and tablets can also be used as a second connection to the virtual classroom, but they come with a few disadvantages, which we'll discuss later in this chapter. If your organization chooses a mobile device as a second connection, be sure to consider both mobile app functionality and internet connectivity requirements. Ideally, the organization, not the facilitator, will provide the funds for a separate device or data plan.

If your organization's IT policies allow only one authenticated login to the virtual classroom per user, be sure to create a second account that the facilitator can use on the second computer. For example, one of my clients created generic trainer accounts to use on the network ("Trainer One," "Trainer Two," and "Trainer Three") so facilitators could easily connect separate devices to the virtual classroom at the same time.

Sample Complete Facilitator Equipment List
- Laptop with the correct specs to effectively facilitate virtual training
- An external monitor connected to the primary laptop
- Another laptop that can be used as a second connection to the virtual classroom, as well as a backup to the primary laptop
- An external HD webcam with a ring light or LED panel lighting
- A noise-canceling headset and an external microphone
- High-speed internet connectivity

Figure 2-1. Photo of a Facilitator's Hardware Setup

More About Mobile Devices

The proliferation of mobile technology in the workplace and the increased capability of software programs that work on mobile devices allows greater flexibility when connecting to a virtual classroom. Most virtual classroom software platforms have mobile apps that correlate to their desktop programs, although some apps have limited functionality. So, while it may be possible to use a mobile device instead of a laptop or desktop computer for virtual training, it's not always recommended.

For example, virtual facilitators often need to share documents, videos, and screens that may not be accessible from a mobile app. They also need to switch quickly from one virtual tool to another while facilitating, which isn't easy to do on a mobile device. In addition, facilitators benefit from a larger screen than most mobile devices have, so they can see participant videos, chat, and other classroom tools. Spatial computing—with its expansive viewing via headset or smart glasses—will eventually overcome this limitation. But it's not yet readily available or widely adopted. Stay tuned for updates in this area, which will open the doors to mobile computing for virtual training.

In addition, participants may struggle to engage fully in a virtual classroom when using a mobile device. The mobile app interface and view may be different than the desktop version and it may not have full functionality. For example, participants may not be able to access whiteboard tools or respond to poll questions. Or more importantly, accessibility features may not work in the mobile app.

Recently, I co-facilitated a virtual class that many participants joined via tablet devices. Connecting to the session was easy because the platform we were using had a mobile app. The participants were able to participate fully in the first few activities, but trouble began when I opened the first multimedia clip. Only those connected by laptop or desktop computer were able to watch the clip; those connected via the app just saw an error message that said, "This feature is not supported." A little later in the session, we began a whiteboard activity. Those connected by computer used the text tool to type on the screen. But those connected from mobile devices could only draw on the screen, and they couldn't add text.

While these two examples of limitations may seem minor, they can make a substantial difference in learning effectiveness. Thus, it's worth noting these kinds of challenges when you're considering the use of mobile devices in your virtual training programs.

Another challenge that can occur with mobile devices is ensuring a stable internet connection with enough bandwidth to handle the learning activities. Participants who use mobile devices will need to ensure they have reliable service or a data plan capable of supporting the program requirements.

If participants are going to use mobile devices, designers and facilitators may need to adapt the activities to accommodate them. Designers should be aware of all mobile features and limitations and design sessions accordingly. In addition, facilitators and producers will have to understand the differences in users' experiences and be able to clearly explain the activity instructions.

In the future, it may become more common to use mobile devices for virtual training if there's a seamless transition when moving between a software's computer and mobile versions, but for now, limited functionality creates challenges. The bottom line is this: In my experience, participants on mobile devices have a diminished learning experience compared with those using a full desktop version, so I don't recommend using mobile apps.

What About Wearables or Car Consoles?

Internet-connected wearables such as smartwatches, smart glasses, holographic goggles, and VR headsets can connect to most virtual classrooms. It's even possible to connect to virtual classroom platforms through internet-connected automobile consoles. But while this capability is *possible*, is it desirable? Will a smart device connection provide the best learning atmosphere for a participant who needs to engage with colleagues, use platform tools, and practice new skills?

As these relatively new technologies evolve, I may eventually answer a resounding yes! But today, wearables and smart devices are still emerging and not yet viable or desirable options.

Participants' Hardware Needs

If your organization intends to create a robust virtual learning strategy, you should not overlook participants' hardware needs. For example, participants need a strong internet connection so they won't spend all their time just trying to stay connected to the virtual platform. They need external headsets for a clear audio connection and webcams for video conversations. These items may be standard issue in some organizations, but they aren't for many. In my annual survey of global training professionals, lack of proper participant resources was frequently noted as a significant challenge (Huggett 2024). We'll take a much closer look at participant preparation in chapter 7 and discuss how to ensure they have the proper setup.

Sample Participant Equipment List
- A laptop with the correct specs to effectively participate in a virtual training class
- Noise-canceling headset and/or an external microphone
- High-speed internet connectivity
- External HD webcam

Hardware for Hybrid Learning Environments

If your organization's virtual learning strategy includes hybrid classes, then pay special attention to the technology you'll need to make that successful. As I mentioned in the previous chapter, the key to making hybrid classes work well is creating a shared experience between in-person and remote attendees. Each participant, regardless of location, should be fully included in the learning experience. A classroom with hybrid-friendly hardware helps.

Several virtual classroom vendors offer hybrid room kits, which include large screens to show remote participant videos, cameras to capture the in-person participants, and microphones to transmit clear audio. Figure 2-2 shows an example of a hybrid classroom setup.

Figure 2-2. Photo of a Hybrid Classroom

Collaborative Software

The most important software decision for virtual training success is choosing the virtual classroom platform. Sometimes it's called a *web conferencing program,* an *online collaboration platform,* or *virtual meeting software.* I typically refer to it as a *virtual classroom* or the *virtual platform.* To select the best software for your virtual training programs:

- Determine what features you need.
- Partner with the IT department in decision making.
- Research vendors who offer solutions that match your needs.

Determine What Features You Need

To help you choose the best platform, start by familiarizing yourself with common features found in virtual classrooms. In fact, everyone who uses or interacts with virtual training should be familiar with platform features and functionality. Administrators need to know the setup and behind-the-scenes operations. IT staff need to know how to install it, integrate it with other software, and enable necessary features for collaborative virtual classes. Designers need to understand how any interaction tools work so they can create engaging activities. Facilitators need to be expert users, and producers need to know how to support and troubleshoot. In addition, participants need to be comfortable using the platform's tools.

Let's review some basic features and functionalities of a typical virtual classroom platform. Please note that each platform has its own nuances and specific functionalities for each feature, and some platforms lack these features altogether. It will be important for you to discover what's included with your selected platform.

If you're already an expert user, feel free to skip this section and move on to the next step—partnering with IT.

Categories of Virtual Classroom Software Programs

Most vendors offer a suite of products to cover a variety of virtual events. For example, you could choose from WebEx Meetings and WebEx Webinars; GoToMeeting, GoToTraining, and GoToWebinar; and Zoom Meetings and Zoom Webinars.

So, how do you know which products to use? As you might guess from their names, each variation of the platform has unique features and functionalities. Just like some restaurants are known for Indian food and others for Thai or Italian, virtual platforms offer unique menus. All restaurants serve food, but you probably wouldn't go to a steakhouse to order spaghetti. Likewise, while you could potentially use any virtual platform to create an online learning experience, some will work better than others depending on what you're building. For example, it's possible to use a meeting or webinar product for virtual training, but it's probably not the best choice.

In general, meeting products are specifically designed for meetings, and usually include discussion, action-item sharing, note-taking, and so on. They may have breakout rooms with limited features for small group conversations. Webinar products have robust presenter features, but attendees stay in listen-only mode without access to most tools beyond chat. As we've already established, meetings and webinars are not ideal environments for virtual training. Because live online learning programs rely heavily on collaboration and conversation among participants, it's usually best to use the training version of your software platform.

One of my global clients once spent considerable time and resources integrating the webinar version of their chosen platform into their LMS and other back-end programs. Afterward, however, they realized that while the webinar features were perfect for giving marketing presentations to large audiences, virtual trainers were struggling to use them for interactive virtual classes. Participant webcams were disabled, breakout rooms were not supported, and everyone was automatically muted upon entry to the classroom and could only speak when invited by the facilitator. The facilitators did their best to overcome these challenges to engagement, but it would have been much easier if they had access to the program's training version.

A product specifically designed for virtual training may be more expensive than the meeting version, but the additional training features offer a substantial advantage if the goal is to create a highly interactive learning program that leads to application and impact. Facilitators don't have to spend so much energy making it work, and participants have a smoother experience. Learning will also happen faster when it's supported by the proper technology.

Integrating Virtual Platforms

Has your IT department stipulated use of a certain platform because it's already bundled with your organization's software of choice? What if that platform doesn't have the training features you need? First, build a business case to select a training platform. If, after doing that, you are still at an impasse, find out if the virtual classroom program you want to use will integrate with the organization's software. For example, if your organization uses Microsoft Teams but you want to use WebEx or Zoom to host virtual classes, it's possible to do so. These programs seamlessly integrate together. This option, if available, may give you a win-win situation and the best of both worlds.

Common Tools in a Virtual Classroom Software Program

Most virtual classroom software programs have similar features and functionality. The following, adapted from my 2018 book *Virtual Training Basics*, explains the tools most often used in virtual training. Please note that this is not an exhaustive list of all features found in every platform, nor is it an endorsement for a particular platform. You should always do your own research to review the pros and cons of any tool you're considering adopting.

Sharing Documents and Screens

Sharing documents and screens is one of the most common features in a virtual class. The facilitator shares a document, an app, or their desktop, which the participants can then see on their own screens. As the facilitator navigates through the shared document, moving from one place to another, the participants' screens follow along in synchronization.

There are two common methods for sharing content: loading files into the virtual classroom software and sharing screens. Nearly all virtual platforms allow for screen sharing, but only some allow files to be uploaded onto the platform. The underlying architecture of the program dictates which type of sharing can be used.

The first method—*loading the documents into the virtual classroom so they are internally hosted by the platform*—is similar to using the File/Open command to open a document on your computer inside Microsoft Word, as opposed to using Office 365 or Google Docs to edit a document saved in the cloud. The advantages of this method include better bandwidth management for all and a clean, focused view of the document. On at least one popular platform, the facilitator can still see chat and participant video feeds (whereas screen sharing hides those features, preventing the facilitator from seeing anything else).

With this method, the virtual trainer will need to prepare ahead of time. They'll need to select the share menu, choose a file from their computer, and then upload it into the system. If they change the original document after sharing it, they'll have to upload it again. Think of the virtual classroom as a container that can hold and display a slide deck. It's fundamentally different from screen sharing, in which the slides stay on the facilitator's computer and participants view that screen.

In addition, if multiple files are loaded into the virtual classroom, it's easy for a facilitator to switch between them. This is useful because most classes include multiple shared documents. For example, one of my virtual training classes on coaching typically has at least five shared documents, which I switch between during the program:

- A welcome slide deck with introductory material
- The class slide deck, which contains program content
- An excerpt from the participant handout
- A short video file that I play during class
- An audio music file I play during reflection activities

Keep in mind that different platforms have different compatibility requirements for shared documents. Most can share Microsoft Office documents (Word, Excel,

PowerPoint), PDF files, and media files (MP3 or MP4). If there are certain file types that you'll need to share, check for file compatibility when considering a platform.

The second method of sharing documents is the *app sharing* or *screen sharing feature* (Figure 2-3). In this method, the facilitator selects the share button and then either selects an open app (such as an internal sales tracking database to demonstrate) or their full screen. Then, remote attendees are able to see whatever file or application is visible on the facilitator's screen, and changes are viewed in real time. While facilitators can switch between the apps they're sharing, it's not always a seamless transition; some platforms require the facilitator to stop sharing the first app and then re-share a second one.

Some facilitators prefer to load their documents into a virtual classroom, while others would rather screen share. Each method has its pros and cons, so it's both a matter of personal preference and functionality. The bottom line when considering virtual platforms is to find out which types of sharing are available, what's recommended by the vendor, and how facilitators will use the feature.

Figure 2-3. Example of Sharing Documents and Screens in Zoom

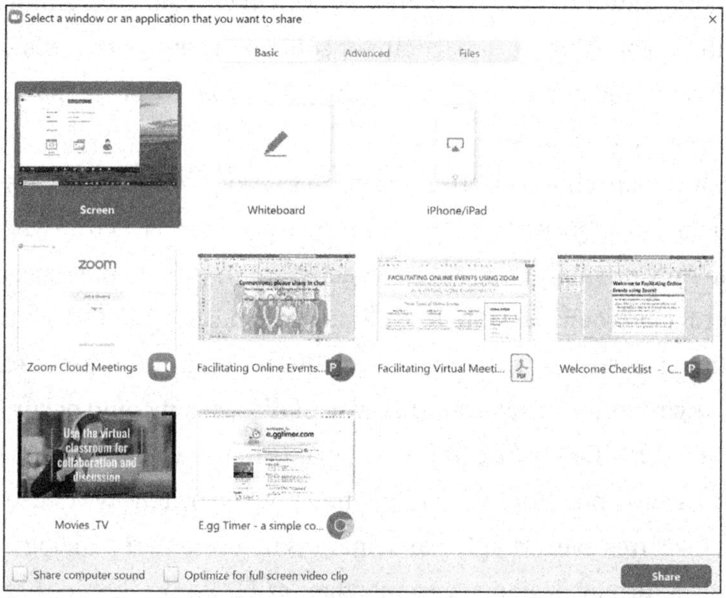

Chat

Chat enables communication between and among participants through real-time typed messages (Figure 2-4). It can be public, so that everyone can see the message, or private messaging between two individuals. Chat allows for more engagement because participants can send feedback, ask questions, and make comments throughout the program. Participants can use the chat window to share running commentary throughout the session and as another option for answering questions and providing input during activities. Facilitators can use chat to pass messages along during activities. For example, they could give timing reminders during a whiteboard brainstorming activity, such as "Three minutes remaining" or "It's time to start sorting ideas."

Most virtual platforms now support enhanced chat features like keyboard

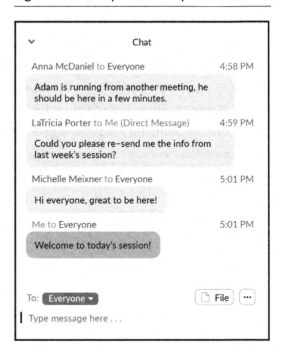

Figure 2-4. Example Chat Responses in Zoom

emojis, GIFs, and real-time participant reactions, which help create more immersion and collaboration. For example, a participant could react with a thumbs-up or heart to another's comment, indicating agreement and emphasis. Or participants could share memes to express their feelings.

Rules about private chat vary from program to program. In many cases, the facilitator or producer can choose whether to allow private chat, as well as whether to allow participants to only privately chat with the facilitator or private message one another.

In a physical classroom session, a facilitator might say, "Turn to the person sitting next to you and discuss your response to this question," but that's not easily possible in the virtual environment. However, this type of discussion could occur in the virtual environment if the facilitator directed participants to use private chat to discuss their responses with a classmate. In fact, this is one of my favorite ways to use the chat feature because it ensures every single participant is involved in the dialogue.

Peggy Page, a former design group manager at TD Bank, shared that she uses the chat feature extensively when designing virtual classes. Because some of her participants are connecting from a wide-open space (their desks are situated in a bank lobby), they can't talk during a session without disturbing those around them. So, they use chat as their primary form of communication. While she wouldn't call these events virtual training because of their limited interactivity, Peggy has found a way to keep each participant's attention via chat during these short virtual sessions.

Annotate

Annotation allows for real-time drawing and typing on top of shared documents, screens, or whiteboards (Figure 2-5). The exact tools available vary from platform to platform, but they typically allow you to:

Figure 2-5.
Annotation
Tools in Zoom

- Highlight words or graphics
- Draw lines and other shapes
- Add stamps
- Draw freehand with an electronic pencil or marker
- Type text on the screen

Most platforms can turn annotation rights on or off for participants and facilitators and let each person choose whether the annotations are anonymous or named. They also include varying degrees of erasers—some allow a person to erase only their own added content, while others only have an "erase all" command.

Annotation tools help keep the screen visually interesting because the facilitator can highlight keywords while speaking. If participants can draw or mark on the screen, it helps them engage with the learning content. A facilitator can also invite participants to type onscreen in response to a question or ask them to highlight something onscreen that stands out to them.

For example, it's common to ask participants to share insights they gained or actions they will take at the end of the program. Participants could use the annotation tools to write these items on the screen for all to see or draw a picture that represents the insight or action. Participants could also go to breakout rooms for a collaborative whiteboard exercise and capture their notes and ideas using the drawing tools. One of my favorite ways to use annotation is to create a grid onscreen and ask each participant to personalize a space on the grid in response to a question I've asked.

Whiteboard

A virtual whiteboard is like a physical meeting room whiteboard or empty chart paper on a stand. It's simply a blank screen on which people can type, write, or draw using the program's annotation tools. They are typically used for brainstorming, debriefing, and other class collaboration activities (Figure 2-6). Whiteboards may be persistent, meaning they are available for continued use after the program ends.

Figure 2-6. Example Whiteboard in Zoom

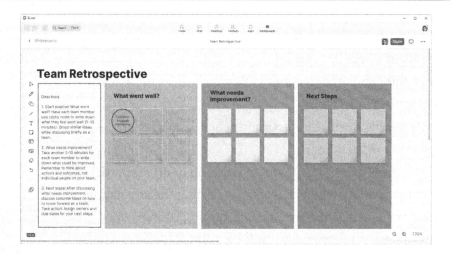

Although the whiteboard screen starts as a blank page, a facilitator can set it up ahead of time by adding drawings or other marks for an activity. For instance, they might draw two perpendicular lines to divide the whiteboard into four sections and write a question or word to distinguish each one. They could then ask participants to fill in details during the activity.

In one of my class activities, I ask participants to think about the benefits to three groups: employees, managers, and the organization. I use a divided whiteboard with one of the three group names at the top of each column. Participants can then type on the screen to brainstorm the benefits.

In another exercise, the whiteboard has a detailed vector graphic with multiple chat prompts. Participants individually choose where they want to contribute and then type their thoughts in the designated spots. Afterward, during reflection time, we review everyone's input and participants are encouraged to stamp items they agree with and circle ones they'd like to clarify or discuss.

As you review your virtual training platform's whiteboard capabilities, check for which participant annotation privileges you can grant. Also, find out if there are any limitations to how many participants can annotate at one time, how many whiteboards can be open or shared during a session, and if the whiteboard will be available after the session.

Reactions and Raise Hand

Reactions, including the one called "raise hand," are some of the simplest and easiest to use virtual classroom tools. Participants who use this feature can click on a button to raise their hand or indicate their current status. Choices typically include options like *agree, disagree, laughter, applause,* and *stepped away*. Sometimes the raise-hand option is bundled with reactions; sometimes it's a separate button (Figure 2-7). Participants use it to indicate agreement or ask a question, so it's often used for responding to closed-ended questions and quick yes/no polls. Facilitators employ this feature to get a quick response from every participant.

Figure 2-7. Example of Reactions in Zoom

On some platforms, only the facilitator can see the participants' reactions. Other platforms allow everyone to see the hand raised or status change. Some platforms place the reaction next to each name in the participant list, some display it on top of the person's video, while others summarize the selected reactions in a list.

Hand gesture recognition, if enabled, can display reactions based on real physical movement. For example, a participant simply needs to clap their hands together to show applause or make a thumbs-up sign to indicate agreement. By removing the step of finding an icon and clicking it, these AI-driven tools allow greater immersion in the virtual experience for learners. This may also help with accessibility because it eliminates extra clicks to use the tool.

Polling

Polls are used to ask participants real-time survey questions, which can be multiple choice, multiple answer, or sometimes even open-ended text responses (Figure 2-8). For example, facilitators can use polls to:

- Quiz participants' knowledge and understanding of a topic.
- Generate discussion using opinion questions.
- Solicit feedback from participants.

Some virtual classroom software allows for multiple questions in the same poll. Other programs limit each poll to one question but allow you to have more than one poll open at a time. Some platforms allow you to create polls before the session and store them as separate files you can launch when needed.

Polling questions can be a fun way to engage participants during class. For example, you might create a contest with points awarded for every correct answer, and then present a virtual prize to the person or team with the most points at the end. Or you could pose a scenario related to the content and ask participants via a poll to select the character's correct course of action. You might also ask for input and use the answers to generate a word cloud to combine everyone's thoughts. The options are limited only by your creativity.

Figure 2-8. Example of Polling in Zoom

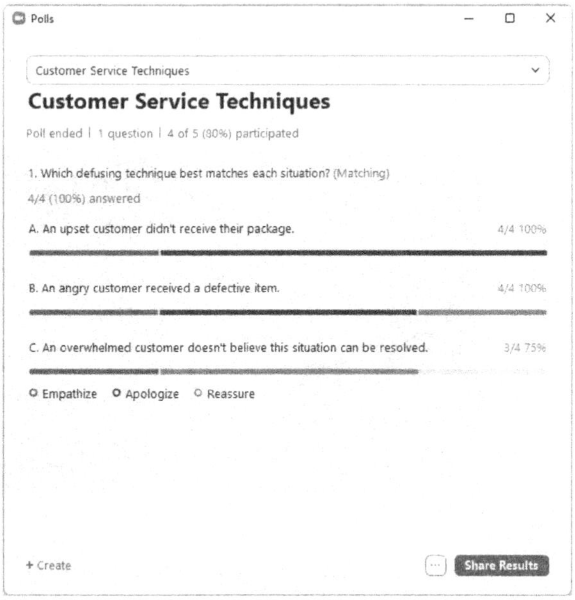

Breakout Groups

Breakout groups mimic small group activities in the traditional in-person classroom. They allow participants to divide into smaller subgroups to complete a learning exercise such as a skills practice or case study activity (Figure 2-9). For example, a class with 15 participants might split into five teams of three people each. The number of breakout rooms available depends on the virtual classroom software. Some platforms allow only a few breakout rooms while others allow 25, 50, or more.

During breakout sessions, participants move into a separate virtual meeting room in which they can have private conversations with one another. In this room, they can share documents and whiteboards and collaborate. Some platforms include a countdown timer for breakout rooms so participants can keep an eye on the activity time. Others allow the facilitator to broadcast typed messages or voice announcements to the rooms. The facilitator can move in and out of the breakout rooms, just like they would walk around the room to check on small groups during an in-person session.

Breakout groups help enable engagement and small group discussion. They can also be used to practice skills learned during the training program. For example, if participants learn techniques for starting a coaching conversation with an employee, they can move to a breakout room and practice those techniques in a small group setting—one participant could practice the new coaching skill, another participant could be on the receiving end of the practice, and a third participant could be a silent observer. The participants could then rotate roles, giving each one a chance to practice the new techniques.

Figure 2-9. Example of Breakout Rooms in Zoom

Integrated Apps

A recent development in most virtual platforms is the ability to use external apps inside the virtual classroom. These apps are a partnership between two or more vendors, creating a simple pathway for seamless integration into the virtual experience. Instead of switching between software programs in a clunky way, apps allow for a smooth, user-friendly transition between tasks (Figure 2-10).

Figure 2-10. Example of Available Apps in Zoom

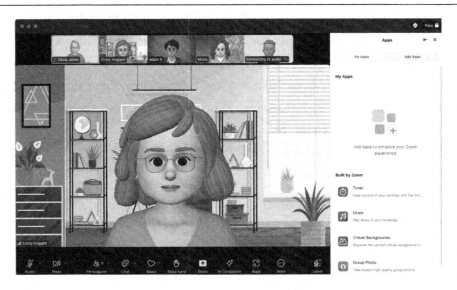

For example, if I wanted to use a survey tool to capture participant evaluation feedback at the end of a virtual class, in the past, I would have shared the survey link with participants via chat. They would then have to click the link, leave the virtual classroom, open their browsers, and submit responses. Now, I can use same survey tool via an integrated app inside the virtual classroom, so participants can take the external survey with the same ease as typing in chat or responding to a poll question.

Today, there are thousands of apps available for virtual classrooms, and that number is increasing every day. From enhanced whiteboard tools to more robust polling features, these apps expand the capabilities of the virtual platform.

For instance, in a recent virtual class, my participants wanted to take a group photo to commemorate their time together. In the past, this meant saying "1, 2, 3, smile!" and capturing a screenshot. And it might take a few tries to get everyone to look at the camera with a smile. But now, there's an integrated app that lets you send a photo request to each participant. They can choose whether to participate, check their camera settings, approve their self-portrait, and retake it if necessary. The app then combines each person's entry into the group photo, creating the appearance of a one-time screenshot. What used to be a cumbersome process now offers easy options for everyone.

Then there are apps that bring virtual and augmented realities to life inside a virtual classroom. Instead of making participants exit the platform to experience an immersive learning scenario, the scene comes to life inside it. Participants can stay focused on learning instead of the intricate and potentially confusing instructions they would need if they had to navigate to an external site.

When evaluating virtual classroom platforms, find out if integrated apps are available, and if so, which ones. Ask questions about any extra costs associated with them, as well as any other settings or restrictions that would get in the way of their use.

Accessibility Features

When comparing virtual platforms, consider their accessibility features. These essential tools support everyone's ability to participate in the learning experience, helping you reach a more diverse remote audience. Settings such as screen reader support, keyboard shortcuts, high-contrast settings, and closed-captioning all contribute to an accessible environment (Figure 2-11).

Figure 2-11. Accessibility Settings in Zoom

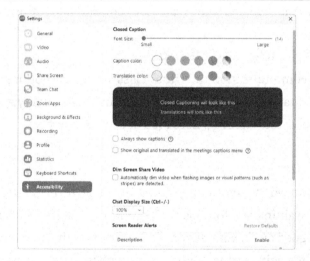

For example, some platforms let you "pin" someone's video to a certain spot on the screen. This feature is helpful if you have a sign-language interpreter for learners who are deaf or hearing impaired. Other platforms have built-in keyboard shortcuts to zoom in and magnify areas of the screen, which helps learners with limited vision. High-contrast options can also help people see the screen more clearly. Additionally, you may find choices for how screen readers interact with the platform (such as which notifications are ignored), granular control over chat and closed-captioned displays, and multilingual support for non-native language speakers.

If your organization is planning to use a platform's language translation capabilities, find out if it's automated through the system or requires a live translator. These subtle differences may determine whether the feature will be useful for you and your participants.

Another tool that may not seem to relate to accessibility but has a definite influence, is the use of video avatars. We'll explore the details of this feature later in the book, but for now, note that avatars allow participants to show up on video for social connection and visual cues without showing their human face. Avatars—which can look realistic or more cartoonish—have virtual eyes that blink and mouths that move to mimic facial expressions while keeping the real person behind the camera hidden from view. This feature provides a way for neurodiverse learners who may not otherwise turn on their cameras to feel comfortable participating.

The importance of accessibility features in virtual classrooms cannot be stressed enough. Virtual training can be accessible to all when it's designed and facilitated well and uses a platform that expands your reach to accommodate a more diverse audience.

Quality Media: Audio and Video

Without two-way communication, a virtual class would be nothing more than a recorded video presentation. Therefore, clear audio and high-quality video contribute to the very essence of virtual training. Let's look at each one in turn.

Telephony Audio

Telephony (pronounced "tel-**eh**-foh-nee") is a broad IT term referring to the overall audio of a virtual training session. It's the behind-the-scenes technology that makes the audio work. A good audio connection allows for smooth verbal communication—a key component of engaging virtual training. Through telephony, a participant can hear the facilitator and talk with fellow class participants.

There are two types of audio connections in most virtual platforms: an actual telephone that's integrated with the virtual platform and computer audio (officially called Voice over Internet Protocol or VoIP). If you use a technology solution that requires traditional telephone conference calling, participants will need a reliable landline connection and a headset for hands-free use. If you use VoIP, each participant's device will need a sound card with speakers and a microphone or a headset that combines these two. In the past, some platforms required all attendees to either join by phone or use computer audio; today, each participant can choose the best connection for their situation.

Figure 2-12. Audio Choices in Zoom

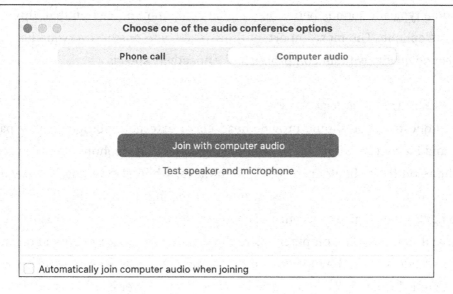

Integrated telephony and conference calling means that the audio and visual components of the virtual class are connected behind the scenes. Participants use their telephones to dial into the audio portion of the call, but the audio commands (such as mute and unmute) can be controlled through the classroom's web platform. Features that use audio, such as breakout rooms, are available to all. It's easy to tell who is speaking at any given moment, provided the platform includes this feature.

Computer (VoIP) audio is currently the most used type of audio connection. It's readily available on most devices, and there is typically no additional cost. Unfortunately, the drawback of computer audio is that it can take up extra internet bandwidth space. In some cases, this can cause considerable quality issues and choppy sound connections.

When using VoIP, the visual and audio portions of the call use the same internet connection, which means that all communication will be lost at the same time if the internet connection fails. For example, if the facilitator's internet unexpectedly drops, they can't continue until they've reconnected to the internet. If the facilitator had been using a telephone for the audio connection, they could at least continue talking with participants and let them know what was happening while they're reconnecting.

Which audio connection type is best? It depends on the virtual platform software you're using, the internet bandwidth speeds available to participants, and your budget. In locations where the bandwidth is unstable, but the telephone system is reliable, conference calling may be a better choice than computer audio. If built-in VoIP includes noise canceling and other quality features, computer audio may be the best choice. The audio typically sounds better on a digital computer connection than through an analog telephone. The most important thing is to try to ensure everyone has crystal clear sound quality without compromising connectivity speeds.

Headsets and Microphones

Without question, you should provide headsets or external microphones for participants and facilitators. If participants are using an actual telephone, they can't cradle the phone on their shoulder for 60 to 90 minutes, while also typing and frequently engaging in a class. It's not a pleasant image or feeling. By investing in better audio equipment, you will give everyone the chance to focus on the learning experience.

In addition, built-in computer microphones are often poor quality and can be a source of audio echo if the input area picks up the surrounding output and causes disruptive audio feedback. You've experienced this if you've ever heard a piercing echo on a conference call or virtual meeting.

Avoid using speakerphones, which can give off an echo, pick up extraneous noises, and generally do not sound good in a virtual classroom. Participants who use speakerphones in an office setting may also distract their neighbors. This is true whether the participant is using a telephone or a device with speakers.

Video and Webcams

Most virtual platforms are now video-first. In other words, the platform expects each participant to connect both audio and video upon joining the online room. The first visible screen after clicking the connection link is an audio and video check—like an actor's green room—so everyone can test and adjust their camera settings.

Using webcams creates a sense of connection among remote attendees if it's done with intention at the right times. For example, at the start of a virtual class, when everyone is meeting one another for the first time, images help encourage relationships. If you've ever heard someone's voice on the phone and pictured them in your mind, only to someday discover that they look completely different than you imagined, then you know the power of both seeing and hearing another person while they are speaking. Webcams also help create a learning experience that goes beyond the two-dimensional screen. Video incorporates multiple senses, which adds depth to discussions because you can see someone using their hands and observe their facial expressions while they talk.

Webcams also allow participants to use filters and virtual backgrounds, which expand their ability to express themselves (Figure 2-13). In one of my virtual classes, participants worked in teams throughout the program on a continuous case study. After the first breakout activity, one group returned to the main room with matching virtual backgrounds. They put together a team identity, adding an element of fun and a sense of shared experience to the program. After seeing the first team do it, most of the other groups copied the idea, fostering shared accountability and contributing to higher engagement levels in the program.

Figure 2-13. Video Settings in Zoom

To overcome the problems of webcams taking up too much internet bandwidth and participants feeling unnatural on camera, many virtual platforms have added new video features. Some allow for lower-resolution video that takes up less bandwidth, while others have a "focus mode" that reduces the number of video streams on view. To help avoid and overcome video fatigue, some platforms include the ability to hide your video (while still seeing everyone else); others incorporate immersive views that create more realistic video scenes (Figure 2-14).

When evaluating platforms for your organization, consider how streaming video will be used and look for robust options that allow for the best communication among all participants.

Figure 2-14. Example Immersive View in Zoom

The Challenges of Webcam Use

Industry experts have debated the increased use of webcams in virtual training and participant expectations for doing so. Some argue that a requirement to be on camera is too invasive and evokes privacy concerns. Others cite studies on video fatigue, while others share concerns over accessibility for neurodiverse learners who don't want to be in the spotlight. These are all valid concerns. And while there isn't one right answer, it's worth noting that solutions exist for each one.

The bottom line is that webcam use should never be required except in rare circumstances, like remote test-taking when visual validation is necessary. That's not to say that cameras shouldn't be encouraged and even expected in virtual classrooms, which is slightly different than requiring them.

Here are some solutions for overcoming webcam challenges:

- To help with privacy concerns, look for platforms that allow for artificial virtual backgrounds or blurred screens, and make sure participants know how to use these features.
- To overcome video fatigue, only use cameras at specific points during the virtual class, such as during small group breakouts or large group debrief discussions. Get everyone comfortable with toggling their cameras on and off during the program.
- To help neurodiverse learners or others who learn better with their cameras off, show them how to use features like hide self-view or video avatars, which help mask a participant's onscreen presence.

Sufficient Internet Bandwidth

Hardware, software, audio, and video all come together over the internet to create a virtual training class. Therefore, you must factor internet connectivity into the technology equation. Without stable, reliable connections with suitable bandwidth for your needs, your virtual training program will not be successful.

The internet bandwidth availability for each participant should be broad enough to support all class activities. There is nothing more frustrating for a facilitator, producer, or participant than when the participant is continuously disconnecting from the platform because their internet connection is not strong enough. The participant gets annoyed and wastes time re-logging in. The facilitator or producer often has to stop and work with that person to get them reconnected. Other participants also may be negatively affected if they have to wait for everything to get back on track. An even worse scenario is if a participant has trouble seeing the screen or keeping track of what's going on because of their limited bandwidth. That experience, from the participant's point of view, is extremely irritating. It's like knowing that everyone else is eating a tasty meal while they're stuck with the leftover crumbs.

Some software platforms have settings that can help with bandwidth challenges (Figure 2-15). For example, built-in bandwidth buffers can play the audio at the same download rate as the participant's bandwidth. Other platforms allow the host to change meeting room connectivity speeds to match the anticipated internet bandwidth, and still others let the platform automatically adjust as needed.

Low bandwidth has several root causes, including:

- Participants are using a spotty, publicly shared Wi-Fi connection or have slow home connection speeds.
- Multiple participants are connecting at the same time from the same location.
- A virtual class makes heavy use of multimedia, such as sharing multiple video streams.
- Other software programs tie up available bandwidth.

The best way to combat bandwidth issues is to educate remote participants about how to make the most of their internet connections. There are several actions they can take to enhance it. If they are working from home, advise them to position their router in the best possible location for reception and to sit as close to it as possible. Better yet, provide ethernet cables so they can connect their computer directly to the router. Some home internet providers have an app that allows you to prioritize one device over another for certain timeframes; I use this feature frequently on my home network.

If participants struggle with connectivity, you can teach them how to pause other, non-essential apps that may be running in the background. For example, they can pause any routine backups to the cloud. And of course, if they are sharing internet bandwidth with others under the same roof, they could politely ask those people not to initiate large file transfers during class time.

Finally, make sure you thoroughly test your program's internet connectivity by replicating the exact conditions under which it will be needed. Run it at the same time of day and with a similar number of users, and make use of any features that will help control bandwidth.

Figure 2-15. Meeting Preferences in Adobe Connect

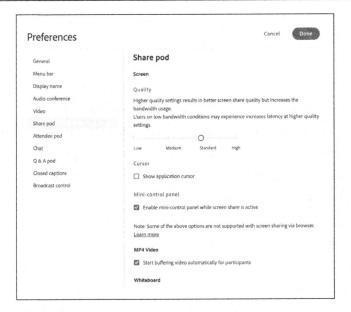

Partnering With IT to Select Technology

"IT Is From Venus, Non-IT Is From Mars" was the headline of an April 2012 *Wall Street Journal* article, and it's still just as relevant today. The author, George Westerman, a research scientist at the Massachusetts Institute of Technology, studied communication between IT departments and other parts of organizations. He recommended, among other things, increased communication and transparency. This truth certainly can be applied to the relationship between training professionals and IT, especially in the case of virtual learning programs. The more communication and transparency you have with the IT department, the more successful your virtual training implementation will be.

In most organizations, IT has control over which software programs are used. Even in a bring-your-own-device work environment, where employees can use personal technology for work-related tasks, the IT department grants access to company systems and software programs. Therefore, you must establish a good relationship with IT decision makers and discuss your virtual training requirements with them. If the IT department purchases a web-based platform, you want it to fit the organization's training needs.

Virtual trainers frequently tell me their IT departments make all the decisions about what software they use. For example, they'll say, "Our IT department purchased the meeting version of the virtual software, and I'm trying to convince them to upgrade to the training version." Nip this problem in the bud by working with the IT team to make a purchasing decision that's right for everyone.

"Partnering with IT can make or break you. You need their support and buy-in to be successful with virtual training."

—Wendy Gates Corbett, author, researcher, and
former Global Training Director

So, you're probably wondering, "How do I partner with IT?" or "How do I create a working relationship with someone?" The best way to build a trusting relationship is to start communicating and listening. Find a person in the IT group who is willing to partner with you and invite them to discuss your common goals and needs.

When training professionals look for software solutions, they often look at the features and benefits first. They'll ask, "What can the software do to help our participants learn?" "Does it have such-and-such feature that we need?"

However, IT may have a different perspective. They'll likely ask questions such as:
- Will it work with our existing systems? Is it compatible?
- Will we buy and install it, or will it be hosted by a vendor?
- If we buy it, who will install it? Maintain it? Support it?
- If it's hosted, will the hosting company protect our data?
- What IT resources—initially and ongoing—will be needed?

When you partner with IT to make your hardware and software selections, you will end up with a choice that appeals to both sides. You will also foster a working partnership that will strengthen your virtual training implementation.

> *"When deciding upon a software solution for training, check to see what already exists in the organization. You may discover a solution in use by another area that would fit your need without having to make an additional purchase. Or if an existing solution does not quite fit because it's lacking a feature or doesn't do what you want, then work with IT and the rest of the organization to find a solution that is a better fit for all parties."*
>
> —Tracy Stanfield, Associate VP, Information Technology, CRB

One Organization's Story
Creating a Conversational Network

Ken Hubbell was the senior manager of learning technology at Ingersoll Rand, a machine manufacturer, for more than seven years. "When we first started, our learning group did not talk to IT," he told me. "And IT only came to us when we pushed bandwidth limits. We had very little communication, and then only if there were problems."

Ken realized it would be better to create a conversational network among three departments—IT, communication, and learning. He saw that they all used the same tools and thought it would make sense to talk about them.

"It's important for us to 'sing off of the same song sheet' and not place demands on the system at the same time," he explained.

So, he invited representatives from each group to meet monthly. This opened a conversation around their departments' needs, desires, and shared goals. It also led to the creation of a technology forecast, which helped ensure that the learning function wasn't getting too far ahead of IT. The group looked at where they were in the present, where they would be in a year, and where they wanted to be further in the future. Their goals were to be ready, informed, and aligned.

Selecting a Technology Vendor

Figuring out which virtual platform to use is like choosing which car to buy. They all have similar features, and everyone has a personal preference. So, if you're selecting a virtual classroom platform from scratch—meaning your organization doesn't currently have a provider—do what you would do when purchasing a new vehicle: Research, shop around, ask for recommendations, read user reviews, take a few test drives, and sit in the passenger seat as well as the driver seat. In other words, take your time deciding, make sure you experience the platform from both the facilitator's and the participant's views, and ask them for their recommendations and advice.

You can research and compare platforms in several ways:

- Participate in sessions offered by vendors—most offer free sessions to help you learn about their platform's features.
- Sign up for trial versions of the platforms you're considering—most offer 30-day trials.
- Search the web for comparative information.
- Check in with colleagues in similar organizations who may have similar learning needs.

People often ask me, "What's the best platform on the market today?" or "Which platform should we choose?" My answer is always the same: "It depends." And again, it's like purchasing a vehicle—each version serves the same basic purpose, just with varying styles and options.

My best advice is to start by listing all the features you need in a virtual platform. Do you need breakout groups so that you can have small group activities? Do you need robust video streaming with customizable virtual backgrounds? Do you need a private chat option for the type of communication you plan to use? Do you need it to be compatible with a specific LMS or LXP? All these questions will help you narrow down which virtual training platform is the best fit for your organization.

Another consideration will be whether you plan to partner directly with the platform provider or go through a third-party reseller. Resellers typically offer additional services to support the programs, such as training, technical support, and event management. They may also package audio conferencing and web conferencing into one bundled solution.

The decision to use a third-party vendor versus going straight to a platform vendor will depend on your organization's overall web conferencing needs. If you need both audio and web conferencing, for example, third-party vendors often provide integrated solutions. But you may not need all the services offered through the bundles. Research thoroughly and decide appropriately.

When partnering with any vendor, whether a software company or a reseller, use the following common-sense guidelines:

- Create a request for proposal (RFP), formally or informally, to document what you need and want from a vendor solution.
- Invite a company representative to demonstrate their software.
- Request a trial version of the program.
- Ask for client references and contact them for details.

When you have selected the right platform, you will be able to design, deliver, and implement virtual training classes tailored to it.

One Organization's Story
Choosing the Right Platform

When Stephan Girard, director of workforce development at PMMI, was searching for a virtual training platform, he had two big selection criteria. First, the cost had to fit within the budget. The investment needed to be the right amount based on the organization's planned use of the platform. Second, because the participants would come from many organizations and have various computer configurations, Stephan had to assume they might not have administrative rights to install software. Therefore, another criterion was that participants wouldn't need software downloads or plug-ins. Facilitators could install software, but participants wouldn't have to.

By homing in on these two important items, Stephan was able to narrow down his choices and work with a vendor to select the right solution for PMMI.

In Summary: Key Points From Chapter 2

- Partner with your organization's IT department to make technology decisions.
- Carefully consider hardware and software needs for facilitators, producers, and participants. Equip them with what they need for virtual training success.
- One of your most important decisions will be choosing which vendor's product you will use for virtual training. Will it be a meeting product or a training product? Select the one that's most closely aligned with your definition of virtual training.
- Most platforms have similar, not identical, features and tools. Find out what's available on your platform.
- Test internet bandwidth for all facilitators and participants to ensure the best connectivity.

Take Action

✓ Analyze the platform your organization is using for virtual training. Talk with your stakeholders—including designers, facilitators, producers, and participants—about their experience with the platform. Is it easy for everyone to use? Does it provide all the necessary functions?

✓ Conduct an internet speed test at various times of the day for facilitators, producers, and participants. Do they have sufficient bandwidth to fully participate in the online learning experience?

Tool 2-1. Technology Requirements for Facilitators and Producers

Use this checklist for the ideal technology setup for facilitators and producers of a virtual training program.

Hardware
- ☐ Computer or laptop with specs that exceed minimum requirements of the selected virtual classroom platform
- ☐ Second computer or laptop as backup
- ☐ External monitor

Software
- ☐ Host account for virtual classroom platform
- ☐ Up-to-date app downloads or plug-ins for a virtual platform

Audio and Video
- ☐ Wired noise-canceling headset or external microphone
- ☐ Reliable VoIP or telephone connection*
- ☐ External HD webcam
- ☐ Adjustable lighting (ring light or LED panel)

Internet Connection
- ☐ Speed test for appropriate bandwidth*

*Note that facilitators and producers may also need to plan for redundancies in internet connection in case of unexpected technical issues. For example, a facilitator working from a home office should have a back-up device (such as a smartphone) and an alternative internet connection (such as a mobile Wi-Fi hotspot).

Tool 2-2. Technology Requirements for Participants Checklist

Use this checklist to identify the technology participants should have for a virtual training program.

Hardware

☐ Computer, laptop, or mobile device (compatible with platform)

Software

☐ Up-to-date app downloads or plug-ins for the virtual platform

Audio and Video

☐ Wired noise-canceling headset or external microphone

Webcam

☐ Adjustable lighting (ring light or LED panel)

Internet Connection

☐ Speed test for appropriate bandwidth

Other

☐ Accessibility tools, if needed (such as screen readers or alternative input devices)

Tool 2-3. Checklist for Selecting a Virtual Training Platform

Features	Supplier 1	Supplier 2	Supplier 3	Supplier 4
Platform Features				
Shared document file type requirements	☐	☐	☐	☐
Media file playback (audio and video)	☐	☐	☐	☐
Chat	☐	☐	☐	☐
Annotation or drawing privileges	☐	☐	☐	☐
Whiteboard features	☐	☐	☐	☐
Polling	☐	☐	☐	☐
Raise hand and reactions	☐	☐	☐	☐
Breakout groups	☐	☐	☐	☐
Integrated apps	☐	☐	☐	☐
Other	☐	☐	☐	☐
Audio and Video Features				
VoIP or integrated conference calling	☐	☐	☐	☐
Desirable audio settings	☐	☐	☐	☐
Webcam streaming	☐	☐	☐	☐
Desirable video settings	☐	☐	☐	☐
Other Features				
Compatible with mobile devices (for participants)	☐	☐	☐	☐
Able to include multiple hosts and facilitators	☐	☐	☐	☐
Immersive tools available	☐	☐	☐	☐
Compatible with your organization's LMS or LXP	☐	☐	☐	☐
Internet bandwidth considerations	☐	☐	☐	☐
Other Considerations Unique to Your Organization				
	☐	☐	☐	☐
	☐	☐	☐	☐
	☐	☐	☐	☐

CHAPTER 3

Design Content

 In this chapter, you will learn how to design effective virtual training:
- Consider three components that will affect virtual design decisions.
- Apply a three-step virtual training design model.
- Incorporate five key design principles into every virtual class.

Virtual training has a reputation as a not-very-engaging way to learn. I think that's because people have attended too many lecture-style webcasts or haven't interacted meaningfully with others online.

Your organization's success with virtual training will depend on having well-designed learning programs. That means a design that engages participants, creates a comfortable space where they can learn, and helps them apply new skills. Good design is about more than just posting slides online and clicking through them while someone talks. It's about creating a high-quality learning experience.

To keep this book within the boundaries of a reasonable scope, I'm not going to address the entire instructional design process in this chapter. Whether you use ADDIE, SAM, or another instructional design model, they all share one thing in common: a business problem to solve (or on the positive side, a business opportunity to capitalize on). The most effective learning designs align with the organization's needs, which have been determined through a needs analysis process.

I will assume that you or someone associated with your organization has gone through the needs analysis process to confirm that training is the appropriate solution. You have identified the business problem or opportunity, recognized the knowledge or skills gap, and written the learning objectives. In the case of converting an existing training curriculum to an online program, someone should have ensured that the classroom program is still in alignment with business needs. Along the way, I also assume your organization concluded that virtual learning was the best modality. Now it's time to design for an online environment. This chapter will specifically focus on what's *unique* about designing virtual training programs.

We'll start with an overview of best practices in virtual training design principles, and then review a three-step design process. I'll also offer tips for converting traditional courses to the online classroom and review the five key elements that belong in every engaging virtual program. Let's start by establishing a few fundamentals.

Virtual Training Design Basics

At the start of a design project, review your definition of virtual training to ensure you're approaching the project in a way that aligns with that definition. While that may seem obvious and unnecessary, it's easy to stray outside the lines when designing learning solutions. By revisiting your definition and making intentional choices, you will set the foundation for a meaningful, high-quality learning experience for all participants.

In chapter 1, you learned about the different types of live online events. Naturally, the design of a 15-person virtual training class will be different from the design for a 75-person webinar. And the design for a small virtual meeting will differ from the design for a webcast with 2,000 people.

> *"When someone comes to our design team with a training request, we conduct a needs assessment to determine our design approach. Based on the topic, the logistics, and the audience, we design different types of virtual experiences. We set expectations of what the learners will receive, from a webinar that has very little participation to an extremely interactive blended solution that includes engaging virtual classes. We distinguish between webinars and virtual training based on the level of interactivity and how immersed the participant will be in the learning."*
> —Peggy Page, former Learning and Development Manager, TD Bank

Next, you'll want to remember four overarching design considerations for each virtual training session: audience size, frequency of interaction, timing, and accessibility.

Audience Size

Most facilitated training classes are small to allow for meaningful discussion and expert feedback on skill practices. Over the years, I've asked thousands of global trainers to share their typical training class sizes, and most say they tend to be under 25 participants (Huggett 2024).

One advantage of using an online learning environment is the ability to scale and reach a larger audience. Virtual platforms allow for hundreds and even thousands of participants to connect at one time. But just because you *can* put hundreds of people into a virtual training class, doesn't mean you *should*.

In his well-regarded book, *Brain Rules,* John Medina (2014) advocates for smaller class sizes because they provide better learning environments. A teacher can pay more attention to each student, which usually contributes to better student performance. We can apply the same education principle to the virtual classroom—the smaller the class size, the better the learning outcomes.

There are certainly times when a substantial number of participants in an online session is a good thing. If your goal is to present information in a webcast format, with one or two people presenting and doing all the talking, then this type of online meeting can help you achieve economies of scale. For example, if your sales organization wants to announce a new product on the market, it makes sense to broadcast this information to the largest audience possible. Or, if your organization holds a town hall meeting with its worldwide workforce, a large-scale event would be appropriate. If you bring in a panel of SMEs to share their latest findings on a topic of interest to a large audience, make use of virtual event technology to make it happen. Remember, however, our definition of virtual training. You must distinguish between these large webcast events and virtual training classes. There is a difference.

If a training class is designed for 20 people, that means it's designed for 20 people whether it's in person or virtual. If you increase participant numbers, you'll likely lose interactivity, discussion opportunities, and the ability to easily coach participants on new skills. Don't upsize the training just because you can. Upsize only when it makes sense to do so—if the topic permits and your design allows for it. For virtual training, my recommendation is to keep your class numbers to a manageable level—ideally less than 25 participants.

Designing for Hybrid Learning

In a standard virtual training class, every participant joins from a remote location. In a hybrid class, some participants are together in person and others are remote. Chapter 1 described the different types of hybrid learning and the pros and cons of this format.

In a *traditional hybrid program*, the design principles are almost identical to an in-person traditional classroom program because most participants are together, but you will need to make a few modifications to include the remote audience. For example, you might start with an opening activity that specifically pairs each remote learner with someone on-site. In the case of a *remote-centric hybrid program*, the design principles are essentially the same as for a fully virtual class with a few modifications to recognize that some participants are together sharing an audio connection.

There are two additional considerations to ponder when designing a hybrid learning event. First, invite everyone to connect individually to the virtual classroom to ensure a similar learning experience for all participants regardless of location. This way, everyone can type in the chat, select reactions, respond to polls, and use the whiteboard. It also allows you to design activities that use those tools.

Second, when planning breakout activities, try to mix the in-person attendees with the remote attendees. It may take a little extra logistical setup time to make this work well, such as reserving another meeting room for the in-person participants to use during small group activities. However, it's worth the effort to help bridge the gap between the on-site and off-site learners.

Frequency of Interaction

Virtual training must engage participants through frequent, meaningful activities that keep their attention. And it's not only about frequent interaction. Responding to one poll question after another will get boring fast, so it's important to be mindful of the variety of interactions and the creative use of virtual tools in your course design. The overall goal isn't interactivity for the sake of it; it's about going deeper to create a purpose-filled learning environment. It's not about keeping participants busy; it's about engaging them in the learning and application process.

Based on what we know about adult learners and our own experiences, there is only so much lecture information anyone can absorb at one time. And lecturing is one of the least effective ways to teach a new skill. When was the last time you paid full attention to a lengthy lecture? If you responded "recently," did that single lecture increase your skills or make you an expert in that topic? Probably not. Most adults learn best through firsthand interaction and practice over time.

A study by physics Nobelist Carl Wieman and a team at the University of British Columbia compared results between learners who listened to lectures and those who participated in an interactive lesson. The differences were dramatic, and the study confirmed that "learning only happens when you have . . . intense engagement" (Mervis 2011).

On top of these truths about adult learning, let's now add the virtual classroom environment. Your virtual participants are surrounded by distractions and competing priorities, especially when they must stay at their desks and use their own devices. Their potentially short attention spans combined with the inevitable distractions can be a recipe for virtual training disaster.

But don't worry—it's possible to create an engaging and successful virtual training program. If you've created a well-designed virtual learning experience, participants can stay fully engaged, learn something new, and apply these new skills on the job. My favorite compliment to receive from a participant in one of my virtual training classes is, "I was so engaged that I didn't have time to check my email." You can achieve this enthusiastic response through a design with frequent, meaningful interactions.

We'll talk much more about helping participants manage their own distractions in chapter 7. For now, let's stay focused on what we can do in our program design to create an interactive learning environment.

Most experienced virtual designers will tell you that you should invite participants to interact every few minutes through virtual tools, with another participant, or with the facilitator. Frequent interaction means the participants are continually involved in their own learning—not just listening to someone else speak.

A foremost authority on participant-centered learning, the late Bob Pike, wrote in his *Creative Training Techniques Handbook* that participants in the in-person classroom "can listen with understanding for 90 minutes, listen with retention for 20 minutes, and that we need to involve them every eight minutes." When applying this same principle to the virtual classroom, he cut this time in half and advised involving participants at least every four minutes (Pike 2011). My own experience in designing and delivering thousands of virtual classes over the last two decades confirms the benefits of frequent interaction.

This principle is rooted in brain research as well as practical experience. Another of John Medina's brain rules is that "people don't pay attention to boring things" (2014). In other words, participants will check out at least every 10 minutes unless you give them compelling reasons to stay tuned into your class. Consider the fact that learners have a hard time paying attention to the multitude of extra distractions in their own environments, and you will realize that frequent, meaningful activities are a must in the virtual classroom.

The bottom line is that your virtual classes should have maximum interaction, with something happening at least every few minutes. These interactions don't need to be lengthy or involved, and they shouldn't feel like interruptions or distractions. For example, you can try a quick check-in, such as, "What's one word you would use to describe this concept? Enter it into the chat." or "Raise your hand if you agree with this statement." These simple touchpoints help keep participants connected to the platform and content.

Timing

I'm frequently asked about the ideal length for a virtual training program, especially in the context of converting traditional in-person classes to a virtual curriculum. Designers often try to move day-long programs (which are typically seven or eight hours long) online. But imagine this timing from a participant perspective: Would you want to spend hours upon hours sitting at a desk, glued to the computer, and interacting every few minutes? Most people couldn't sustain their attention span for that long, even with the most interesting content. To keep participants fresh, comfortable, and open to learning, virtual sessions should happen in short bursts of highly interactive time; 45 to 60 minutes is ideal, and 90 to 120 minutes is the maximum. Designing for this length of time also helps you avoid triggering cognitive overload. When the training curriculum is chunked into manageable pieces, participants are better able to learn and retain content.

If you have a lot of content that requires more time to cover, break the program into short chunks and sequence them into a series of events. For example, schedule part 1 from 8:30 to 10 a.m., give participants an assignment to complete from 10 to 11 a.m., and then reconvene from 11 a.m. to 12:30 p.m., repeating this process throughout the day. The participants' calendars will be blocked off for the entire eight-hour timespan, but the facilitated online learning events will be spread out. And the in-between assignments give participants a chance to continue learning and practicing through self-directed activities.

Always include a break when sessions are on the longer side (90–120 minutes). If you don't schedule an official physical and mental break at least every 45 to 60 minutes, your participants will take one anyway. They will check out when they need to, and depending on when that is, they could miss the most important learning point of the session. So, design your programs with an eye on the clock and your participants' attention spans. For example, in the middle of my virtual classes, I often ask participants to move their bodies and stretch and then raise their hands in the platform to indicate they are ready to continue. This brief physical and mental break takes only a few seconds, but everyone returns to the session refreshed. In a longer session, I'll set an onscreen timer with music for five minutes—I'll invite everyone to pause their webcam and step away from their devices as long as they stay connected to the platform. When the timer ends, so does the break.

Because virtual training classes are often part of a blended learning journey, the overall curriculum might contain several short sessions strung together over time paired with asynchronous activities and other components. The program run time may total many hours, but they're spread out with plentiful breaks in between. For instance, a cohort might meet for two hours each afternoon on Tuesday, Wednesday, and Thursday, or they might meet for 90 minutes at 10 a.m. on six consecutive Fridays.

If you are converting an in-person training program to a virtual classroom, know that your overall class time probably will be shorter. The platform's tools usually help virtual classes move at a faster pace, which also helps keep participants engaged in the learning content. Your timeframes will also be shorter for most of the in-person exercises you convert to the virtual classroom. For example, a traditional class activity might call for participants to watch a brief software demonstration, answer questions about what they saw, and then try it on their own. This classroom sequence might take 45 minutes. In the virtual classroom, however, you can ask the same questions via polling and display multiple polls onscreen at the same time—now the activity may only take 20 to 30 minutes. Or, in a traditional class, you might have participants go around the room and introduce themselves one by one, which could take upwards of 20 minutes. Participants in the virtual classroom, on the other hand, can type their introductions simultaneously into the chat window, cutting the time required down to two minutes.

Accessibility

Accessibility is often an afterthought in training. It's not an intentional slight, but it happens when we haven't learned how to fully accommodate a variety of learners. For example, a designer might create a slide deck and then run it through an automated accessibility checker during final edits. While this isn't a bad thing to do, a better choice is to design for accessibility from the start. In other words, try to begin as you mean to end—creating a virtual learning experience that's available to all who need it.

For virtual training, this means that you should:

- **Determine in advance that accessibility is an important goal.** Don't wait until the end of the design phase to consider your learners and what they might need to fully participate in the experience—lead with this thought. Including accessibility as an initial goal means it will be on everyone's minds from the start.

- **Invite conversations about accessibility by including a diverse group of stakeholders in planning and design testing.** The development of accessibility and inclusivity guidelines is still a new concept for many people, especially related to online events. We can learn from one another by discussing accessibility issues and looking for collaborative solutions.

- **Choose virtual classroom platforms and other online tools with built-in accessibility features.** In the previous chapter, we reviewed accessibility tools that can enhance an online learning experience and discussed the importance of choosing platforms with these features. Having access to these tools can mean the difference between participant success and failure.

- **Design learning exercises with accessibility in mind.** Consider the learner experience when making your initial choices about what topics and activities belong in the virtual classroom. For example, would a certain skills practice exercise work better as a self-directed assignment between virtual classes to accommodate neurodiverse learners? Also, think about the inclusiveness of your activities. Ask, would it be better for all your participants to write on a whiteboard or type in chat for a case study exercise?

A Virtual Training Design Model in Three Steps

Based on my experience designing hundreds of interactive virtual training classes over the past 20 years, I've developed and refined a three-step design process:

1. Select the best format for the content.
2. Shape appropriate learning activities.
3. Support the learning.

In this section, I'll break down each step in detail.

Step 1: Select the Best Format for the Content

For any training program to be successful, the learning outcomes must be paramount. What do learners need to know or do at the end of the program? What skills should they have? How should their behavior change? What do they need to start doing or stop doing?

By focusing on these outcomes, designers have a sense of what they should cover in the training curriculum. One way or another, the learning outcomes reveal what learners should accomplish. They establish a solid foundation for what content belongs in the learning experience. And they help differentiate between *need-to-know* and *nice-to-know* information.

Once you confirm the learning objectives, you can select the best format for each one. By format, I mean the basic design plan for the class or the delivery modality for each piece of content. When considering the format, I ask questions such as:

- What's the best way for a participant to learn the content?
- Could they read a job aid and gain enough understanding of the topic to act on it?
- Does the content warrant a discussion with a SME or practice in a simulated environment?

As you closely examine the content, decide what belongs in a facilitated virtual class versus what might translate better as asynchronous self-directed activities. In other words, will learners need a facilitator to help them or could they learn it on their own? Could participants read a case study as prework and then have a small group discussion about it during the class? Or could they watch a demonstration video on their own and come to class prepared to role-play the situation?

"Every time I design a virtual class I ask, 'What do the participants need to know to do their job?' Then, when looking at content and materials, I ask, 'Is it necessary for participants to do this in class? Where's the value?' If there is no value in doing it in a group setting, then there's no value in including it in the virtual class."

—Jennifer Newton, Instructional Designer

This is one of the greatest benefits of virtual training—flexibility. You can mix and match various learning formats into one comprehensive training curriculum, and you can combine asynchronous assignments with synchronous events to create a blended learning journey. No rule says you must put everything into one long continuous virtual training class. It's the opposite. You might have four virtual sessions that make up a series or two virtual sessions with a learning assignment in between, or any other combination of components. You can also break down larger pieces into smaller chunks of learning content and then arrange them in the best way possible.

This first step also recognizes the realities of modern learners. Many people are simply overwhelmed with work and have competing priorities that consume their time. It's difficult to stop in the middle of the workday and focus on learning, especially if people can't see the immediate benefit. It's not that learning isn't important to them; it's just not the most urgent concern. So, you're showing respect for your adult learners by only bringing them together for facilitated learning when necessary. When you let learners do as much as possible on their own and at times that are convenient for them, commitment levels are typically higher and the program is more likely to realize learning results.

In addition, by recognizing that some learning activities are more accessible when done offline, you'll create a better program. For example, a neurodiverse individual will be able to take more time to process new content when working offline. And a visually impaired learner can benefit from shorter bursts of collaboration with rest time in between.

If you are concerned that your learners won't complete the self-directed, asynchronous components, build in safeguards to overcome this challenge. For example, start with a facilitated kickoff session to set expectations and create social commitments. Clearly communicate requirements and time commitments. Include required knowledge checks that they must complete within a certain timeframe. Integrate facilitated sessions or coaching checkpoints throughout if it's a lengthy curriculum. Add knowledge checks and other assessments that learners must complete before moving on to the next step. And partner with the learners' managers to help with accountability.

I recently designed a change management curriculum that included three virtual classes and four self-directed application assignments. I spread the overall program across eight weeks to give participants time to apply what they were learning between each facilitated session. It started with a short, facilitated online orientation to establish expectations. I then used a learning experience platform for participants to track their progress over the course of the journey. The system sent reminders, and I held participants accountable for their learning. Some participants found the learning experience to be more challenging than others, but most appreciated its flexibility. Figure 3-1 provides an illustration of this program.

Figure 3-1. A Sample Blended Learning Journey

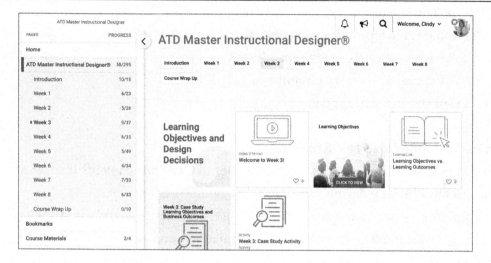

Converting Lengthy In-Person Classes Into Virtual Classes

"How do you convert a lengthy face-to-face class into a virtual one?" I hear this question frequently from designers. So, what should you do with a two-week orientation program? What about a six-week in-depth technical series?

No matter the starting point, you'll always follow the same process:

- Select the best format for the content.
- Shape appropriate learning activities.
- Support the learning.

I'd recommend breaking the virtual training class into many smaller chunks. For example, the two-week orientation may become 10 live online sessions with assignments in between. And the six-week technical series could become a short in-person class followed by virtual sessions and on-the-job coaching.

The possibilities are endless as long as you engage participants in their own learning using all available tools.

When this type of program design is done well, it's an art form. It's like a child's building block set that you can pull apart and put back together in dozens or hundreds of ways. As you build the curriculum, combine the learning chunks in ways that make the most sense for your learners and the content at hand. You can also include more application exercises, which lead to better learning transfer.

You should ask four main questions when choosing the most appropriate format for your content:

1. Do participants need to be together?
2. What is the type of learning objective?
3. What are the technology capabilities?
4. What are the trainees' circumstances?

Let's review these in more detail.

Do Participants Need to Be Together?

Would participants benefit from being together to learn this content? If so, then you may want to address it during a facilitated live online session.

Some topics are just more natural for participants to learn when they're together. Interpersonal skills such as communication and negotiation, for example, need to be practiced with someone else. Or learners might benefit from learning a specific topic in an synchronous live discussion with a facilitator or each other. Maybe the topic is complicated and requires significant explanation. Or the topic could be sensitive and result in emotional reactions that participants could talk through with others.

For example, a brand-new standard operating procedure will require participants to learn the procedure and be willing to stop following the old process. Because there may be some resistance to this change, you want participants to be able to discuss and mentally process the new procedure with others. If participants benefit from being together, it makes sense to put the content into a live online virtual session.

What Is the Type of Learning Objective?

Knowing the *type* of learning objective can give you some insight into which topics belong in the virtual session and which ones can be moved to another type of assignment or out of the curriculum.

If the learning objective only requires recognition or rudimentary comprehension, then it may not need to be covered during the live online class. Instead, it might fit better as a self-directed reading assignment or post-session activity. For example, if participants need to identify parts of a machine before they can operate it, they could learn this by watching a video before class or navigating through a self-paced lesson. Or if participants need to recognize which type of eye protection to wear when performing a specific maintenance task, they could learn to identify it by reading a job aid.

While it may sound complicated, you are probably familiar with this model of taking knowledge objectives out of the classroom. You may have had this experience while learning a technical skill like how to change a tire or drive a car. You first needed a general understanding of the basics, such as how to use a wrench or what the road signs mean, before you moved on to learning the actual skill required for the task. You may have acquired these fundamentals by reading a book, watching a video, or simply watching someone else do it. Armed with this prerequisite knowledge, you then continued to learn and perfect the skill through hands-on practice. For example, I picked up the basics of cooking (like how to measure ingredients and read a recipe) by spending time in my grandmother's kitchen and watching her work. But I really learned to cook once I started making meals for my own family.

To apply this principle to your virtual training design, look at the objectives to see what the participants need to know or understand. Do they have to identify parts of a spreadsheet to enter data? Or what form to use when a customer files a complaint? Or recognize which questions they can and cannot ask during a hiring interview? Consider turning these and other knowledge-only learning objectives into self-paced activities for participants to do on their own.

Of course, sometimes it makes sense to cover basic knowledge in a facilitated class. For example, if the topic is short, you can quickly review it during class time. Or if the concept is a little complicated, participants may benefit from being able to ask questions while learning.

When considering the types of learning objectives in your curriculum, remember that many virtual training classes are part of a blended journey. The knowledge-only objectives become asynchronous self-directed assignments, while the skill and application objectives are addressed during the live online virtual classroom sessions.

Effective Learning Objectives

The best learning objectives are ones that specifically tie to what the learners need to know or do on the job. According to Julie Dirksen's fantastic 2016 book, *Design for How People Learn*, well-written learning objectives should indicate "something the learner would actually do in the real world" so you can "tell when they've done it."

Even if you have a situation in which knowledge is the outcome, learners will usually still need to act upon that knowledge in some way. Therefore, the learning objectives should use action verbs. One sign of a weak learning objective is the use of "know" or "understand" because those actions can't be measured. Consider the difference between these examples:

> *At the end of this training session, the participant will know three techniques for responding to an upset customer.*

versus

> *At the end of this training session, the participant will be able to:*
> - *Recognize three techniques for responding to upset customers.*
> - *Select an appropriate technique based on an upset customer's situation.*
> - *Use the appropriate technique to respond to an upset customer.*

The second example is much richer, ties to what the learner would need to do on the job, and enables the designer to plan out in more detail what the training program needs to cover.

What Are the Technology Capabilities?

Next, consider your organization's technology capabilities, as well as those of your participants. Some of the virtual program design will be driven by these technology opportunities and limitations.

In the previous chapter, we addressed selecting a technology platform based on the organization's needs. The virtual training platform should not be a limitation. However, sometimes technology factors into the choices you make in a virtual program design. For example, if you want participants watch a live demonstration but internet bandwidth gets in the way of high-quality streaming video, you might need to find another option, such as showing screenshots while the facilitator talks through the topic. Or let's say you want participants to practice a new skill by role playing in small groups. If your virtual classroom platform does not support breakout groups, you might need to design the training as a blended curriculum, assigning small groups to meet on their own after a virtual class and then report back to the large group during the next session.

As we discussed in the previous chapter, to ensure that your technology capabilities match your training needs, partner closely with your organization's IT department to select and implement the appropriate technology.

What Are the Trainees' Circumstances?

The final important consideration in the design format is to think about the typical participants who will be in the virtual classes and design with them in mind. Do they have limited time available during the day to attend training? That restriction may influence the length of your sessions. You may decide it's better to hold three 75-minute sessions on the same day, with plenty of break time in between. Or your participants may benefit from having five 45-minute sessions spread out over several weeks.

If your participants are brand-new users of the virtual platform, make sure to include activities to help them learn how to use the tools. For example, use an opening activity to familiarize participants with the platform's simple annotation tools, and then introduce the more complicated electronic sticky note features later in the session.

Do some or all of your participants speak another language? If so, you might need to allow for extra reading and typing time during a session. Or you might need to include a glossary of terms along with the participant materials, and include time for learners to look up unfamiliar words before class.

To meet the needs of diverse learners, you may need to find ways to release control during the program, allowing them to learn on their own time, at their own pace, and in their own space. If your tech doesn't support accessibility requirements or you don't have the resources to create different activity streams for different learners, these limitations will factor into your design decisions.

For example, years ago, I hired a transcriptionist to caption the conversation during one of my virtual classes in real time. A certain breakout activity was essential to the learning outcomes, but I only had the budget for one person to transcribe the entire virtual class. Because this meant I wouldn't be able to transcribe more than one breakout room, I spent some time redesigning the activity as a two-part exercise. I started with a whiteboard and then gave an individual assignment for learners to complete during a 10-minute interlude before the next topic. As another option, I could have worked with my team to create a separate, self-paced e-learning module for this topic.

3 Conversion Mistakes

Designers make three common mistakes when converting traditional in-person training classes to the synchronous live online environment:

- **Taking an interactive in-person classroom session and turning it into a presentation-style webcast.** Just because participants are dispersed instead of together doesn't mean that your live online class should be a lecture. Remember what you know about adult learning principles and how to engage participants. Those guidelines apply to all types of training, including virtual.

- **Thinking that an eight-hour in-person class will become an eight-hour live online virtual session.** One minute of classroom time does not equal one minute of virtual time. Technology often saves you time, which is one of the many benefits of virtual training.
- **Inflating the number of participants in the live online class.** Most traditional in-person training classes are designed for small numbers of participants. Yet the temptation to vastly increase participant numbers in the equivalent live online class is difficult to resist. As I've said before, just because you *can* put hundreds of participants in an online classroom, doesn't mean you *should*.

Step 2: Shape Appropriate Learning Activities

Once you have determined what content to cover within each virtual training session, the next step is to shape the program by selecting appropriate activities that lead to learning and application.

The process of selecting activities for virtual training is like designing a traditional in-person class. You design a learning experience that incorporates adult learning methods and real-world application. You also motivate participants to learn by helping them see the importance of the content. You find learner-centered ways to present content and provide relevant practice opportunities. And finally, you focus on real-world application and learning transfer.

Again, this isn't a book on instructional design basics—so I'll assume you have foundational knowledge you can apply when selecting learning activities. If instructional design is not your strong suit, check out the resource list found at the end of this book.

What's important for our purposes in this chapter—and this section in particular—is what's *unique* about shaping an engaging virtual class. In short, it's the tools available to you in the virtual classroom platform (such as chat, polling, and breakout rooms) and how you use them to achieve the desired learning outcomes. It's also about holding remote participant attention despite many distractions and competing priorities surrounding them.

Ruth Colvin Clark and Ann Kwinn (2007) put it this way: "Virtual classroom software tools actually offer instructors more opportunities for frequent learner interactions than do most traditional classroom settings. Frequent and effective use of these response facilities is the single most important technique for successful virtual events." Review your learning outcomes and select the virtual classroom learning tools and methods that will enable participants to achieve them.

Let's say they need to learn how to resolve conflict in a team setting, and the learning objectives include how to "facilitate a dialogue" and "respond to emotional reactions." You would shape learning activities around these topics. Participants could learn by watching a facilitated demonstration, discussing their past experiences, and practicing real-world scenarios. Or they could review the steps, work through a case study, and then receive facilitator feedback on practice situations.

There's no single way to select activities that lead to good learning outcomes. Different designers create activities according to their own preferences and experiences. Just remember to design engaging activities that drive toward learning outcomes, not just busy work for the sake of interactivity. As we established earlier, interactive virtual classes should frequently engage participants. Use platform tools to involve participants in their own learning, and use your own creativity to design unique interactions. In addition, ensure that you incorporate the five principles of engaging design, which we'll cover later in this chapter. These key elements belong in every virtual class.

If you are converting an in-person class, some activities will be easy to translate into the live online environment. For example, a classroom paired discussion activity could become an online paired chat activity. Or a classroom competition between teams to answer questions could become an online competition using poll questions. And a live demonstration could become a live demonstration using screen sharing.

Always keep in mind that it's not just about keeping participants busy; it's about engaging them in the collaborative learning experience.

Learning Objectives in Converted Classes

If the in-person class you're converting to virtual doesn't have learning objectives or has learning objectives that don't describe what a participant needs to do on the job, go back to the analysis phase of your instructional design process to determine what your learners need to know or do.

In fact, it's always a good idea to quickly review the learning objectives of a traditional training program before converting it to a live online program. Check in with a SME to ensure that each objective is still valid. This brief review may uncover more significant challenges that you can address before converting to the live online format.

For example, when Danielle Buscher, former director of global learning at Marriott International, worked with her team to convert a traditional classroom curriculum to a blended one, they took the time to partner with SMEs to ensure the messages were engaging, relevant, and up to date. This step required extra design time, but it resulted in an exceptional virtual training program.

Be resourceful when designing activities for the live online classroom. Only your imagination and creativity limit your use of the tools. For example, if your hot potato activity usually involves tossing a foam ball from one participant to another, how could you do that in the virtual classroom? You might "toss" the virtual ball to the first person by typing their name in the chat window and then ask them to select the next person, and so on, until everyone has a turn.

Also, think about how participants can use the available tools. If you use PDF handouts, for example, have participants "raise their hand" when finished with an electronic worksheet exercise. When asking questions, direct participants to respond via reactions or chat. When surveying the group, create challenging poll questions to check for knowledge or get participants thinking. In an online survey compiled by virtual training expert Roger Courville, attendees rated multi-select polling as the most engaging activity in a virtual session, closely followed by single-select polling. (You'll find Roger's research on his website, thevirtualpresenter.com.) One implication of his study is that the design will be more engaging if you directly involve participants in the learning.

Table 3-1 outlines some ideas for using common virtual classroom tools. For illustrative purposes, I only provided one example of how each tool could be used in a coaching skills class. In reality, you could use these tools repeatedly and in various ways throughout an entire class.

Table 3-1. Ideas for Using Common Virtual Classroom Tools

Tool	Virtual Classroom Activity Idea for a Coaching Class
Share document	Open a document that contains a written script of a dialogue between a manager and an employee. Ask participants to use their annotation tools to highlight words and phrases that should not be used in a collaborative coaching conversation.
Chat	Post a poorly worded example of a manager's coaching statement onscreen and ask participants to rewrite the statement using coaching techniques they just learned.
Media	Show a short, prerecorded video example of a manager demonstrating a coaching skill that participants are learning. Before the video, ask participants to be on the lookout for specific examples of the skill used, and invite them to take notes on their handout or in the chat.
Whiteboard annotation	Ask participants to think of challenging statements employees might say in response during a collaborative coaching conversation. Have them type their responses on the screen. Then, categorize these statements by highlighting or some other indicator for use in discussion and a practice activity.

Table 3-1. (cont.)

Tool	Virtual Classroom Activity Idea for a Coaching Class
Reactions	Make a persuasive statement about coaching, and ask participants to indicate agreement or disagreement with the statement by choosing the appropriate status indicator ("raise hand" or "agree" or "disagree").
Poll	Post a list of challenging coaching situations, and ask participants to select any that they have experienced.
Breakout groups	Divide participants into groups of three. Assign a role-play exercise in which one person plays the manager, one plays the employee, and a third person observes. Have the observer take notes and lead a coaching conversation before the group switches roles, giving each person a chance to practice.

The next chapter provides more ideas for using virtual classroom tools.

Content Type

It doesn't matter what type of training you have to deliver—technical, interpersonal, or something unique to your organization—just about anything can be taught in the live online environment. It's possible to deliver technical training, software training, interpersonal skills training, communication skills, or even sales training using the virtual classroom. Here are some special design considerations for technical training and interpersonal skills training topics.

Technical Training

It may seem natural to use technology to deliver technical training. The connection seems obvious, doesn't it? However, the reality is not so simple. It's easy to conduct software demonstrations online and straightforward to show a website. Yet an engaging, interactive training program requires more than just watching a demonstration. Therefore, when delivering technical training in the virtual classroom, try the following tips:

- Show the software through screen share, demonstrating its features while asking participants to follow along and take guided notes on an electronic handout you have provided.
- Give a participant control of the cursor and let them drive the software.
- Take screenshots of the software. Ask participants, "Where should I click for the next step?" and have them use annotation tools to mark onscreen where they would click to perform a function.
- Use real-world (not hypothetical) examples. For instance, use the exact form template participants will use on the job instead of one you've created.

- Incorporate real-world stories to bring the content to life. For example, instead of "Click here to X," you can try, "Let's say Layla encounters a customer who needs ABC. The first step to help the customer is . . ."
- Use frequent polls and chat questions to check for comprehension.
- Use a virtual classroom platform that has a hands-on lab feature so multiple participants can use the software at the same time.
- Send participants into individual breakout rooms to complete hands-on practice exercises. Have them share their screens in the breakout rooms so the facilitator can see their work and jump into the different rooms to answer questions and assist when needed.

Interpersonal Skills

Conventional wisdom says you can't learn soft skills using hard devices. But that sentiment doesn't consider the collaborative nature of the virtual classroom. Given the tools available on most platforms—notably small group breakout rooms—meaningful dialogue and practice conversations can happen easily. So, don't shy away from delivering interpersonal skills topics in the virtual classroom. Try the following strategies:

- Ask participants to share their experience with the topic using poll questions or through small group discussion.
- Set up case study scenarios that participants can relate to, and ask them to weigh in on how they would approach the situations. Do this in both large and small group settings.
- Have participants use the whiteboard to brainstorm challenging ideas.
- Group participants in pairs or trios and use breakout rooms to practice new skills.
- Use immersive scenarios available via integrated virtual classroom apps.

Step 3: Support the Learning

The final step of the design process recognizes that there are other program components needed to ensure learning success. These components surround the facilitated virtual classes and support the learning outcomes.

You should consider the overall structure of the program from a big-picture perspective. Then, you'll need to create the program elements; for example, develop ancillary activities, create facilitator and participant materials, and include assessment methods.

Structure of the Program

There are two levels of structure to a virtual training curriculum: the big picture and the small details. The big-picture structure determines how many components make up the course, including the exact number of virtual sessions, any offline or self-directed participant assignments, and how these components fit together. At the detail level, you choose how the activities flow from one to the next, or the sequence of learning content within a session.

A typical virtual training class sequence begins with an overview of the content, an assessment, practice opportunities for participants, and application exercises for when they're back on the job. Each activity flows naturally from one to the next, in a logical progression for learning. If you have a lot of content—too much to put into one short virtual session—you should structure the curriculum into a series of sessions, as I mentioned earlier in the chapter. Sequence them in a logical progression. The amount of time between sessions depends on the topic and your audience. You could create three 60-minute sessions in a day with a 60-minute break between each one, or host 10 sessions spread out over 10 weeks. Of course, you'll structure the curriculum in the way that makes the most sense for your content, your participants, and your organization's needs.

Sequencing the Content

When sequencing learning events in a virtual class, I follow this simple structure:

- Introduce it.
- Practice it.
- Apply it.

If you are covering multiple topics, this three-part sequence would repeat over and over throughout the session. So, if participants are learning how to enter data into an online purchasing system, they would learn the fundamental process, then practice those steps, and then apply them to specific purchasing scenarios they encounter on the job. This helps avoid cognitive overload by allowing time to *practice* and *apply* before moving to the next topic. It also provides a chance for practice, which should lead to real-world use back on the job.

While this sequencing pattern is common for designing any type of learning experience, there is a nuance that's unique for virtual classes: the way you incorporate your virtual platform's interactive tools into the activity flow. For example, when introducing a topic, instead of asking questions for an open general discussion, it would be better to use directed poll questions for clarity.

Darlene Christopher, former knowledge and learning officer at the World Bank Group, used this introduction technique in one of her virtual training classes for managers. To spark a class discussion about what worked in the previous year's talent management process, she created a poll question asking participants to anonymously rate how successful they thought last year's process was using a 5-point scale. This gave the group a starting point for discussion, which then led everyone to share examples of how they had used the process. Darlene's design created much better learning outcomes than she would have gotten by just starting with the open question, "So what did everyone think about last year's talent management process?"

For practice, make liberal use of your platform's interactive tools for participant feedback opportunities. Learners could answer questions through the status indicators, a series of poll questions, or in a whiteboard activity. Or they could complete worksheet exercises on their own and compare answers with a partner.

Finally, for the application stage, participants could work together in breakout groups on scripted case studies. Or they could create their own practices based on previous experiences. You could place them into small groups for fishbowl-style activities or ask them to individually apply new skills and receive feedback from the facilitator. These are just a few examples of how to engage participants. Use your creativity and the ideas in the next chapter to come up with even more!

Once you have sketched out the flow of the class, it's important to look at it through your participants' eyes. Is there enough variety among platform tools? Does anything feel abrupt, or do you have gradual transitions from one activity to another? You don't want to create six poll questions in a row or ask participants to raise their hands repeatedly. Ask yourself and trusted stakeholders, is it accessible to all? Are there more ways you can increase accessibility while still meeting the learning outcomes?

The bottom line is that your sequence, while sharing commonalities with any type of training class, should foster an engaging learning experience for all participants. The success of your virtual training class will depend upon it.

Developing the Program

The next chapter will take a deep dive into developing your program, including how to use the platform tools for engagement. It will also cover creating program materials like facilitator guides, slides, and participant workbooks. These supporting elements enhance and enable learning and are critical components of the program.

One Organization's Story
The Nugget Approach to Online Learning

Dan Gallagher, former vice president of learning at Comcast and author of *The Self-Aware Leader*, converted a two-day traditional classroom-based performance management class to the live online environment. The new program included both virtual classes and self-study components. The live online sessions were held once per week for six weeks, and each one was 90 to 120 minutes long.

"We took the nugget approach," Dan said, "and we learned many lessons along the way.

"We had to redesign the classroom exercises for the virtual environment," he continued. "We kept the core learning model but added new activities and ways to engage the learners. While the delivered solution created efficiency for the learners, it increased the amount of work for the trainer and the project manager. We had to create additional documentation for the curriculum.

"Finally, we had to have influence over the class size to keep it to an appropriate level for the curriculum. It's key to manage class size. While you may be able to increase the numbers from a technical perspective, you can't from a learning perspective."

Five Key Design Principles That Belong in Every Virtual Class

Effective virtual classes engage participants, create a comfortable space for learning, and provide opportunities to apply new skills. They do this through a well-thought-out, intentionally planned design centered on learning transfer. If participants aren't paying attention and actively engaged in the learning experience, they won't be able to apply their new knowledge and skills on the job.

To ensure an engaging learning environment, you need to follow five essential design principles in every facilitated virtual class:

- Set expectations in advance.
- Start strong.
- Select activities for maximum involvement.
- Seek and sustain engagement.
- Create a social experience.

No matter the topic, class size, platform, or duration, these design principles will lead to higher participation levels, which in turn leads to better learning outcomes and ultimately results.

Principle 1: Set Expectations in Advance

Remote participants are notorious for multitasking during virtual events. Most people are used to attending passive webinars and boring online meetings, so it may come as a shock when you ask them to actively engage in a virtual training program. Therefore, it's important to clearly set expectations well before the training session begins.

An interactive virtual class should be engaging from the start, as early as the registration process because that's when participants begin forming their impressions. The program description, invitation, welcome, and initial instructions play an important part in how participants perceive the training, so you should intentionally plan these as part of the design process.

Program descriptions should be carefully crafted to emphasize interaction. Designers can establish these expectations through course communications, including custom registration and reminder messages, as well as scripted emails sent from the virtual facilitators to build rapport and relationships before the class starts. (We'll learn more about this in chapter 7.)

The more participants get involved in the virtual experience, the more likely they will reach the desired learning outcomes. In other words, if participants will need to collaborate on a case study and practice new skills with a partner to achieve the learning objectives, they should come ready to actively contribute. Don't leave this important detail to chance. Let participants know at every opportunity that the program will be an active learning experience, not a passive presentation.

When you communicate participation requirements in advance, everyone will know what they need to do to achieve the learning outcomes. Gallup's research on employee engagement has found that employees who know what's expected of them are more engaged and productive at work (Gallup n.d.); I've found that this applies to the virtual classroom as well. Expectations can alleviate stress by eliminating the unknown while setting the tone for collaboration. It's also simply good manners to let people know what to expect.

You show respect for participants by clearly establishing guidelines and expectations prior to the program. Some participants may want to prepare their workspace in advance by moving their main webcam to a different spot or making another change. Other participants may appreciate having extra time to consider what questions to ask their peers or to make other preparations so they'll be more comfortable in a collaborative online setting. Advance communication also gives participants the chance to opt out of the program, or at least talk with their manager about whether the learning format is the best fit for them.

If, for any reason, you are not able to communicate with participants in advance, use virtual platform tools to help share expectations with program participants as soon as possible. For example, use custom messaging in the waiting room or virtual lobby, or display a set of guidelines onscreen upon entry. These tools also let you re-inforce the messaging before each virtual class. Figure 3-2 demonstrates one way to establish expectations at the beginning of a virtual event, as participants log into the virtual classroom.

Figure 3-2. Sample Opening Slide to Set Expectations

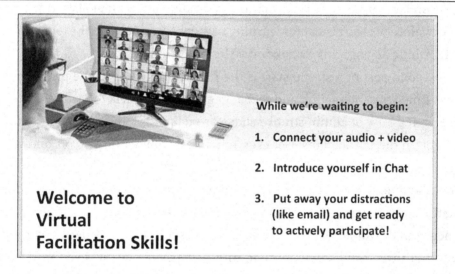

Chapter 7 is devoted to preparing participants for the virtual session and provides more information on this principle. For now, just recognize that setting expectations in advance puts everyone on the same page for an interactive learning experience.

Principle 2: Start Strong

A virtual class often interrupts the participant's workday. They may get a calendar reminder at 9:50 a.m. to join an online class starting at 10 a.m. When that happens, they'll have to pause what they are doing and switch from working mode to learning mode. Most of the time, participants will join the virtual event without stopping what they are doing and will continue to multitask until the learning experience begins.

Setting expectations in advance (principle 1) helps participants anticipate interaction, but it may still come as a surprise for those who don't realize what that entails. A strong start captures your participants' attention and gets the program's momentum going in the right direction.

The first part of the strong start begins when participants join the virtual classroom. What they see should pique their interest and invite them to engage immediately. If the audience is new to the platform, engagement could be as simple as answering a question using reactions or hand gesture recognition to learn how that feature works. Or it could be responding to a poll question, writing on the whiteboard, or typing in the chat. I call this time the "start before the start." Its primary purpose is to set the tone for an interactive, engaging virtual class while participants are connecting and settling in. Its secondary purpose is to teach participants about the virtual platform, if needed. The start before the start is not for learning new content related to the topic; it's simply for establishing an engaging, collaborative learning atmosphere.

The second part of a strong start is the first five minutes of the program. Front-load this time with interaction and focus on getting the learners involved. Instead of starting with a slew of administrative slides or facilitator announcements, open with a spotlight on the participants. Get everyone interacting with the tools and with one another right away.

For example, ask everyone to respond to a question via chat (even before the facilitator's introduction). Or ask everyone to answer a poll question about their experience with the topic. Or post an image on the screen and ask participants to type out the first three things that come to mind when they see it. Use those words to jump-start your conversation about the training topic. At a minimum, ask participants to introduce themselves in the chat window or respond to a multi-select poll question that requires some thought before answering. The point is to get everyone typing, clicking, or talking within the first few minutes, and before the lengthy facilitator spiel.

This critical first five minutes or so is when participants will decide whether to stay engaged or turn their attention to other things. Not only will this get the class started on a positive note, but it will also set the tone for an interactive session.

Principle 3: Select Activities for Maximum Involvement

In any group setting, some people will feel more comfortable speaking and sharing than others. This fact also holds true in virtual classes. In a group of 15 learners, some may show up excited to learn but some may have a million other things they would rather be doing. Some will be uncertain about the expected social norms in a virtual class, so they'll stay silent to avoid embarrassment.

Every virtual class participant needs to learn the content, and if they aren't paying attention, they aren't learning. And if they aren't learning, they cannot apply the new knowledge and skills back on the job. It's not enough for only 10 of 15 participants to engage in the learning experience. All 15 are important. Therefore, virtual class activities should be designed to include everyone.

Some virtual classroom tools are better than others for encouraging involvement. For example, in a verbal discussion, only one voice can be heard at a time. But everyone can simultaneously type in the chat, making it a more inclusive tool. Likewise, poll questions are accessible to every learner. And breakout activities give space for multiple conversations. When you have a choice among tools for an activity, pick the one that allows for maximum involvement.

Let's say the learners need to identify safety hazards in an office environment. You've staged a photo and placed it on a slide. To have participants note the visible hazards, you could:

1. Ask them to raise their hand and verbally share what they see.
2. Ask them to type a description of any hazards they see into the chat.
3. Send them to breakout rooms in pairs to discuss the hazards they see with a partner.

Each option progressively includes more participants. Personally, I would almost always choose option 3 so that everyone has a chance to do the activity and be involved in the learning. Again, it's not enough for only a few participants to practice a new skill. If they are registered for the right program, each participant will need to apply the knowledge and skills back on the job.

Another example, which I'll repeat in chapter 5 as a facilitation technique, involves using reactions. When writing questions for the facilitator to ask, one option is to have them ask participants, "Have you experienced this challenge before? If so, click on raise hand." However, another option, which involves everyone, is to ask, "Have you experienced this challenge before? If yes, click agree; if not, click disagree." The latter choice expects everyone to respond in some way. It invites involvement from every participant, creating a more inclusive environment.

Principle 4: Seek and Sustain Engagement

This principle flows naturally from the previous ones. You have set the stage for interaction, created a strong start that engages everyone from the beginning, and used tools that maximize involvement. Now it's time to continuously deliver on that promise. Don't give false hope of a collaborative learning experience only to deliver a passive one.

Fortunately, today's virtual classroom platforms provide an abundance of ways to involve a remote audience, including learners with disabilities or those who are neurodiverse. By using these tools creatively, you can engage participants in the content, which leads to deeper learning. And deeper learning leads to better learning outcomes. For example, you can use:

- Polls for conversation starters
- Chat for group conversations
- Webcams for deeper dialogue
- Whiteboards for team collaboration
- Breakout rooms for practice and feedback

Remember that it's not about using the platform tools just to use them. It's about using them to further the learning outcomes. For example, if participants must learn a new job-related technique, they can respond to a poll question about their experience with it, see a short demonstration via video, brainstorm application ideas with their peers on a whiteboard, and then go into breakout rooms to practice the new technique.

It's also important to maintain interest by not repeatedly using the same activity. Participants will get bored quickly if the only activity you offer is "Type your response in the chat." Chapter 4 provides more ideas to help you use the tools creatively.

Principle 5: Create a Social Experience

The very nature of virtual training means that participants are remote and isolated from one another. But remember that we're talking about synchronous virtual training, which means that participants are joining at the same time to learn together. Make the most of that opportunity. The program should take advantage of the ability to collaborate and encourage conversation.

As we've already established, engaged participants are more likely to learn and apply their new knowledge. Therefore, design virtual training classes that allow for, and even emphasize, participant-to-participant interaction. Participants learn from one another through shared experiences and robust conversation. They also feel less isolated when they realize they're part of a group. By designing conversation and team-work into the program, participants become part of a community. When they feel connected to others, they are more likely to participate. On the other hand, if a participant stays anonymous, they are more likely to tune out and multitask. Simple ways to increase social engagement include:

- Encouraging small talk among participants
- Using poll questions to gather input and share those results for all to see, commenting on the group's responses
- Using breakout groups for deeper discussion and dialogue
- Allowing time for conversation by not cramming too much content into a session
- Assigning participants to teams at the start of a session and encouraging the teams to work together
- Asking participants to choose a learning partner with whom they can privately chat throughout the session to share insights

Tips for Designing Presentation-Style Webcasts and Webinars

In chapter 1, we distinguished between webcasts, webinars, and virtual training classes by the amount of interactivity in each one and the number of typical participants. If you need to apply the virtual training design principles found in this chapter to a presentation-style webcast or webinar design, keep these additional points in mind:

- Find out as much as you can about the audience ahead of time so you can tailor the content and make it relevant to them.
- Add as much interactivity as possible by making full use of the available web platform features.
- Insert question-and-answer segments throughout the session instead of waiting until the end. For example, instead of a 45-minute lecture with 15 minutes of questions, intersperse shorter question opportunities throughout.
- Use a webcam for presenters to add a personal touch.
- Make the screen as visually appealing as possible through creative use of slides and graphics. Also, create enough slides so that the onscreen display will change frequently and help maintain visual interest.

In Summary: Key Points From Chapter 3

- Well-designed classes are a key to virtual training success.
- Design virtual classes for maximum learning interaction, engaging participants frequently.
- It's not about keeping participants busy; it's about engaging them in their own learning.
- A virtual class begins the moment a participant logs in to the session, even if that's before the official start time.
- Plan a meaningful, engaging activity within the first few moments of a virtual class. Then keep the momentum going with thoughtful activity sequencing.

Take Action

- ✓ Audit several virtual training programs to look for the five principles of engagement. Which principles are already in place? Which ones are missing? Which ones can be improved?
- ✓ Ask yourself if accessibility has been an afterthought or an integral part of your virtual training strategy. What can you do to improve?
- ✓ List steps you can or should take to educate stakeholders on the importance of accessibility in virtual training.

Tool 3-1. Sample 75-Minute Virtual Class Outline Using the Five Principles

Estimated Time	Activity Type	Notes
	Welcome activity on-screen before the start time	Poll questions or other activity onscreen as everyone joins, along with administrative and tech logistics.
5 min	Strong start	Welcome to the event on topic ABC. Introductions via chat and webcam sharing.
5 min	Breakout team check-in	In groups of three to four people, say "hello" to your teammates and create a team name!
5 min	Agenda and poll	Today's agenda is ABC. Which of these topics are you most interested in? Respond via poll. Share the "What's in it for me?" for attendees, what to expect, and how the program is extremely relevant to them right now.
10 min	Whiteboard challenge	"What's challenging for you related to topic ABC? Let's brainstorm a big list on the whiteboard." After the board is full of ideas, tell participants to use markers to put a dot next to the ones that resonate with them as well.
5 min	Presenter lecturette	Brief lecture on topic A; include at least one raise-hand question.
10 min	Breakout brainstorm	In breakout groups (same groups as before), review assigned challenges in light of topic A. (Option to provide additional relevant scenarios prepared in advance for groups to consider.)
5 min	Presenter lecturette	Brief lecturette on topic B; include at least one chat question.
15 min	Breakout case studies	In breakout groups (same groups as before), review assigned case studies in light of topic B. Create relevant solutions and present out to large group.
5 min	Presenter lecturette	Brief lecturette on topic C; include at least one poll question.
10 min	Partner action planning	In paired partners, use private chat (or breakouts, if preferred) to create action plans for applying the content and solutions learned from topics ABC.
	Close	Thank everyone for their active participation. Share job aids and other takeaways.

Tool 3-2. Five Principles of an Interactive Virtual Class Worksheet

Use this planning worksheet to ensure your live event includes the five critical design principles of engagement.

1. Set expectations.	
Ensure everyone knows what's expected by having an accurate event description, sending appropriate communication to attendees, and preparing them to get involved.	
Example: *Change event description to include words like "interactive" and "hands-on." Send an email with all prerequisite tasks and ask attendees to respond with confirmation.*	
2. Start strong.	
Capture attention as soon as attendees enter the live event by including onscreen interaction.	
Example: *Opening slide includes a "while you wait" activity that captures attention.*	
3. Select opening activities with maximum involvement.	
Involve everyone in the opening activities that begin right at the event start time.	
Example: *Within the first 2 to 3 minutes of the event start time, use a poll question to gather input and ask attendees to select yes or no to a question.*	
4. Create a social environment.	
Find ways for attendees to connect, communicate, and collaborate with one another.	
Example: *After initial introductions via chat, place everyone into small (3 people) breakout rooms for a quick meet and greet.*	
5. Seek and sustain engagement.	
After the initial whole-group interactions, invite frequent engagement throughout the event.	
Example: *Use a variety of platform tools (such as chat, polls, annotation, and breakout groups) to enable attendee involvement at least every 5 minutes.*	

CHAPTER 4

Develop Activities

 In this chapter, you will learn how to develop engaging activities and other resources for virtual training:

- Creatively use virtual classroom tools for interaction and collaboration.
- Generate ideas for opening and closing activities.
- Ensure that virtual activities are inclusive and accessible.
- Create virtual program materials.

In most traditional instructional design models, such as ADDIE, development follows design. A blueprint, known as the *design document*, guides the development process. It outlines the program's components, establishes the overall flow, and indicates which practice exercises and application activities need to be done. The design document is also used for necessary approvals among stakeholders and becomes an essential guide for the next phase: development.

During development, the design springs to life. You flesh out activities, script role plays, write scenarios, and create materials. Think of it this way: A designer provides a sketch of the big picture, and then the developer colors in all the details. Or consider design as your home's blueprint and development as its construction and interior decorating.

This design-to-development sequence is true for nearly every instructional design project, whether you're creating a traditional classroom program, a self-paced e-learning program, or a blended curriculum. So, what's different about virtual training? You have to account for the virtual platform's tools, the different types of collaboration, and the amount of interactivity needed to make the learning experience

99

successful. Developing virtual training requires a different mindset about participant engagement and a new approach to using virtual platform tools to create an interactive learning experience.

Remember, our definition of virtual training means *that the learners are individually connected from dispersed locations*. Because they'll likely be at their desks or another remote location, their learning environment is probably far from ideal. As I mentioned in the previous chapter, participants may be surrounded by distractions and will be tempted to multitask throughout the event by checking their email or working on other projects. Interactive program design and fast-paced activity sequences are essential for developing a successful virtual learning experience.

Your program must keep participants' attention and engage them fully in learning the material. And in the case of hybrid learning—when some participants are together in the classroom and others join from remote locations—designers need to place extra emphasis on developing program activities that include both audiences.

In this chapter, we'll review creative ways to use common virtual classroom tools, as well as how to design activities that are inclusive for all attendees. I'll share tips for creating facilitator guides, participant takeaways, and supporting documents like slides and visual aids.

Using Virtual Platform Tools Creatively

As we've already established, virtual classroom platforms are full of features that allow for participant interaction. When these platform tools are combined with engaging activities, the result is a participant-focused learning experience.

Designers can take creative license with their tools as long as the goal is to create learning content that leads to on-the-job application. There may be times when it makes sense to do an energizer just for the sake of taking a much-needed mental break or to establish rapport among learners to help build trust. For example, after an intense, realistic practice activity, participants may need a minute to relax before moving on to the next topic. Or you might follow an activity that involved concentrating and looking at various diagrams onscreen for an extended time with a short, lighthearted, exercise off camera. These kinds of activities have a purpose, even if they aren't directly tied to a specific learning objective. Use your platform tools to help participants engage, learn, and apply.

Just as there is more than one way to design any learning experience, there is more than one way to do most activities. You may prefer to get participant input via chat while another designer would use polling. Your virtual platform may have a robust collaborative whiteboard that's always included in a program design, but in a different platform, you may instead need to rely on breakout rooms. If the learning outcomes are the same, it usually doesn't matter which tool you use. For instance, let's say your program design includes a case study activity. You could:

- Post the case study description onscreen and ask participants to talk about it via chat.
- Share a series of thought-provoking poll questions related to the case study and then discuss the responses.
- Provide the case study details in an electronic handout and use breakout rooms for small group discussion.

These ideas would all work, and your decision about which method to use will depend on a variety of factors, including the content flow and the available platform features. Your choices will be based on a combination of art (your design preferences and creative touches) and science (facts about your participants, your program, and the desired learning outcomes).

"Listening is not enough. Learners need to be doing something to maintain attention. Without their attention, you cannot have engagement. No engagement? No behavior change. No behavior change? No impact on performance. If they aren't doing something meaningful in the learning environment, you will lose their attention. Engagement starts with good design.

—Katrina Kennedy, experienced learning professional

To help you think through these design decisions, here are a few ideas for using the most common virtual platform tools to create an engaging learning environment. This is not a comprehensive list; it's simply a starting point to help get your creative juices flowing. (You may also want to revisit chapter 3 for a description of each tool and how they're typically used.)

Chat

Chat lets everyone engage in meaningful ways. The facilitator can invite participants to send feedback, ask questions, and make comments during the program. They can use it for specific, pointed input at designated times, or it can hold a running commentary from participants who want to communicate throughout the session.

Participants can also use the chat to give quick, typed responses to a question from the facilitator. From "Share three words that describe your thoughts on this topic" to "What should Adam say next in this conversation?" the chat allows participants to contribute their ideas while simultaneously scanning and reacting to input from their classmates (Figure 4-1).

Figure 4-1. Example Chat Activity in Adobe Connect

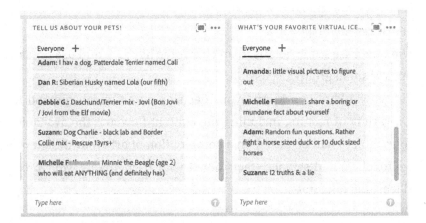

You may use the 3, 2, 1, go! method if the activity calls for everyone to give input without influence from other commenters. For example, when I teach virtual facilitators how to ask inclusive questions, I'll post an incomplete phrase on the screen and ask everyone to finish the statement by typing in the chat. But I give explicit instructions not to press Send or hit Enter until they hear me say, "3, 2, 1, go!" That way, everyone's response appears in the chat at the same time, and we can discuss similarities and differences in the answers.

Since most platforms allow graphical input, such as keyboard emojis and GIFs, it's easy to incorporate them into participant responses. Let's say a lesson on leadership involves putting yourself into someone else's shoes. A facilitator could lead a discussion on the topic and then ask participants to either type a descriptive phrase into the chat or share a GIF that illustrates their thoughts. The visual responses are often faster and may convey meaning better than text alone.

You can use a private chat to create a paired discussion opportunity in the virtual environment. For example, a facilitator in an in-person classroom session might say, "Turn to the person sitting next to you and discuss your response to this question." While this would be impossible in the virtual classroom, a facilitator could direct virtual participants to discuss their response to the question in a private chat. To ensure this activity works well, make sure you provide clear, step-by-step instructions. First, ask participants to find their partner by typing "hello" in a private chat and raising a hand once both partners complete the task. This step helps the facilitator and producer identify anyone struggling to connect with their assigned partner. Next, share the specific discussion question and allow two to three minutes for private partner conversation. Give time prompts as needed, and then ask everyone to return to the public chat and type "I'm back!" in the window. You can then debrief the discussion by asking pairs to share their key insights with the larger group.

Over the years, I've heard from many facilitators who don't like using chat as an input tool because they have trouble keeping up with it—there are too many entries and they go by too fast. However, you can overcome this challenge with deliberate practice, effort, and perhaps a few tricks. Don't be afraid to ask for help by getting producers or other learners involved in watching the chat window. Or you could set designated times, such as when participants are in breakout rooms or doing a whiteboard activity, to review any chat entries you missed. Also, remember that you don't have to read every message aloud or comment on each one. Instead, you can ask participants to summarize their statements or verbally expand upon their written comments. The bottom line is that the potential fast pace of a chat should not be a reason to shy away from using it for training activities.

Reactions

Participants can quickly share a visible, onscreen reaction by clicking on a button to display their choice. The most well-known reaction is *raise hand*, but there are also options like *yes and no* (or *agree and disagree* depending on the platform) as well as emoji smiley faces and other symbols. On most platforms, a small icon will show up next to the participant's name whenever they click on a reaction (Figure 4-2). Facilitators often use this feature when asking participants to respond to simple questions and quick yes-or-no polls. They might ask, "Who has seen this feature before? If you have, please virtually raise your hand; if not, just click on no."

Using reactions is one of the fastest, easiest, and best ways to infuse a virtual session with interactivity. At any point, facilitators can ask for participant input, and it will be immediately displayed on the screen. The key is to keep it seamless, so it's part of the conversation, rather than stopping the flow. For example, when transitioning to a new topic, the facilitator could post a relevant but provocative statement onscreen, asking participants to choose *agree* or *disagree*. This simple gesture involves everyone, piques interest, and can lead to meaningful dialogue.

Facilitators may also use reactions to encourage applause, laughter, or other status reactions during group discussions. To help create a more social environment and deepen the conversation among attendees, I frequently ask participants to react positively to their colleagues' comments, cheering one another on. After a few prompts at the start of a session, this collaborative atmosphere continues organically throughout. Designers can write these prompts into the facilitator guide as a reminder to use the tools.

In addition to the standard one-click reactions, many platforms now have AI-driven hand gesture recognition. When enabled, participants can simply clap their hands together to show applause or give a thumbs-up to indicate agreement, and the platform translates that to an onscreen reaction, just like if they'd clicked the button. These tools allow greater immersion in the virtual experience because participants no longer have to pause and find the right button to react. Instead, they can just react naturally, confident that the platform will translate their reaction and respond. This may seem intrusive at first, but it opens the door to a more immersive learning experience. This feature also enhances accessibility by removing potential barriers like the extra clicks needed to participate in the discussion.

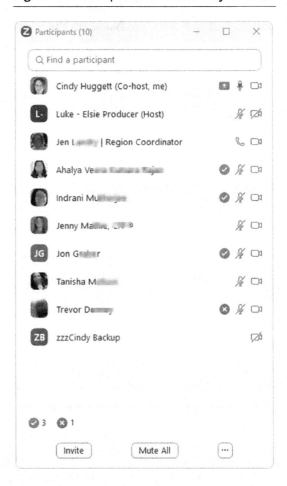

Figure 4-2. Example Reaction Activity in Zoom

Polls

Polls ask participants survey questions in real time. Depending on the virtual platform, your polls may use multiple choice, multiple answer, short answer, ratings, rankings, word clouds, matrices, and more. These polls may be built directly into your platform, or they could be part of an integrated app that incorporates external polling software. This versatility means you have almost unlimited options for how to use them in learning activities. From inviting input on a topic by asking a thought-provoking question to testing knowledge by asking quiz questions, polls are useful, multipurpose tools.

The best polls get learners thinking—not just responding. They ask meaningful questions that require participants to mull over the options before selecting their answers. Poll questions should be well-written and should not try to trick the learner.

Facilitators can use polling to start a robust discussion by asking for everyone's opinion on a particular topic. After the collective group has finished responding, invite those who chose answer A to share why, then ask those who chose answer B to explain their reasons, and so on. This often leads to lively conversations and eye-opening insights.

Another polling activity develops a connective thread throughout the entire class by inviting participants to keep track of their points for correct answers. Points can add up quickly when a program includes several polls. A twist on this activity groups participants in pairs or small teams, allowing them to combine their point totals and awarding prizes to the winning team. This creates a social network of loosely connected participants who are primed to cheer one another on.

One of my favorite polling activities invites participants to contribute answers to a word cloud (Figure 4-3). It's generated in real time and displayed on the screen—graphically emphasizing repeated answers. After the responses appear, the facilitator can invite participants to share what patterns they see and which words stand out to them.

Figure 4-3. Example Word Cloud Activity

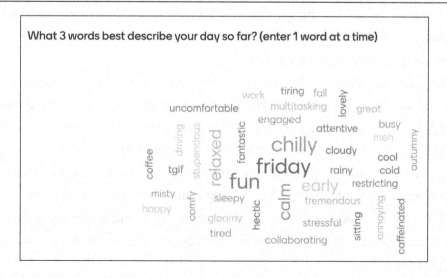

I frequently use poll questions to help debrief breakout activities. Instead of asking each group to report out on their discussion topics, I post a poll question listing the most discussed topics for that activity, as well as an other topics or something not listed response option. Participants select the choices that surfaced in their breakout group, and the poll quickly summarizes all the conversations. I then ask those who selected other to elaborate. This debrief method includes everyone in the report-out poll activity and shortens the time needed to process breakout discussions.

Video

The ability to see faces on camera during a virtual program enhances the quality of communication. In the early days of virtual training, it was audio only. Now, with better internet speeds and the proliferation of webcams, video has become a vital part of most virtual experiences. It's both expected and beneficial.

The increase of video streaming and webcam access in the workplace means that most virtual training platforms now operate with a video-first approach. In other words, the system immediately prompts a participant to enable both their audio and video when they log in to the platform.

Although I discouraged webcam use in my first book, the 2009 edition of *Virtual Training Basics,* I now embrace it wholeheartedly. When a virtual class has 20 or fewer participants, I often prefer the opening screen to be nothing more than a gallery view of everyone on camera so that we can quickly build rapport (Figure 4-4). Following my own advice from the previous chapter, I always set expectations in advance, telling everyone that the training program will use video. That way, no one is surprised when I ask them to join with their webcam on. However, I don't use words like *required* or *mandatory* because my goal is simply to explain that webcams will be used in the program. This allows grace when it's needed. I also share tips for using avatars and filters. (We'll discuss this more later in this chapter.)

Video can help establish communication norms, which leads to deeper collaboration opportunities. For example, you might ask participants to vote by holding up their fingers in response to a multiple-choice question—"On a scale of 1 to 5, what do you think about X?" Or participants could use breakout groups with their cameras on for a directed conversation. Another fun activity asks participants to turn their cameras on if they would answer "yes" to a question, but to turn it off if their answer is "no." A rapid-fire question series, reminiscent of the popular "Have you ever . . . ?" game, brings the screen to life as participants appear and disappear in response to each question.

Figure 4-4. Example Gallery View During an Opening Activity

When using webcams for activities, make the experience as accessible as possible. Teach participants about the platform's available camera and display settings. For example, show learners how to avoid video fatigue by using focus mode or the hide self-view option. Participants may be more comfortable if the program blurs their background or smooths their skin tone, so show them how to use these features. If your virtual platform supports avatars, participants may want to make use of these digital twins, which use their computer's camera to read and display their movements (like blinking eyes and moving mouths) to create a realistic, but also artificial image (Figure 4-5). As we discussed in chapter 2, avatars and filters increase accessibility options by providing camera-shy participants a way to engage with video without revealing themselves on a webcam.

Figure 4-5. My Avatar in Zoom

Remember, you don't have to use video for the entire program. You can toggle it on and off, only using cameras when they benefit the learning activity. It's a good idea to write prompts in the facilitator guide as a reminder.

Using Webcams to Increase Physical Movement

One advantage to using webcams is that it's easier to incorporate physical movement in learning activities. Most people assume that, when taking a virtual training class, they'll be sitting passively behind their desks for the duration of the program. But webcams open up opportunities to move.

For example, you could ask participants to jot down a response on paper and hold it up to the camera for all to see. Or you might ask a true-false question and have participants give a thumbs-up if it's true or a thumbs-down if it's false. Similarly, you could ask a numerical quiz question like, "Use your fingers to show us how many minutes a facilitator should pause after asking a question." These physical movements help keep energy levels high.

In a more involved activity, participants with access to an external, mobile camera could take it with them on a purposeful scavenger hunt. In a technical training class, I've asked participants to walk over to a piece of equipment and practice using it with the camera positioned on them. I've also asked participants using mobile devices in a new-hire orientation program to go discover important places in their location.

Whiteboards and Annotation Tools

Whiteboards and their associated drawing tools are part of the original toolset found in most virtual classroom platforms. They mirror the traditional classroom's chalkboards, whiteboards, and chart paper, and you can use them in similar ways. Facilitators and participants can type or draw freehand onscreen, either on top of slides or on separate whiteboards. Note that this book uses *annotation* and *drawing* interchangeably to describe the tools available for onscreen marking because these terms often vary by platform.

Facilitators can use annotation tools to highlight words and phrases on slides, which helps keep participant interest focused on the screen. They can also ask participants to read the screen, inviting them to circle, stamp, or highlight anything that stands out. This helps with participant engagement because it keeps the learners actively interacting with the program's content.

Traditional and virtual whiteboards are both used for capturing notes or brainstorming activities. The whiteboard screen in a virtual class can be a blank page or it can be customized ahead of time by adding drawings that correspond to the activities (Figure 4-6). In one of my programs, I draw a straight line down the center of the screen, splitting the whiteboard into two sections, which are labeled pros and cons. Then, when it's time for the activity, I ask participants to add text in the appropriate section of the whiteboard. Sometimes I divide the group into two teams and assign each one to the pro or con side. Or I allow participants to choose where to record their answers. The larger the group, the more likely I will assign participants to specific areas of the board to help manage the logistics.

Figure 4-6. Whiteboard Activity in Adobe Connect

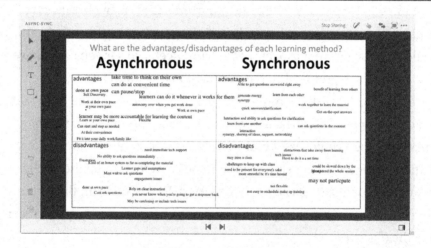

Note that in some platforms, it's easier to use blank slides in place of whiteboards, and in other platforms, it's better to use the actual whiteboard feature. Usually, this is a matter of personal preference and may depend on whether you have a large group activity in which everyone could easily use the slide or a small group breakout in which separate whiteboards are useful. If you want to be able to reference the whiteboard during post-program application or reflection activities, it's important to use a separate whiteboard (not a slide), because they can stay available to participants perpetually.

Breakout Rooms

Breakout rooms allow for small group activities to occur within the larger virtual class. They're essentially subconferencing spaces, in which only the other occupants can hear or see one another. They can use this space to collaborate on documents and whiteboards, brainstorm ideas, discuss challenges, or practice new skills together.

Breakout activities encompass at least three of the five design principles discussed in the previous chapter and are the foundation of all modern virtual classes focused on the learner experience.

- They allow for maximum involvement.
- They create a social environment.
- They help participants engage with the content and with one another.

To maximize engagement and involve everyone in virtual breakout rooms, most activities will work best with small groups of three to four people (as compared to the common recommendation of five to seven people in a traditional classroom setting). However, you can also use breakout rooms for pair discussions or even individual activities.

Case studies and scenarios are prime opportunities for using breakout rooms. Each group could discuss the same case study and then compare notes afterward. Or each group could discuss different aspects of the same scenario. Or you could have a different case study for each group, either assigning it to them or allowing them to choose.

You can also use breakout rooms for participants to practice the skills they've learned. For example, if they learn about specialized interviewing techniques to use with applicants, they could use breakout rooms to practice. One participant could practice the new interviewing skill, another could pretend to be the applicant, and a third participant could serve as a silent observer. Have them run through a scenario and then rotate roles so that each participant has a chance to practice and receive feedback from the observer.

If participants are learning tech skills, you can send them to individual breakout rooms to complete hands-on practice exercises. In each solo breakout room, the participant will share their screen while working on the activity. That way, the screen is available for review if the facilitator drops in to check on them. It's like an in-person lab where the facilitator can look over the learner's shoulder and provide feedback.

From a design perspective, going into breakout rooms should feel smooth and seamless to participants, without bumpy transitions or awkward pauses. Activity instructions should be displayed on the screen, along with any tech tasks that must be done for the breakout rooms to work well. This allows participants to focus on the task instead of the technology.

If the activity directions are detailed, lengthy, or complex, share them in smaller chunks, checking in with participants each step of the way. For instance, if participants first need to read a scenario, then discuss it with their teammates, then answer questions and take notes on their responses, then role play parts of the scenario to practice new skills, and then select a spokesperson to report their insights back to the large group, you could break this activity into three parts:

- In part 1, explain the breakout room mechanics (how to get into the room, where to find the scenario, and how long to spend reading it).
- In part 2, tell them how and where to take notes.
- In part 3, give details about the role play and report out.

The instructions could be on a PDF handout, on a slide, typed into the chat, or broadcast into the breakout rooms by the facilitator or producer. Or you could do all of these ideas! The main point is that participants should always know exactly what to do, when to do it, and how to go about doing it.

When participants return from small group activities, it's important to recognize the need for reflection and debriefing discussions without repeating the entire breakout conversation. If deeper learning will occur when each group reports out, you'll want to build in enough time for a debrief conversation. Use interactive debrief methods to keep everyone engaged in the conversation instead of giving the microphone to one person at a time. And remember, it's not always beneficial for participants to rehash the entire breakout conversation, especially if it's a larger class with multiple groups. Streamline the process by having the facilitator invite each group to share just one or two highlights from their breakout discussion. Or create a poll question with common answers, and invite participants to select which topics their group discussed during the activity. Then reveal the post-poll results and patterns, as well as any additional topics that arose. If groups need to share a whiteboard, ask their spokesperson to be specific: "Tell us one place on your board we should look." This way, the debrief will stay focused on essentials.

Opening and Closing the Learning Experience

While all activities are an important part of the learning experience, you should pay extra attention to activities during virtual class openings and closings. At the start, you are capturing learners' attention and laying the foundation of the program. Participants will decide quickly how engaged they plan to be. As brain researcher John Medina (2014) says, "If you are trying to get information across to someone, a compelling introduction may be the most important single factor in the later success of your mission."

The program's closing activities provide a transition back to the real world. Virtual classes shouldn't end abruptly based on when the session timer runs out. Instead, closing exercises should allow for reflection, action planning, and application. You want participants to take the learning with them instead of leaving it at the proverbial exit door, and an intentional shift from the virtual classroom back to their jobs can help make this happen.

Opening Activities

In the previous chapter, I established the importance of a strong start and shared how to create one. To support those techniques, try using some of these opening activities.

Introductions

To set the stage for interaction, help participants get to know who else is in the virtual classroom. You can invite introductions in the chat, in response to poll questions, or by video. Or you could place everyone in small breakout groups at the start of the event to have a quick, five-minute introductory conversation. Alternatively, you could post a discussion question onscreen and ask each person in the program to answer via reactions or a quick verbal response. To promote a learner-first mentality, do the participant introductions before the facilitator gives a lengthy spiel about themselves.

Commonalities

Establish trust and rapport by uncovering something everyone has in common. One way to do this is with a series of poll questions to home in on the answer. For example, you might ask "How many years have you been in your role?" followed by "Which of these challenges (about today's topic) have you encountered?" A rapid-fire polling series can be fun if the platform allows it; otherwise, create a multi-question poll (Figure 4-7).

Figure 4-7. Example Opening Activity

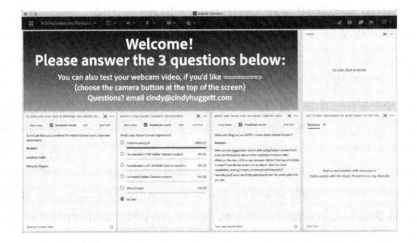

Social Networking

Create a social experience as soon as you can so participants realize they are in a virtual room with others and conversation is encouraged. Unless they'll serve a specific purpose, avoid using frivolous icebreakers. Instead, you may start by getting participants to talk about their work history at the organization, finding common threads such as who has served on a corporate committee. You can ask participants who arrive early to help you greet people who arrive later by typing personalized greetings in the chat. Or post a slide full of images and ask participants to share which image they relate to most and why.

Teach Platform Tools

One of the worst ways to open a virtual class is to blandly demonstrate the platform's features. It's boring for those who can already use them and too passive for anyone who needs to learn how to use them. A better approach is to teach the tools just-in-time, as needed. For example, say, "Click on the three dots in your video square to find viewing options like gallery or speaker-only view; choose the one you like best." Or "Look for the pencil button in the bottom left corner and raise your hand once the drawing tools appear."

If you must teach participants how to use the platform tools at the start of the virtual class, do it in an engaging way by allowing them to actively use the tools. One of my favorite methods for introducing the hand-gesture recognition feature is to ask participants a few questions, inviting them to raise their physical hands in response, so they are visible in their video squares. We then look at the toggle switch that enables recognition to demonstrate its usefulness.

Agenda Review

Adult learners typically need to know what they're doing—and more importantly, why they are doing it—before they'll engage fully in a task. This means it's ideal to include the learning objectives and planned agenda for the program during the opening activities, along with sharing the benefits of active participation. But instead of just posting a slide onscreen, find a creative way to share this information. For example, display the agenda graphically on a slide and ask participants to use their annotation tools to highlight any topics they have questions about. Or open a multi-answer poll question with the topics listed and ask participants to select the ones they are most looking forward to exploring. Sharing this information in a more interactive way helps set the stage for participant involvement, gives the facilitator useful information, and increases learner buy-in.

Closing Activities

A powerful, intentional closing activity acts as a bookend to an interactive virtual training class. It concludes the experience and sets up learning transfer and application. The closing can include a series of activities, gradually leading the participants to an endpoint. Or it can be a single comprehensive activity that combines closing elements. Let's look at a few options.

Self-Reflection

Kolb's Learning Cycle insists that if application is the goal, reflection must be included in a learning experience (Kolb 1984). The challenge of self-reflection in a virtual class is designing an activity in a way that doesn't encourage multitasking. To help participants prevail over the temptation to disengage, try one of these tactics:

- Place a countdown timer on the screen so participants can see how much time to take for each self-reflection question.
- Put each participant into a separate breakout room with an individual activity whiteboard. Watch as they complete the questions.
- Inform participants that they will be reporting out the results of their self-reflection to a partner, small group, or the larger group.

Action Plan Presentations

Action plans involve asking participants to list the steps they will take to use the content they are learning in the program. This gives them a path forward and motivates them to take ownership of using what they've learned. It's important for the action planning process to occur during the facilitated virtual class; don't save it for a post-program activity. Ideally, action planning should happen about three-quarters of the way through the session so that adequate time and attention can be given to it. Learning transfer expert Emma Weber (2018) puts it this way: "The creation of the action plan needs to happen towards the end of the training program, but not at the very end of it. Too near the end and people are out the door."

The added accountability that's fostered as participants create and present their plans to others increases commitment and leads to a higher likelihood of implementation. Learners can give their presentations in several ways, including asking each participant to share with the larger group or a partner or small group through a breakout session.

Call to Action

Participants should leave your virtual class knowing exactly what to do next. If there's an application assignment to complete before the next session or another program component, everyone should be aware of these expectations. Beyond recognizing what to do, participants should also know why they need to do it. Include a specific call to action near the end of each virtual class, and try one or more of these ideas:

- **Accountability pairs.** Assign partners or ask participants to select a partner from the attendee list. Ask partners to exchange contact information through a private chat and arrange a follow-up conversation to discuss how they are applying the content.
- **Note to self.** Ask participants to use a private chat to send the facilitator their email address and a brief note to themselves about how they will apply what they've learned. The facilitator can save those notes and send them to the participants after the program is complete.
- **Red light, yellow light, green light.** Use a slide or whiteboard divided into three sections labeled red light, yellow light, and green light. In the red section, ask participants to list anything that will stop them from implementing what they've learned. In the yellow section, ask them to list any potential roadblocks that could get in their way. And in the green section, ask them to list action items or ideas for applying the content.

Checks on Knowledge, Understanding, and Ability

Incorporate evaluation (which we'll cover in much more detail in chapter 9) by checking for knowledge and understanding. Do this through poll questions and skills checks, but be sure to go beyond simple poll questions focused on recall. Instead, use relevant application questions or create more hands-on activities. For example, participants in a customer service program could review challenging customer situations and role play their responses. This activity mirrors what they'll do back on the job and allows the facilitator to gauge their ability to use and apply the material.

Feedback Collection

Many virtual platform tools allow you to collect participant feedback, and this should be part of every online class. Use polls to collect hard data and use the chat or whiteboards to collect open-ended or anecdotal data. Chapter 9 offers a detailed look at measuring the success of virtual training.

More Ideas on Ensuring Inclusive and Accessible Classes

We've already discussed several ways to ensure that your virtual classes are accessible and inclusive for all participants. Accessibility can and should be factored into your virtual training classes from the start. In chapter 3, we looked at developing an inclusive mindset in your program design, ensuring that accessibility and inclusion are top of mind instead of an afterthought. Now, as you develop activities, have empathy for diverse participants and proactively work to select tools and activities that are available and valuable for all.

Here are a few more specific tactics you can use to infuse accessibility into your online learning activities:

- Most virtual platforms include accessibility features such as closed-captioning and high-contrast mode. Find out which tools are available on your platform and make sure they are enabled.

- Invite participants to share in advance any special adaptations they might need. Ask for this information at registration, or before the program, so you can add or research options for reasonable accommodation.

- Add descriptive alternative text (alt text) to all displayed visuals so participants can use screen readers. Follow current guidelines for alt text (such as not using emojis), which should help avoid bogging down the reader with extraneous words.

- Use compatibility checking tools for any documents you plan to display onscreen. For example, run your slide deck through the Office 365 compatibility checker.

- Pay attention to the color contrast (the difference in brightness between the foreground and background colors) on slides, documents, and visuals. Higher contrast is usually better.

- Avoid fast flashing animations on slides or other visuals because they can be triggering to some individuals and may cause dizziness, headaches, or discomfort.

- Always share activity instructions and content in multiple ways. For example, place instructions on slides so participants can see them onscreen while the facilitator also verbally explains the activity's directions.

- If participants are using screen readers, consider minimizing the use of the chat between program activities or show participants how to temporarily disable notifications.

- Distribute class materials in advance so participants can read and review them at their own pace.

- Ensure all distributed participant materials are shared using accessible file formats. For example, if you convert a word processing document to a PDF, use the "export to PDF" method instead of "print to PDF" to preserve important accessibility file tags.

- Encourage participants to share any feedback that will help you continuously improve the program's accessibility.

Creating Virtual Program Materials

Facilitators, producers, and participants depend on good program design to do their jobs well. Thus, a well-crafted, interactive virtual class design will set everyone up for success. To help them, you should:

- Write facilitator guides with explicit instructions on how to lead activities and enable learning.

- Design slides and other visual aids to help illustrate lessons and exercises.

- Create participant resources with class content (not just a copy of the slides).

Facilitator Guides

Virtual training facilitator guides help the facilitator and producer know how to set up, manage, and debrief each class activity. Because an interactive design requires action on their part as well, facilitators and producers need to know what is expected of them. A guide can be fully scripted, with instructions for the facilitator to "say" statements and "do" activities. Or it can be as simple as bullet point lists with general instructions for managing activities. What's most important is that the instructions include enough information for the activities to run as planned and in the expected timeframe. Participants should be able to complete each learning activity easily because the facilitator and producer had enough information to make it run smoothly.

If you are both the designer and the facilitator, you might take shortcuts when creating the facilitator guide; for example, you might use abbreviations and notes that only you understand. Unfortunately, this means that if anyone other than you needs to deliver the program, they won't know what you meant. That's why you should always create a facilitator guide with clear instructions for reference and consistency. It's also best practice to have a producer who follows along with the instructions. Therefore, be sure to include notes for the producer as needed.

I included a sample page from my virtual training facilitator guide template at the end of this chapter, and it's available for download on my website (cindyhuggett.com).

Visual Aids

On many virtual classroom platforms, the largest part of the screen is set aside for document sharing. Therefore, the facilitator's materials should include at least one set of visual aids, which is most commonly a slide deck. But virtual training is not the same thing as lecturing, presenting, or reading a set of slides. Not every piece of training content belongs on a slide, and the facilitator should not read every word. Slides are not a teleprompter!

Virtual training slide decks have a few specific purposes:

- They help present and visually enhance the training content.
- They help maintain learner attention with interesting graphics and a frequently changing screen.
- They provide direction and guidance as participants move through learning activities.

One of the most common design mistakes in a virtual training class is not having enough slides. If a slide stays on the screen for too long, participants will grow visually tired and start to look away—and when they look away, they stop paying attention and stop learning. Every time the screen changes to a new visual, it attracts the learner's attention. A virtual class typically has at least *twice as many slides* as its in-person counterpart, partly to maintain attention and interest among participants.

For example, if an activity calls for participants to privately chat with one another in a paired or partner exercise, you might use four or five slides just to set up the discussion. One slide introduces the topic, the next shows instructions for how to privately chat, the next helps establish the pairings, the fourth offers timing information and activity instructions, and the fifth displays the discussion question.

Slides should enhance content and provide activity instructions. Best practices for slide design include:

- Convey one thought per slide, without making them text heavy or laden with bullet points.
- Use sans serif fonts, which are easier to read onscreen.
- Use photos or vector graphics, not clip art, to enhance the visual appeal.
- Ensure slides can be read easily by screen readers.
- Include alt text for all graphics.
- Use high-contrast colors.

Remember the difference between visual aids and reference material? The best slides make the worst handouts, so make sure to create separate participant guides that are distinct from the facilitator material. For example, your slide deck may have more than 90 slides, but it translates to a two-page takeaway document summarizing the key points. Job aids or other documentation are best for technical content, with the slides serving to highlight key content.

Finally, because your participants may join from a variety of devices, each with a different screen size, pay attention to the font sizes. The smaller the screen, the larger the font needs to be for readability. As a general guideline, fonts should be *at least 34-point* to be read easily on most screens. One of my favorite activities to do in my Designing Engaging Virtual Learning workshop is to ask participants to guess the font size on a particular slide based on how it's showing up on their screens. Most say they are looking at a 20- to 30-point font and are shocked when I reveal it's 72-point.

Participant Resources

Participants will benefit from any reference material you can share that's related to the training class content. This is true in both the in-person classroom and the virtual classroom. You may choose to send documents to participants ahead of time (which we've already established is best for accessibility needs) or use the platform's material sharing capabilities.

Handouts (also called *participant guides* or *workbooks*) may include the main training content, exercises, activity instructions, and reference material. They allow participants to take appropriate notes, just like they would in an in-person class, without feeling compelled to write down every key idea or point made during the learning experience. Handouts often include job aids, as well as any additional resources, tips, techniques, content, and information, that participants can use on the job. Always distribute electronic handouts in an accessible format, such as a fillable PDF.

"For our single two-hour virtual classes, we provide a PDF that's up to 20 pages long, which participants use to fill in and take notes. For longer sessions that mirror our full-day classes, we ship the same materials that participants would receive if they took the in-person program."

—Treion Muller, CEO and Founder, The Modern Learning Architect; former Chief E-Learning Architect, Franklin Covey

---

Shipping Participant Materials

Sending materials to participants via email or another digital distribution system (such as an LMS or LXP) is common practice; however, it places the burden on participants to ensure the materials are available for reference during class. If your handout happens to include electronic worksheets or other activities that require editing, create fillable PDFs. Be sure to let participants know well in advance if they'll need to print out any of the material to use during the program.

A business or learning need may require you to ship preprinted materials to participants ahead of time, rather than sending electronic files. For example, you may want to use this option if learners are using a lengthy printed book or a document with specially formatted pages that may not display accurately onscreen or may be difficult for learners to print themselves.

The advantage of shipping materials is that you can choose your shipping date and be relatively sure participants will receive them in advance of the virtual program. The other advantage is the ability to include fun tactical items, such as "do not disturb" door signs, sticky notes, colorful pens, or branded tchotchkes they can use during the class. If there are no shipping restrictions, you might even send a tea bag or a nonperishable snack. The disadvantage to shipping materials is the potential high cost and the associated administrative time.

Carefully consider which option will work best for your virtual training curriculum.

Remember, a participant handout should never be a straight replica of the facilitator's slides. Just like you wouldn't hand over the facilitator guide to participants in an in-person class, you shouldn't send your facilitator slides to participants in a virtual class. The facilitator slides are part of the facilitator's materials—they include activity instructions, copies of poll questions, and other items participants won't find useful.

A well-designed participant handout should be all your learners need, and it will be far more useful than a deck of reference slides.

Designing Participant Materials for Blended Learning

If your virtual training class is part of a larger blended learning journey, participants will find it helpful if you create a checklist or road map to help them see the big picture. Give them an overview and let them know which components they will complete, as well as any resource requirements, including class expectations, deadlines, dates, and times of facilitated sessions.

You could create a calendar showing participants what to do during each week of the curriculum. Or give them a job aid listing every component of the blended journey and asking them to make notes as they complete each one. The purpose is to guide them through the program and make it easy for them to follow along.

The beginning of a sample checklist could look something like this:

- Week of February 9:
  - ▷ Introduce yourself on the program portal.
  - ▷ Attend virtual kickoff meeting with your direct supervisor.
  - ▷ Begin first assignment (found on the program portal).
- Week of February 16:
  - ▷ Complete the first assignment and post responses to the portal.
  - ▷ Meet with your direct supervisor to discuss learning goals for the program.
  - ▷ Attend the first class scheduled on Thursday, February 19, at 11 a.m. [*Link found here.*]

In Summary: Key Points From Chapter 4

- Creatively use platform tools to engage participants.
- Pay special attention to opening and closing activities.
- Consider accessibility options when creating virtual training.
- Design facilitator and participant materials that are useful for everyone.

Take Action

✓ Look at the materials you are creating for virtual training programs. Talk with your facilitators and producers to find out what's most useful in the facilitator guides and what could be improved.

✓ Check to see if your virtual training programs are incorporating reflection and action planning as part of the agenda. If not, find opportunities to add these essential components to the learning experience.

Tool 4-1. Virtual Class Activity Planner Template

Use this worksheet to plan out a virtual class activity tied to a learning objective.

Learning objective or topic:	
Virtual tools used:	
Activity description:	
How will you debrief the activity?	

Tool 4-2. Template for a Designed Hybrid Class

In this content outline, notice how the virtual classroom tools are used for both the on-site and off-site audiences.

Time	Activity Type	Details	Hybrid Considerations
	Welcome activity onscreen before the start time	Poll questions onscreen as everyone joins the virtual classroom	Every participant, both on-site and off-site, should join the virtual classroom.
5 min.	Strong start	Welcome to the hybrid event on topic XYZ. *Introductions via chat and webcam sharing.*	Acknowledge the presence of remote attendees, inviting them into the conversation.
5 min.	Breakout team check-in	In groups of 3 to 4 people, say hello to your teammates and create a team name!	Group remote attendees together and in-person attendees together.
5 min.	Agenda and poll	Today's agenda is XYZ. Which of these topics are you most interested in? Respond via poll. *Share the WIIFM for attendees, what to expect, and how the program is relevant to them right now.*	
10 min.	Whiteboard challenge	What's challenging for you related to topic XYZ? Let's brainstorm a big list on the whiteboard. [*Once the board is full of ideas*] Use your marker to put a dot next to the ones that resonate with you as well. *Ask for someone in the remote audience to summarize key themes and ideas.*	Note that everyone, both on-site and off-site, has access to the same whiteboard in the virtual classroom. Ask learners to "raise their hand" once finished typing onscreen, to ensure everyone has equal opportunity to respond.
5 min.	Presenter lecturette	Brief lecturette on topic XYZ—include at least one "raise hand" question	
15 min.	Breakout case studies	In breakout groups (the same groups as before), review assigned case studies in light of topic XYZ. Create relevant solutions and present them to the larger group.	
10 min.	Partner action planning	In paired partners, use a private chat (or a breakout room, if preferred) to create action plans for applying the content and solutions learned from topic XYZ.	
	Close	Thank everyone for their active participation. Share job aids and other takeaways.	Thank everyone, including the remote audience, for their active participation. Keep the virtual classroom open until all have left the room.

Template 4-3. Sample Facilitator Guide Page

Facilitator Notes

WELCOME participants to the program. If bandwidth allows, turn on webcams during introductions to briefly give learners a visual of you and of one another.

HAVE participants introduce themselves using CHAT, sharing their name, their role, their current location, and the length of time they've been with the organization.

Comment on introductions as appropriate. Encourage participants to chat with one another to begin building a comfortable learning environment.

INTRODUCE yourself to the group. Include the following information:
- Your name and location
- Your role and experience with the training topic

ASK participants to "Raise hand" if they have the handout available or to click on the red X (disagree) if they do not. For those who need it, draw their attention to the File Share pod where this handout is uploaded.

MOVE TO the "Guidelines" slide.

SAY: On screen is a short list of guidelines for our success in today's online class.

ASK: Who's willing to follow these guidelines to help make our program successful? Please select the "Agree" status (or "Raise hand"). {Acknowledge responses.}

SAY: It looks like we have an eager group who is ready to learn! We will continue using the chat window, as well as the status indicators and verbal dialogue throughout today's session. Your active participation is both requested and required!

Facilitator & Producer Guide
10 min

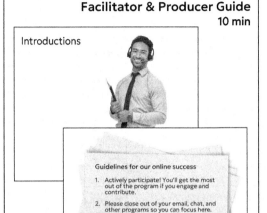

Introductions

Guidelines for our online success

1. Actively participate! You'll get the most out of the program if you engage and contribute.
2. Please close out of your email, chat, and other programs so you can focus here.
3. State your name before speaking so that we can get to know your voice.
4. Be prepared to be called on.

Producer Notes

ASSIST participants with chat introductions as needed.

ENSURE the "Introductions" slide is displayed.

INTRODUCE yourself both verbally and in the chat. Let everyone know you are available to assist with any technical issues.

ENSURE the handout is uploaded into the File Share pod for those who might need it.

ALLOW participants to clear their own status. If needed, clear it for them.

ANNOTATE the "Guidelines" slide by using the pointer or highlighter to note key words as they are spoken.

SWITCH to "Program Overview" layout before moving to the next slide.

CHAPTER 5

Prepare Facilitators

 In this chapter, you will learn how to prepare facilitators to deliver engaging virtual training:

- ○ Identify the facilitator's role in the virtual classroom.
- ○ Review selection criteria for facilitators.
- ○ Prepare and upskill virtual facilitators.
- ○ Master the art of online facilitation.

A well-designed program is essential to the success of your virtual training classes, but it's only half of the equation. The other—and equally important—half is excellent, engaging delivery. When combined, interactive design and effective delivery create a positive learning experience for participants that leads to learning transfer and on-the-job application.

In one of my train-the-trainer workshops, I ask participants to work in groups to create a list of characteristics describing the best and worst training classes they have ever attended. Under the "best" category, I usually see responses like "great facilitator," "got everyone involved," "relevant, practical information," "hands-on practice," and "enthusiastic trainer." And under the "worst" category, the responses almost always include "boring trainer who just read from notes," "unprepared speaker," "no engagement," and "just listened to lecture."

In the same exercise, I also ask participants to sort their statements into two categories: related to program design and related to delivery. Responses like "getting everyone involved," "including relevant practical information," and "providing hands-on practice" are typically associated with design. However, some argue that the facilitator is also responsible for those factors. Everyone usually agrees that the facilitator brings the design to life, enabling and supporting the learning. In other words, it's the facilitator who can make or break the learning experience for participants.

In this chapter, we will look closely at the facilitator's role—how to select the right person, how to prepare them, and how to set them up for success. By the end, we will answer the question, "How does a great facilitator create an engaging virtual environment that enables learning and leads to on-the-job application?"

The Facilitator's Role in Virtual Training

Whether you call them a *facilitator*, *trainer*, or *instructor*, this person is the leader of the virtual learning experience. They manage the classroom, teach content, guide everyone through learning activities, and facilitate discussion among participants. They speak, listen, direct, plan, lead, encourage, observe, and guide—all the actions necessary for learning to occur in a classroom and be transferred to on-the-job application.

Effective facilitators enhance the virtual training experience for everyone in a way that motivates participants to learn. They ask questions to provoke thinking. They present content in ways that are easy to understand. They connect new material to post-program actions. They give instructions to complete learning exercises. They encourage participation from everyone. And they create a comfortable and safe learning environment where participants are free to explore and practice new skills. The facilitator's ability to help participants realize their learning potential is paramount in ensuring the success of any virtual class.

While facilitators may occasionally have to present content more formally, they always stay focused on the participant experience. They are more concerned about the learning—and the transfer of that knowledge to the workplace—than they are about their own speaking skills. They recognize when to let go of *presenting* and focus on *facilitating*.

You can think of the facilitator as the conductor of an orchestra. A conductor leads the show, but the players make the music. A conductor enables the musicians to play beautiful music together and individually, and in the same way, a facilitator leads the program, but the learning happens through participant involvement and engagement.

AI's Impact on the Facilitator Role

As we move into the age of generative AI, you might be wondering whether the facilitator's role will soon be obsolete. It's no secret that advancements in AI technology are changing the L&D landscape. With the help of AI, designers can script an entire learning program from a few well-crafted prompts. Developers can use it to quickly create a slide deck full of amazing and relevant graphics, and then preprogram entire dialogues with realistic conversations and artificial human-like characters. This growing collection of technological advances is promising, and it's possible that it may one day reach the point of replacing virtual facilitators.

However, if you've ever argued with Siri or Alexa—gotten frustrated over their inability to understand or their not-quite-on-target responses to your queries—then you've experienced first-hand the current limitations of AI. Now imagine those obstacles appearing in the middle of a learning experience. You would certainly not achieve your desired results.

Thanks to research-based evidence (as well as our own intuition), we know that human facilitators add value to many learning experiences and support participant learning in ways that AI cannot currently provide (Chernikova 2020). While the role of AI in virtual training will certainly evolve, there will always be a place for traditional facilitators in virtual training programs.

What's in a Name?

My preferred term for the person who conducts virtual training is *facilitator* because it keeps the emphasis on the participants. Instead of presenting information, a facilitator encourages discussion and dialogue.

Compare the word *facilitator* to the word *instructor*. Although these terms can be used interchangeably, instructor implies teaching or imparting knowledge to the learners. While that task is certainly an important part of many training classes, it puts too much emphasis on the idea of an expert teacher. Unless this is a deliberate choice to establish credibility with the audience, I still prefer the word facilitator.

The word *trainer* is used in this book occasionally because it's part of the common vernacular among training and development professionals; however, when asked to choose between the two, I'll usually go with facilitator.

The current preferred title for instructional designers is *learning experience designers*, so I'll also advocate for calling facilitators *learning experience facilitators*. (I give a more detailed breakdown of this job title in my 2022 book, *The Facilitator's Guide to Immersive, Blended, and Hybrid Learning*.)

Selecting Facilitators

The first step in facilitator preparation is careful selection. The best traditional classroom trainers don't necessarily make the best virtual training facilitators. Success in virtual training requires a different mindset and an updated skill set.

What qualities and characteristics should you look for? The best virtual facilitators possess a unique blend of training aptitude, facilitation abilities, and technology skills. In addition, they:

- Can apply adult learning principles to the virtual classroom
- Are tech-savvy (or willing to learn)
- Can easily engage a remote audience
- Make learners feel comfortable with the technology and the virtual learning environment
- Encourage dialogue by willingly sharing airtime with participants and being comfortable with silence
- Can multitask effectively
- Have a solid knowledge of the program content

"Effective virtual trainers are prepared but also able to think on their feet. They have a vibrant voice and are able to build rapport with participants. They also have command of the virtual platform's tools."

—Wendy Gates Corbett, author, researcher, and
former Global Training Director

Some organizations have a cadre of facilitators who specialize in virtual training, and that's all they do. Other organizations want every facilitator to do it all well, whether the program is in person, hybrid, or virtual. Neither method is right or wrong. Those who facilitate frequently in the virtual classroom keep their skills fresh, and those who work in all environments may keep their fingers more firmly on the pulse of the organization. I recommend seeking virtual training specialists who master the necessary skills and continually improve them—it's better to have a few experts than many generalists.

Once you have selected the facilitators, the next step is to ensure they are prepared for effective delivery.

Facilitator Preparation and Upskilling

As soon as a facilitator has been identified or self-selected to deliver live online learning, the preparation and upskilling should begin. It's not automatic that someone will be a good virtual facilitator, even if they are proficient with technology. It takes more than a tech background to lead an effective online learning experience. The good news is that if the person has had any classroom training experience, the task will be more like an upgrade than a brand-new start. It's like learning how to drive a truck if you already know how to drive a car. There are significant differences between traditional and virtual learning, but the basic rules of the road are the same.

When you think about facilitator preparation, consider how an Olympic athlete prepares for the games. Through a disciplined diet, exercise, practice, and sport-specific routines, they prepare themselves to win a medal and stand on the podium. In the same way, the best virtual trainers prepare relentlessly for live online events. The tongue twister, "proper preparation prevents poor performance," is just as true in the virtual classroom as it is in the athletic arena.

To effectively deliver virtual classes, facilitators need to master:

- The essentials of live online delivery
- The technology they will use during the learning experience
- The content and design of the training program

On top of these three items, facilitators also need to develop contingency plans in case of technology problems or other unexpected occurrences.

Mastering the Essential Techniques of Online Delivery

Many facilitators are tossed into the virtual classroom and expected to thrive immediately. The assumption that virtual facilitation is easy and anyone can do it is counterproductive. In my work with thousands of facilitators over the years, I've discovered that even experienced facilitators can benefit from professional development. Their independent efforts to master virtual facilitation may fall short, not from a lack of trying, but from a lack of awareness. They think they know what it takes to engage a remote audience, but their efforts don't always lead to the desired results. To carry the earlier sports analogy further—even championship-winning, world-class athletes return to basic training camp at the start of every season. Why? Because they recognize that the foundation of mastery is the *consistent performance of the basics*. Great athletes are willing to spend time reviewing, practicing, and tweaking their skills in pursuit of continuous improvement. Great facilitators can and should do the same.

Some organizations have formal train-the-trainer programs to help virtual facilitators learn the nuances of delivering online training programs. Others pair a new facilitator with a more experienced facilitator to learn the ropes. Periodic refresher workshops fill in the gaps for those who need to stay current. The key to preparing trainers is giving them enough time to learn the technology and enough practice to get comfortable engaging participants in the virtual classroom.

When Darlene Christopher, senior knowledge and learning officer at the World Bank Group, identifies new virtual facilitators, she works with them individually to show them how to deal with limited visual cues from the audience. She uses a fantastic technique to help them get comfortable—she calls them on the telephone and tells them to ask her a question. Then, she asks them to mute their phone line and count to 10. This simple practice helps a new facilitator get used to having a few seconds of silence before anyone responds, which is typical in a virtual class.

In a more formalized train-the-trainer program for virtual facilitators held by Yum! Brands, each participant completed three, 20-minute, self-paced e-learning modules: leading virtually, content development, and platform basics. Then, participants applied what they learned by creating a short virtual lesson. Finally, they attended a two-hour virtual class with a small group to practice their short virtual lesson and receive feedback from others. Upon finishing the program, each participant received an account on the online platform so they could continue practicing. They also gained access to an internal site with additional tools, job aids, and a forum for asking questions.

My own Beyond the Basics workshop for experienced virtual facilitators begins with a knowledge and skills assessment so I can focus on the gaps. Facilitators work together in groups to fine-tune their delivery skills, taking turns practicing and receiving expert feedback. They explore creative ways to use platform tools and spend time planning for their continued development.

Scheduling Facilitators: How Many Sessions per Day?

Whenever someone asks me, "How many virtual classes can a facilitator deliver in one day?" I tell them there are several answers!

From a timing perspective, facilitators should log in to a virtual class approximately 30 minutes before the start time, and they'll need 15 to 30 minutes at the end to debrief the experience and complete administrative tasks.* This means that for a 90-minute virtual class, the facilitator should block off close to three hours on their calendar. This translates to a maximum of two or three virtual classes in a day if they're scheduled back-to-back. Of course, the number of classes any facilitator can do varies depending on class length. Also, please remember that facilitators need to be able to take breaks between sessions so they can stay sharp in the virtual space.

From a workload perspective, a facilitator can handle as many classes in a day as their stamina allows. Delivering a virtual class well requires enthusiasm and energy. Some facilitators may drain their internal reservoirs too much during a session, making them fatigued and less alert, which has a detrimental effect on their ability to deliver multiple virtual classes effectively.

Some platforms allow setup in advance of the session, while other platforms require setup at the beginning of each session. If the virtual classroom and all its activities can be set up before the day of the class, then logging in 20 minutes before the start time is probably fine. If the virtual classroom must be set up from scratch at the start of each session, then it's better to log in closer to 45 minutes in advance.

Learning the Technology

The second part of facilitator preparation for virtual training focuses on technology. The best virtual facilitators are experts in the virtual platform. This means they know the software and all its features in-depth. They know what every menu command means and what every button does. They know how the program works from the host's or presenter's view, and they know how it works from the participant's view. They are familiar with the mobile app version of the platform, have used it, and can explain to others how to navigate it. They can use all the tools available and help participants use them as well. Effective virtual facilitators don't stumble around trying to find a command; they move with ease from one tool to the next.

How do virtual facilitators learn the software platform? Mostly through practice—by clicking on every button and trying everything out. They set up virtual sessions with multiple laptops and practice using the tools from both the presenter's and participant's viewpoint. They watch how-to videos and review the vendor's online help site to read detailed instructions for each tool. They may also attend formal training sessions offered by the software vendor. And they get tips from other facilitators while sharing ideas and resources online.

The bottom line is that learning how to use the technology takes time, play, and practice.

Given all this emphasis on time with the technology, you might be wondering how long it takes to learn a platform. That's like asking how long it takes to learn how to ride a bike or drive a car. It varies from person to person, depending on prior knowledge, their confidence, whether they learn on their own or work with someone, and how much practice they put in.

Technology Resources for Virtual Facilitators

While we are on the topic of technology, let's explore the resources facilitators need. In chapter 2, we explored most of the technology needed for virtual training. Let's now return to this discussion from the perspective of facilitator preparation and setup. All facilitators must have the resources they need to properly deliver training.

The first and most important thing a virtual facilitator needs is a computer from which to deliver the training class. This could be a desktop computer or laptop, as long as it is powerful enough to run the full (not mobile) version of the virtual class platform. Most facilitators use laptops because they are portable and more commonly available than desktops. The computer also needs a reliable internet connection—preferably wired instead of wireless. Even though most wireless connections are dependable, when delivering a live online class, you're better off erring on the side of caution. If there is any chance the Wi-Fi could be unstable or experience interference, use a wired connection.

Second, most virtual platforms are easier to use when an external monitor is connected to the facilitator's laptop. In some platforms, you can "pop out" classroom tools like chat and video and move them around on a larger screen. The external monitor also provides more space to display participants' videos and other classroom features. I recommend using external monitors for virtual facilitation whenever possible.

A facilitator should also have an HD webcam placed at eye level, which is why I prefer to use an external webcam for maximum flexibility. The built-in laptop webcam is not ideal, but you can use it if you put your laptop on a raised platform (if you do this, you'll probably need to get an external keyboard). If the facilitator's workspace isn't well lit, then a ring light or LED panel is a necessity. See Figure 5-1 for an example webcam setup.

The next essential item is a quality, hands-free wired headset or an external microphone with a pop filter to ensure a good audio connection. This setup allows you to type and talk easily at the same time. It also provides a crystal-clear connection, unlike the laptop's built-in microphone, which often has an undesirable echo. Wired connections will have the best quality, even better than Bluetooth, so use wired headsets and mics when possible.

Some facilitators use external consoles with buttons to trigger preprogrammed actions like switching between devices, adjusting lighting, playing music clips, and so

Figure 5-1. Example Facilitator Webcam Setup

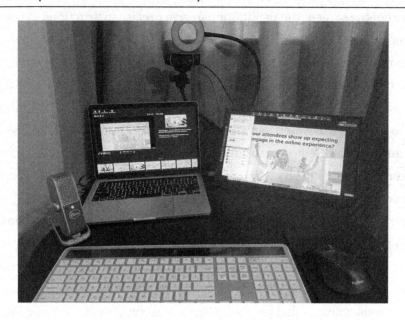

on. These consoles are widely used in video production studios and have now found a place in virtual training. A console can be helpful if you are using multiple webcams or working without a producer and want to inject a slick, automated production feel into your virtual classes. For me, it falls into the "nice to have" category because the console's best use case is a virtual presentation (as opposed to a facilitated learning experience). But some experienced facilitators consider them a must-have accessory.

If your virtual classes use immersive technologies such as augmented reality (AR) enhancements or VR simulations, facilitators will need access to the corresponding equipment. For example, to display AR objects in high-quality resolution, you may need a tablet with plenty of memory available. Or to facilitate an immersive simulation activity during a virtual class, you may need a VR headset with haptic controllers. The items you need will depend upon your activities, but they shouldn't be overlooked if they are part of the learning experience.

The final piece of hardware that can elevate a facilitator's setup is a second computer. Again, this could be a desktop computer or a laptop, provided it can run the software and has a solid internet connection. This second computer has a dual purpose. First, and most important, you can use it to log in to the virtual classroom as a participant to see what they see during the class. Because the view on most virtual classroom platforms is different for facilitators and participants, being able to see what the participants see will help you guide and direct the experience in a way that makes the most sense to them. For example, if a class activity calls for participants to annotate a specific part of the screen, the facilitator can give precise instructions to complete the activity—including exactly where to find a button.

My second computer came in handy during a recent class. I had given instructions for a whiteboard activity, but nothing was happening. At first, I thought the participants didn't understand what to do, but then I glanced at my second computer with the participants' view: there weren't any annotation tools! I immediately realized that my producer and I had neglected to unhide the participant drawing tools, which we had hidden after a previous activity. A quick click of the button fixed the situation, and this new whiteboard activity began right away.

Another purpose of the facilitator's second computer is as a backup connection to the class in case of emergency. For example, if the first computer were to crash or have some other problem, you could still communicate with participants and continue delivering the session on the second one. Depending on which software platform you're using, your producer can either promote the second computer to become the host with full facilitator privileges or, as the facilitator, you can reclaim the host role using a special code that is generated when you set up the class. Either way, the second computer serves as a safety net, and any facilitator who operates without one runs the risk of disrupting a virtual class if an unexpected technology problem occurs.

I don't recommend facilitating from a mobile device because, at the time of this writing, the mobile versions of most virtual classroom platforms are limited in their features, and a facilitator needs full functionality. However, using your mobile device (such as a smartphone or tablet) as a second computer is better than nothing, and if it's the only option available, you should use it. When I am facilitating online, I like to connect a mobile device to the session in addition to my second computer. That way, if any of my participants are connecting via tablet or smartphone, I know what they see onscreen. This also gives me one more contingency option. To give you a visual idea of a facilitator setup, Figure 5-2 is a photo of what my desk looks like when I'm delivering a virtual class.

As we've discussed, beyond a standard technology setup, virtual facilitators must be prepared for contingencies and unusual situations. Because virtual classes rely so heavily on technology and the internet, you should always create redundancies and backup plans just in case. It's the reason you see extra items on my desk in Figure 5-2.

Usually, virtual classroom platforms function normally and internet connections are strong and steady. And if you've got a reliable platform, you never expect anything to go wrong. That's exactly why virtual facilitators need to prepare for the unexpected. By taking the extra step of thinking about and preparing a backup plan, you can ensure

Figure 5-2. My Facilitator Setup

that any unforeseen challenge is just be a temporary nuisance. For example, if you are a facilitator working from home and the internet connection unexpectedly goes down during a session, how will you reconnect? Think about this contingency ahead of time and create a backup plan. What if your headset loses battery power during a virtual class? You should have a second headset or a mobile phone nearby and ready to use.

By taking just a few extra steps to plan tech backups for contingencies, an effective virtual facilitator can always be prepared.

Learning the Program Content

Finally, virtual training facilitators need to realize that it's important to learn class content and design, just as they would for an in-person class. Some facilitators read the guide several times, some like to observe the class as a participant, and others practice facilitating to an empty virtual classroom. Regardless of your method, as a facilitator, you should be a content expert before delivery.

In addition to mastering the content and class design, virtual facilitators should also get to know the audience so they can tailor the program accordingly. For example:

- Who are the participants? What are their names, roles, locations, and other relevant demographic information?
- Do the participants know one another, or are they meeting for the first time? If they know one another, what's their relationship? (Are they managers and employees, peers, or something else?)
- Why are they taking this program, and what do they hope to gain from it?

- What are their experience levels? Will the content be brand-new information, or are some of them already knowledgeable enough to be teaching the course? Are they somewhere in between?
- What types of questions will they have about the material? What concerns will they have? What challenges will they have in applying the content?
- What accessibility needs might they have? Will they be using assistive technologies like screen readers? What additional accommodations, if any, will help them have a better online learning experience?

The amount of time needed for facilitators to become familiar with the content and audience will vary depending on several factors including previous familiarity, complexity of the topic, and quality of the facilitator materials. A general guideline to follow for in-person training is three days of preparation for one day of class time. For virtual classes, this translates to three hours of prep for a one-hour program. While this is only an estimate, it's a starting point to help you schedule enough time to learn the content. If needed, grant additional time to learn the technology platform. And for a brand-new virtual facilitator, be generous and allow as much time as possible to feel comfortable delivering the content online.

Partnering With Producers and Co-Facilitators

The smoothest virtual classes have multiple leaders—a facilitator and producer or two co-facilitators who take turns supporting each other. The producer is the designated technology specialist and is responsible for making the tools run smoothly, assisting the facilitator behind the scenes, and helping participants get (and stay) connected to the virtual classroom. In the case of co-facilitators, one person takes a turn leading the discussion and collaboration while the other is producing. It is possible for a facilitator to deliver virtual classes solo, but it may not result in the best learning experience for participants. In the next chapter, we will thoroughly review the producer role. For now, however, we'll focus on the facilitator's preparation step involving a producer.

A good partnership between the facilitator and producer is grounded in excellent communication and a clear division of responsibilities. Both are determined in advance with intentional planning. Your organization may have standards in place, such as a required prep meeting for program leaders before every class. You may also have a detailed facilitator and producer guide that spells out everyone's role. Working out the small but important details, such as who will greet participants when they log in to the virtual classroom, shouldn't be left up to chance. When planning, be sure to factor in enough preparation time to have these discussions.

Ongoing Preparation and Development

As a virtual facilitator, after you learn the content and the platform, it's important to continue learning and practicing. The more time you spend in the online classroom, the better you will be. A facilitator who delivers every day or every week will become much better at it than someone who delivers only once every few months. It's also valuable for the facilitator to receive periodic feedback to improve their skills.

To help facilitators receive feedback and improve their delivery, I've created a facilitator observation form to provide ongoing skills coaching. (This is found in Tool 5-2 at the end of the chapter.) The observation form measures both technical proficiency and facilitation skills.

Are You Preparing to Facilitate Hybrid Learning?

You'll need a special type of preparation to facilitate hybrid learning. For in-person classes, facilitator preparation focuses primarily on content. You need to learn the material, plan activities, and tailor everything for the audience. For virtual classes, the focus shifts to include technology. All the traditional preparation steps are still important, but platform planning takes center stage. You need to ensure virtual classroom tools and activities are set in advance.

For hybrid classes, your preparation emphasis should be on the participant experience. Because your goal is to create an atmosphere that equalizes the participants' experience regardless of their physical location, you must ensure that everyone has what they need in advance of the class and all expectations have been established.

Hybrid facilitator preparation tasks include preparing the:

- In-person hybrid classroom to ensure the technology setup is conducive to mixed-audience collaboration
- Virtual classroom that will be used to connect the mixed audiences via audio, video, and other interactive features
- Participants, so remote attendees are ready with their webcams, in-person attendees bring their devices, and everyone's clear on expectations

The Art of Online Facilitation

Effective virtual delivery is more than just presenting content from a set of slides. Just because a facilitator says it, doesn't mean participants learn it. As we've discussed in previous chapters, a virtual class should be designed with high interactivity and focused on participant learning and application. It's a social experience with conversation, collaboration, and discussion. Successful virtual facilitators create interactivity using the 10 techniques described in this section:

1. Build rapport with and between participants.
2. Create community.
3. Show up on video.
4. Have a clear voice.
5. Read the virtual room and respond accordingly.
6. Manage group dynamics.
7. Involve participants.
8. Debrief activities.
9. Manage technology with effective multitasking.
10. Validate learning.

1. Build Rapport With and Between Participants

The best facilitators recognize the importance of connection and communication, shining the spotlight on participant input. They intentionally build rapport with participants, striving to make a good first impression and following up with authentic interest. As the saying goes: People don't care until they know how much you care. Showing an interest in each participant goes a long way toward ensuring they feel like part of the group and are engaged in the learning experience.

One of the best ways to build rapport with the audience is to ask questions. Ask about your learners and their experiences, their work, or their interest in the program. Use active listening skills to hear what they say, reflect on their comments, and ask appropriate follow-up questions.

Another way to build rapport in the live online classroom is to listen carefully to what participants say and incorporate their thoughts and ideas into the conversation. When participants feel heard, they are more likely to feel comfortable and connected to the facilitator and the class. For example, when greeting participants at the beginning of a class, make a point to find out something about them and their experience with the training topic. Then, during the session, refer to relevant details. This creates a connection and helps participants realize you heard what they had to say. In short, it builds rapport.

Another technique is to say participants' names. Think about how you react whenever you hear your name mentioned from across the room. Your ears perk up, and you become a little more interested in that conversation. It happens in the virtual classroom as well! Effective virtual facilitators use participant names frequently and with sincerity. For example, "Julio, thanks for adding your thoughts to the chat. You've got a great point." They also make connections between the content and participant comments; for instance, "Earlier, Sophia asked about the challenges of using this technique. Here's a solution you can try." You might also want to incorporate participant names into examples, such as, "So if Aisha were a manager, then . . ." When participants hear their own names during a session, they pay closer attention, and it helps build rapport among the group.

Should You Call on Participants by Name?

Some facilitators are taught to avoid directly calling on participants by name because putting people on the spot can create an uncomfortable learning environment. The solution to this dilemma is easy. As a facilitator, use these three guidelines whenever you plan to pose direct questions in the session:

- Let participants know at the beginning of class to expect direct questions, and that it's OK to say, "pass" if they aren't ready to answer.
- Make sure your direct questions don't have a single correct answer. For example, instead of asking for a fact, such as, "Camille, what's the next step in the process?" you might ask for an opinion, like, "Camille, what thoughts do you have about this process?"
- Take turns with the direct questions. For example, "Let's hear from at least three of you on this next question. Let's start with Emma first and then Jose."

The goal of calling on participants by name is to encourage participation, not to put someone on the spot or embarrass them. If you use this technique, use it only in a way that maintains a comfortable and safe learning environment.

Two common misconceptions about building rapport with an audience are that facilitators don't have time for it because there's too much content to cover, and icebreakers are a waste of time. Both sentiments have a hint of truth in them, but neither is fully true and both can be overcome.

If there's too much content to cover, then there is a problem with the program design. It's important to make space for conversation within the program's allotted timeframe, so add some relationship-building time to the agenda. The benefit of the live online classroom is bringing learners together, so there should always be time for social connections and discussion. If you're not planning to include interaction, then stick with asynchronous, self-paced learning.

Regarding icebreakers: Switch to openers instead. An opener serves a purpose similar to an icebreaker—to interrupt preoccupation with outside influences and capture attention in the virtual classroom. However, instead of somewhat random getting-to-know-you questions, openers feature content-related discussion starters. For example, at the start of a customer service virtual training class, instead of asking, "What did you have for dinner last night?" ask "What is your favorite restaurant and why?" Then use this restaurant discussion to lead into the topic of memorable customer service. The activity suddenly becomes an advance organizer instead of a time filler.

2. Create Community

When geographically dispersed participants join a virtual class, they are isolated from the group and often—even if subconsciously—feel alone. The facilitator needs to make special efforts to draw the participants together into a community so they feel like they're having a shared collective experience. When participants become part of a connected community, even briefly during a short virtual session, they become more accountable and have a better overall experience.

Research shows that connected participants learn more and have higher satisfaction rates. Manuel Cebrian at the University of California San Diego analyzed 80,000 interactions among 290 students in a collaborative learning environment and found that the more a student interacted with other students, the higher they scored in the course (Jacobs School of Engineering 2013). Researchers at the University of North Carolina-Wilmington examined interactivity in the virtual classroom, including learner-to-learner interactions. Their findings concluded that "interaction is crucial to student satisfaction in online courses" (Martin et al. 2012).

There are several ways a facilitator can help create community. From a simple poll question that asks participants to share their common experiences to putting participants in pairs or trios to discuss a topic, any time the facilitator connects participants, they create community. One-on-one conversations between participants can happen through a private paired chat activity or in small group breakout rooms. The more the facilitator creates a positive environment in which this networking can happen, the better the experience will be.

One of my favorite ways to open a virtual class is to establish pair partners within the first five to 10 minutes. I'll send these pairs into breakout rooms, asking them to start with introductions and then discuss a specific question. The initial conversation may be only four or five minutes long, but it immediately increases participant interest and engagement, setting the tone for the remainder of the session.

3. Show Up on Video

Whether or not participants use webcams (a topic we'll address more in chapter 7), a facilitator should be well versed in how to use video to enhance the virtual learning experience. Your ability to show up on camera influences the group dynamic and enhances learning with visuals, body language, eye contact, and human connection. It's one of the best ways to increase communication and dialogue in a group.

Your video setup is essential for showing up on camera professionally. My ABCD method will help you remember each item:

- **A = angle.** Put the camera at eye level. Move the camera angle so you look straight forward into the lens. You may need to reposition your laptop, get an external webcam, or adjust your chair so you can do this more comfortably. If you look down on the camera lens, your audience will subconsciously feel like you are looking down on them. It sends the message that you are trying to dominate the conversation. Instead, show up as their guide by using an appropriate camera angle.
- **B = background.** Try to have a clean, uncluttered scene behind you. You don't need a perfectly curated background, but it should not be distracting. Most platforms allow virtual or blurred backgrounds, which can conceal imperfections in your environment. However, those digital overlays take up extra bandwidth, which could be problematic for some facilitators. Virtual backgrounds can also get fuzzy if the lighting isn't just right. Use the best and clearest background for your environment.
- **C = clarity.** Place lighting in front of you. One of the most common mistakes facilitators make is hiding their faces in shadows. This happens if you sit in front of a window or don't have good lighting. If your office has overhead fluorescent lights or you don't have a place to sit with light in front of you, invest in a simple system to create a well-lit space. Ring lights and LED panels are relatively inexpensive and readily available.

- **D = distance.** Position yourself at the correct distance from the camera. Participants should be able to see your head and shoulders in the shot, with some space above the top of your head. If you are sitting in front of the camera, use the same rule of thirds as a professional photographer: Place yourself so that your eyes are about a third of the way down from the top of the image your viewers see. A quick way to measure? Check to see that there's enough space for your hand to rest on top of your head with your palm facing the camera. If you are standing, position yourself so the top part of your body is also visible.

Figure 5-3. The ABCD Techniques in Action

It doesn't matter whether you sit or stand on camera, or do a combination of both. If you're struggling to find the right angle, lighting, or distance, think about joining the virtual classroom from a mobile device perched on a tripod stand that's positioned at a prime spot for showing up on a webcam.

A common concern about using video is maintaining eye contact while facilitating. It looks more natural to your participants when you look at the camera lens. It takes practice and determination to do this when there are so many other things to look at on the screen. First, remember that as a learning facilitator, you are not reading from a script or teleprompter. Instead, you're leading a discussion or having a conversation with the participants. Therefore, the most crucial time to be looking into the camera lens is when other people are talking. Second, there will be natural times to glance away from the lens, just like glancing in a rearview mirror while driving a car. Your primary focus is on the participants, but you can look elsewhere on occasion. Use conversation transitions to adjust your line of sight or while participants are working on an activity. Set up your delivery workstation in a way that lets you easily see the entire screen at the same time as the camera lens. Or consider using virtual camera add-ins that mimic eye contact.

4. Speak With a Clear Voice

Beyond having good quality audio equipment as described earlier, an effective virtual facilitator makes the most of their voice's tone, volume, rate, and pitch to connect with participants in the virtual classroom. Your voice should be engaging enough to keep participants paying attention, but without becoming distracting. It should be crisp, easy to understand, and neutral—avoid using filler words. It should also be energetic enough to sound enthusiastic through the computer screen. Having a positive tone will enhance the learning experience.

Facilitators who talk too quickly are difficult to understand, and those who speak too slowly will lose participants' interest. The ideal voice speaks around 164 words per minute, pausing for less than a second between sentences (BBC News 2008). At the end of a sentence, your tone should fall instead of rise. A voice tone that lowers at the end of a sentence sounds declarative, like the speaker is making a statement. But when your voice rises at the end of a sentence, you sound uncertain, like you're asking a question. While not every voice matches this ideal, it's good to strive for something similar when seeking to improve your delivery style. You should sound energetic, enthusiastic about the topic, confident, and pleasant to the listening ear.

If you've never heard your own voice recorded, make a point to do so. Does your voice include variety and emphasis on the appropriate words? A common mistake is using too many filler words, which waste audio space and make it more difficult for participants to listen to you. Another common mistake is the intentional use of vocal fry—a creaky voice that can sometimes be interpreted as boredom—for emphasis. Listening to a monotone or difficult-to-hear speaker is exhausting in an in-person environment; it's even worse online.

A recent study found that highly qualified SMEs were perceived as lacking credibility if their audio stream wasn't clear. Same message, same content, same speaker; the only variable was audio quality (Newman and Schwarz 2018). This is why it pays to ensure your audio connection is as crystal clear as it can be. Effective virtual facilitators listen to their voices and adjust as necessary. They seek feedback and apply it.

Some facilitators have told me that they avoid using headsets because they don't want to feel a heavy band over their head or thick speakers over their ears. If this is your reason for not using a headset, I recommend you try out a different style, such as a behind-the-neck headset or a standalone microphone. Just be sure to position the mic so it doesn't catch your breath sounds while speaking, or use a pop filter to avoid sounding like you're in an air tunnel.

Fortunately, most virtual classroom platforms include built-in noise-canceling features that provide an extra layer of protection on top of your headset. Ensure you are familiar with these controls and how to use them. Again, these small but significant tactics will help your participants hear you better and help them learn.

5. Read the Virtual Room and Respond Accordingly

A common sentiment among frustrated virtual facilitators is that online classes are difficult because they lack body language cues. Webcams can partially overcome this challenge. However, here's a better response: Shift your mindset to read the room in other ways. The best virtual presenters can still read a virtual room, with or without everyone on a webcam. They simply use other techniques to gather feedback on participant engagement and learning.

Let's consider the skills you need to read a physical room. You observe the environment and pay attention to details. You use sensory perceptions to get a feel for the energy levels. You watch the body language, listen for audio clues, and take in all the other sights and sounds. Collectively these inputs give you a sense of the room's atmosphere.

It may seem more difficult to do all that in a virtual classroom, but you still observe the environment, watching for cues and paying attention to details. You're looking for inputs—verbal or physical (such as typing in the chat, writing on the whiteboard, and responding to poll questions)—and actively listening to those responses. You're carefully observing the audience and their actions. If learners are on camera, you can also watch their facial expressions and reactions.

If you are uncertain about the cues, interpreting them the wrong way, or not understanding cultural or other differences, simply ask the group for feedback. Post a poll question to gauge how they are feeling about a topic. Encourage the use of emojis in the chat. Invite them to share their thoughts. Use this input to adjust your facilitation style. For example, if energy levels have dropped, take a short stretch break to revitalize the room. It's okay to say something like, "You are all doing great, and you deserve a stretch. Let's all move our bodies before moving on to the next topic. Roll your shoulders, move your head from side to side, or do something that feels comforting to you." By paying close attention to your participants, you can read their digital cues and adapt appropriately.

When I was a child, I used to think my parents had eyes in the back of their heads because they always seemed to know when I was doing something I wasn't supposed to. One time I distinctly remember my father telling me I couldn't have a cookie before dinner, but I got one out of the cookie jar anyway. Somehow, he knew right away, even though he wasn't in the kitchen with me when it happened.

In some ways, a virtual facilitator's ability to read the audience is like my father's ability to sense that I had eaten the forbidden cookie. He knew because the evidence gave it away. I was probably silent for too long, or he heard me chewing loudly. Maybe he saw crumbs on the counter or on my face. A skilled and experienced facilitator uses the same sleuthing techniques to know when participants are connected and engaged in the class or have drifted off. They pay attention to the clues.

Some virtual classroom platforms have an "attentiveness indicator" feature. This tool shows the facilitator which participants are in the room, and which are not, by placing a symbol next to their name if they click away from the web platform. While the theory behind this feature is great, it's imperfect because it relies on the participant's active window. Anytime a participant stays on the virtual classroom window, they are considered "attentive," and anytime they click to another window, they are "not attentive." But this isn't a very accurate measure of engagement.

Just because a participant's active window is the virtual classroom doesn't mean they are truly engaged. And the same goes for the reverse. They may have clicked away to adjust the volume of their speakers or to look up something relevant to the content. They may be using an assistive device or taking notes in word processing software. Clearly, the attentiveness feature does not really measure participant engagement or learning. An engaged facilitator who is acutely tuned into participants is the best measure of levels of engagement.

Finally, when thinking about learner engagement, remember that silence is not necessarily bad. Natural pauses occur when speaking. And participants may need time to think before responding onscreen. In addition, many of the best virtual classes incorporate purposeful silence in the form of reflection time as a learning tool. Silence for the brain is like sleep for our bodies. It's a necessity—a chance to renew and recharge. So be careful not to equate silence with a lack of engagement. It's possible that the opposite is true.

6. Manage Group Dynamics

During an interactive virtual class full of engaging discussion, facilitators will need to manage the dynamics effectively. Good group relations are established at the beginning of a virtual class and supported by the facilitator throughout. This includes keeping track of time and process, involving everyone in the dialogue, and managing the planned learning activities. At the same time, facilitators work to increase trust, encourage dialogue, and build consensus.

An effective facilitator ensures that activity instructions and expectations are always clear. Participants are never left wondering what they should be doing at any given time—they always know what to do, when to do it, and what their current role entails. It's not that the facilitator becomes dictatorial, they're just being a clear communicator. If activity instructions are lengthy or detailed, as the facilitator, you can artfully share them in smaller chunks, both visually and verbally.

Facilitators also need to keep track of time. Because virtual classes are usually 60 to 90 minutes long (or shorter), every minute counts. Even a five-minute unexpected delay could affect the program's flow. During discussions, skilled facilitators actively listen while monitoring input signals (like time, topics, and so on). They may need to shorten a conversation, move a topic to the "parking lot" for later discussion, or ask permission to take the group in a different direction.

Skilled facilitators include everyone in activities and work with their producers to enable accessibility tools (like closed-captioning). They deliberately phrase questions in ways that invite all to participate. For example, instead of asking, "Who else has a comment about this topic?" they say, "Raise your hand if you have a comment; otherwise, click on the no reaction." Or they might say, "There are 11 of you, so let's get 11 responses in the chat before we continue." This simple rephrasing leads to massive changes in participation levels because it expects responses from everyone, not just the extroverted few. As a facilitator, it's vital to keep track of participation, openly ask for input, and seek everyone's involvement in the learning experience.

At the start of my virtual classes when we talk about participation guidelines, I'll sometimes tell participants to "Manage the distractions you can and minimize the ones you can't." I then invite them to choose an emoji to symbolize their agreement. Other times, I'll ask participants to choose their role for the class, with options such as "chat champion," "hand-raise monitor," "notetaker," and "active participant." Or, I may propose a set of agreements and invite the group to comment on and adjust them before we put them to a vote. Regardless of the actual method, the essence of these early activities is about gaining agreement on how the group will work together to achieve the learning goals.

Another technique to manage group dynamics is to assign partners or teams with intention. For example, it may make sense to group participants by region or department for one class, but in another class, it could be better to diversify the groups. Skilled facilitators also pay attention to how well the groups "gel" and adjust accordingly.

For breakout activities, purposefully assign a team leader or someone to start the discussion so groups don't waste time figuring out roles and responsibilities. For example, you may say, "We're now transitioning into breakout groups. If your name is alphabetically listed first in your breakout room's participant list, please jump in to be the team leader. This means you get to talk first and help the group keep track of time."

When a skilled facilitator successfully manages group dynamics in a virtual classroom, the participants typically won't notice, because it just becomes part of the overall learning experience.

Managing Group Dynamics in Hybrid Classes

While proper hybrid room technology makes it easier for everyone to have a shared experience, it's your skill as a facilitator managing hybrid group discussions that can make or break the learning environment. A hybrid facilitator's job is to enable relationship building among all participants, despite location differences, so everyone can learn together.

It may seem counterintuitive, but to create space for conversation as a facilitator, you need to be more prescriptive, direct, and structured than you would be in other settings. For example, when asking discussion questions, you need to specify how participants should respond. This helps keep the in-person participants from jumping in and dominating the conversation, which could easily happen without the extra direction.

Instead of simply asking, "Who has prior experience with this process?" say something like, "Do any of you have prior experience with this process? If yes, click on raise hand, and if not, just click on no." From there, the discussion can proceed based on the input you receive. Or, to help guide a conversation while also avoiding uncomfortable audio lags, you can designate the order in which participants speak. Keep in mind that it's not about controlling the conversation; it's about enabling it. When you provide boundaries, participant dialogue can flourish.

In the hybrid environment, facilitators should always have a remote-first mindset, giving priority to off-site attendees in conversation. This preference helps balance the disadvantages of not being in the room with everyone else.

This type of facilitation doesn't happen by accident; it requires planning. Facilitators who successfully bridge the gap across locations are the ones who carefully consider the methods they will use to generate conversation.

7. Involve Participants

One of the most important but difficult virtual facilitation skills is to release control and involve participants—to let go of your need to exert power and to allow it to shift to the learners. It can be challenging to do this in person, and it's even tougher to do it online. The fact that participants aren't always visible, and even if they are, it's harder to know if they are fully engaged in the learning, creates an extra hurdle for many facilitators.

One reason facilitators are unwilling to transfer power to remote participants is the fear of silence, because they think silence means participants are not paying attention. However, silence can mean many things. Participants may be reflecting on a learning point, formulating their next response, or taking notes on an action they want to take.

Some facilitators also fear silence because they think if they aren't talking, they aren't doing their job. One common mistake is keeping up a running commentary while participants are doing an activity. If you ask participants to brainstorm on a whiteboard, you may be tempted to start talking as soon as the first item appears. Or if participants are responding to a question via chat, you may want to start reading the comments as they come in. But no one is listening to you in that moment—they're all focused on typing in their own responses and reading the others. The better choice is to wait until most responses have appeared before discussing them.

Now consider a whiteboard activity. A facilitator sets the stage, provides instructions, and ensures that everyone is equipped with drawing tools. Then, they stay silent while the participants work. As the whiteboard contributions start to wane, the facilitator might ask participants to make sure their text is visible to all and then raise their hands when they're finished typing. The silence allows participants the time and space they need to do the activity without facilitator interruption. Skilled facilitators are comfortable with this type of silence.

Two key facilitation methods that involve participants are sharing airtime and allowing choice:

- **Sharing airtime** is when skilled facilitators actively involve participants in the discussion. Rather than reading exactly what's written on a slide, they may post a slide and ask participants to raise their hands when they're finished reading it or ask them to comment on the content. Skilled facilitators don't read every chat comment aloud or whiteboard entry verbatim. Instead, they let participants elaborate on their own words as part of the discussion and dialogue.

- **Allowing choice** reflects the fact that most adults don't like to be told what to do and instead prefer to have a say over their environment. Skilled facilitators let participants choose at every opportunity. This can be as simple as using an invitation instead of a command, like asking, "Will you join me on page 7 to review the case study instructions?" Or it can be more complex, such as letting participants choose which case study to use in small group work. They may say something like, "The conversation in scenario A takes place in an in-person office environment and scenario B has a remote employee in a hybrid workplace. Use the scenario that more closely matches your reality." You can also take advantage of the "choose your own breakout room" feature that some virtual platforms have.

For my own virtual classes, I pre-plan ways to release control to participants. I go through the facilitator guide looking for opportunities to open the dialogue. I review the slides to see where I might be tempted to talk too much. I search for ways to involve learners and provide choices. Afterward, I reflect on the experience to discover where I could have improved. My goal is to keep the participants immersed in the conversation and collaboration so they can learn from one another and apply the content back on the job.

8. Debrief Learning Activities

A classic facilitator responsibility is guiding participants through an experience, and then helping them process and learn from it afterward. Skilled facilitators ask a series of intentional questions designed to help participants reflect and respond. This essential process is called *debriefing*. The facilitator's primary role in debriefing isn't exclusive to the virtual classroom, but the methods used are unique.

One popular debriefing technique is the "What?" "So what?" "Now what?" series of questions (Driscoll and Teh 2001). In this method, the facilitator asks participants to reflect on what happened during the learning experience, then asks them questions about the importance of the experience, and finally, probes them about future application opportunities. Another popular debriefing technique is to ask reflection questions such as, "What's a new insight you gained today?" and "How will you apply this information after you leave?" No matter the technique, debriefing's goal is always to ask questions that encourage contemplation, reflection, and learning.

In the virtual classroom, it's important to keep our participants' attention during what can be lengthy debriefing discussions. If only one person is speaking at a time, everyone else may be tempted to tune out of the conversation. Skilled facilitators will keep everyone engaged by asking for responses from the entire group via chat, poll, or other methods. You may also use guided breakout group conversations in which the participants process the learning experience in small teams. Pay extra attention to timing to create an appropriate balance and keep energy and engagement levels high.

Another distinction in the virtual classroom is the number of tools available. As I've already noted, the ease of involving everyone in a poll, chat, whiteboard, or breakout group creates more opportunities to include all participants in debriefing discussions. It also allows for additional creative debriefing methods.

For example, after a whiteboard brainstorm, you can ask participants to review the board and mark or stamp anything that resonates with them. That way, participants can silently review the class input and reflect upon it. Once the stamps appear, ask the group to look for patterns and themes, drawing out key learning points from their observations.

When participants return from breakout activities, you have several debriefing options. The round-robin report-out method is the most common ("Let's hear first from group 1, then from group 2, then group 3, and so on"). However, as I've said previously, avoid this method if you want to keep engagement levels high. Let's take a look at a few more effective debriefing methods:

- Invite each group to share one single highlight from their discussion, avoiding anything that another group has already said. Instruct all participants to raise a virtual hand if they hear something their group also discussed.
- Post a poll question with discussion topics that likely surfaced during the breakout activity. Invite participants to select which topics their group discussed, so you can reveal the post-poll results and examine patterns. Be sure to include an "other" response option to capture any unique topics.
- Invite each group to share their whiteboard or other electronic notes, asking the spokesperson to "Tell us one place on your board we should look at."

- On a shared collaborative whiteboard, conduct a digital gallery walk so each group can scroll around the board and review what everyone else said. Then invite discussion of patterns and themes.

Traditionally, debriefing questions are open-ended. You'll find most open-ended questions are met with silence in the virtual classroom, however, because they're not specific enough to jump-start the conversation. Virtual facilitators get much better responses when the initial question is both *precise* and *prescriptive*. In other words, ask a specific question that includes directions on how to respond. For example, instead of asking, "What did you observe in this demonstration?" it's better to say, "What one event stood out in the demonstration? Please type it in the chat." Or, "Raise your hand if you noticed ABC happen during the demonstration." From there, you can use the typed comments or raised hands to ask follow-up questions and get the conversation going.

Skilled debriefing is especially important when immersive simulations are part of the virtual learning experience. VR usually lives up to its name, creating a realistic virtual environment. Participants who become fully immersed in a scenario will feel like it's really happening to them. If the simulation is dangerous (a safety simulation, for example) or full of conflict (like a crowd-control scenario), then emotions may run high. Facilitators should allow learners enough time to reflect (and possibly decompress) individually or in small groups before discussing what happened. The richer the simulation, the more or longer participants will need to talk. Experienced facilitators can help participants process their feelings and de-escalate emotions.

To successfully debrief learning activities in the virtual classroom, facilitators need to be active listeners who can draw out meaning from both written and verbal comments and keep participants engaged so they can translate what they've just learned into on-the-job application.

9. Manage Technology With Effective Multitasking

Expert facilitation looks like a duck gliding across a pond. An outside observer sees smooth sailing, but underneath the duck is paddling furiously to propel itself forward. Similarly, an effective virtual facilitator must juggle many tasks with ease. There's always a lot going on at once in a virtual classroom, and facilitators must pay attention to content, activities, timing, participant comments, and the platform. Effective multitasking comes from a combination of preparation and speed. Virtual facilitators who do it well are prepared, practiced, and proficient:

- **Prepared.** One benefit of having enough preparation time is that it contributes to effective multitasking. Take time to prepare your workspace, removing any unnecessary documents from your desk so you can give your full attention to the screen. When you are fully prepared, you won't have to use extra energy to remember what comes next.
- **Practiced.** Effective virtual facilitators practice interacting with all their tools and using their facilitation techniques. Just like a world-class musician who plays a song over and over again until it sounds perfect, an effective facilitator practices as much as possible to improve their skills. The more experience you have with multitasking, the better you will be.
- **Proficient.** By having in-depth knowledge of all their tools, effective facilitators won't have to hunt for menu commands or stop to think about where to find an item. They are also skilled typists who don't need to watch the keyboard to type. As a virtual facilitator, your proficiency comes from diligent practice, which leads to easier multitasking.

Unforeseen challenges can occur during virtual classes—a participant may disconnect, an activity might not go as planned, or a distraction (such as a barking dog, thunderstorm, or other background noise) might need to be addressed. You should expect one or more challenges to arise during each class; it's part of the territory. If you prepare relentlessly, you will be able to rely on your backup plans for any unexpected technology challenges. For example, if you lose internet connectivity, you can switch to your backup provider. If an activity doesn't work as planned, you can respond with flexibility and good humor and switch to something else. Challenges are an opportunity for you to stay calm, handle things gracefully, take care of the issue, and return focus to the learning as quickly as possible.

10. Validate Learning

The ultimate measure of a successful learning experience is participant behavior change and the transfer of their new knowledge and skills to on-the-job results. All virtual class activities and facilitation techniques should lead to these outcomes.

The virtual facilitator's job is to ensure that participants are following along the expected learning path and that they understand and grasp the program's topics. You'll need to validate their learning and ability to apply their new skills.

First, make sure the design has built-in knowledge checks throughout the event to assess understanding and comprehension. Knowledge checks can go beyond polls and quizzes focused on recalling facts to include hands-on activities and other practical application exercises. As a facilitator, it may be tempting to bypass these if you are short on time, but they are an essential part of the learning experience. For example, in one section of my Virtual Facilitation Skills workshops, each participant must rephrase a question, using a specific skill they just learned. This activity mirrors what they'll do when facilitating and helps me test their comprehension and application abilities.

Second, you can use very small group breakout activities, with two to three attendees per group, for application conversations. By working in pairs or trios, everyone has an opportunity to be involved and engaged. It's much harder to stay silent.

Third, you should have extra examples and scenarios you can share if participants have questions or need additional explanations. The ability to flex the agenda as needed comes from a combination of active listening and reading the room. If you predetermine what's need-to-know content versus the nice-to-know content, it will be easier for you to adjust the program's timing by decreasing the amount of time you spend on the less important information.

Finally, you should carefully monitor participant involvement in the learning activities. It's easier to hide and remain anonymous in a virtual class, so facilitators need to ensure each person is connected and engaged in learning. If they choose to remain passive, find out if that choice is affecting their ability to learn. And if technical problems or accessibility roadblocks are getting in the way of learning—such as a participant who can't stay connected due to bandwidth issues—be ready to reschedule them to the next class, or have other backup learning activities you can give them.

A quote famously attributed to Albert Einstein is, "I never teach my pupils; I only attempt to provide the conditions in which they can learn." This sentiment summarizes the role of a skilled virtual facilitator. And as we've discovered, it's the unique combination of your mindset, tool set, and skill set that creates conditions in which your participants can thrive.

One Organization's Story
A Train-the-Trainer Approach With High-Quality Results

Dale Carnegie Digital has an extensive train-the-trainer process for new virtual facilitators. They begin with trainers who have already gone through the rigorous certification process required to deliver Dale Carnegie content. Then, potential virtual trainers must be recommended by someone in their organization who can attest to their excellent delivery skills.

The virtual train-the-trainer process includes four live online sessions totaling 12 hours of learning time. Topics include how to facilitate online and how to engage participants in their learning. The virtual trainer candidates practice delivering content using a teach-back methodology through which they receive feedback and coaching from an expert trainer. The next step is to co-facilitate at least three classes, totaling nine hours of delivery. They receive feedback and coaching on these co-facilitation sessions.

After a virtual trainer has been endorsed to deliver online, they are required to attend refreshers each year to stay up to speed on both technology and content. The time, effort, and resources invested in Dale Carnegie's virtual facilitators lead to high-quality results.

In Summary: Key Points From Chapter 5

- Effective virtual facilitators create an environment that's conducive to participant learning.
- Successful virtual facilitators know the virtual classroom platform inside and out—every feature, tool, button, and command.
- Facilitators need sufficient technology resources to do their jobs well.
- The art of online facilitation includes 10 distinct and powerful techniques.

Take Action

✓ Review your organization's facilitator selection process and upskilling methods and compare them with the recommendations in this chapter. If you have experienced virtual facilitators, is there an ongoing development and continuous improvement process in place for them?

✓ Use the observation form in Tool 5-2 to provide encouraging feedback and constructive advice to your virtual facilitators.

Tool 5-1. Virtual Delivery Tips for Success: A Quick Reference Guide for Facilitators

Facilitators can use this quick reference chart as a job aid while delivering a virtual session. Hang it in a conspicuous place (like clipped to your monitor) so that you'll easily see these reminders just before every virtual delivery.

- ☐ Create a comfortable environment for participants.
- ☐ Establish clear expectations for interaction and engagement.
- ☐ Help participants learn to use the tools as needed throughout the session.
- ☐ Create a sense of community among all participants.
- ☐ Give specific directions on how to answer questions. (Chat? Poll? Verbal? Other?)
- ☐ Drive toward the learning outcomes by helping participants see the connections between the content and their working environments.
- ☐ Keep the focus on participants throughout class with a learner-first mentality. It's about them, not about you.
- ☐ Share airtime by releasing control to participants as much as possible.
- ☐ Minimize the impact of any technical difficulties.
- ☐ Be confident in your knowledge of technology and the content.
- ☐ Create enthusiasm and excitement using your voice and attitude.

Tool 5-2. Virtual Facilitator Observation Form

Continuous improvement should be a goal for all virtual facilitators. If you are evaluating facilitators, use this observation form to monitor performance, enhance and coach delivery skills, and provide feedback.

Virtual Facilitator Observation

Facilitator:	Program:
Observer:	Date observed:

Skills	Observed	Comments
Opens with interactivity	☐ Greets learners upon entry ☐ Invites immediate interaction at the start of the session	
Creates a comfortable learning environment	☐ Creates a welcoming and inclusive online environment ☐ Teaches how to use platform tools as needed ☐ Adapts content to make it relevant to learners through stories and examples	
Engages learners	☐ Limits own airtime by inviting learners into the conversation ☐ Creates opportunities for discussion and dialogue ☐ Draws out learners who are silent	
Asks questions	☐ Asks specific, precise questions ☐ Gives instructions for how to respond to each question via poll, chat, raise hand, verbal response, or other means	
Facilitates	☐ Refers to, but doesn't read, slides ☐ Maintains a learner-centered mindset	
Builds rapport	☐ Shows interest in learners ☐ Uses learners' names	
Makes the most of the media (e.g., voice, webcam, and VR)	☐ Speaks clearly and audibly ☐ Conveys enthusiasm for the topic ☐ Sounds energetic and confident ☐ Appears confident and professional on webcam	
Uses technology effectively	☐ Uses platform tools with ease ☐ Handles technology challenges without disruption	
Partners with producers or co-facilitators	☐ Has established clear roles and responsibilities ☐ Has seamless conversational transitions	

Additional comments:

CHAPTER 6

Support Producers

 In this chapter, you will learn how producers support virtual training:

- Identify the producer's role in virtual training success.
- Recognize three types of producers.
- Employ techniques to support facilitators and participants.
- Troubleshoot common tech issues.

If you have experienced a smoothly delivered virtual training class without any tech hiccups or glitches, it was probably supported by a producer. The best virtual experiences don't happen by accident; their delivery teams carefully and intentionally choreograph them. The work of these teams usually goes unnoticed because it is executed so flawlessly by producers working behind the scenes from start to finish.

Consider how important behind-the-scenes preparation is to countless positive experiences in our everyday lives. For example, when you place your regular order at a favorite coffee shop and walk out with a tasty beverage, you don't give it a second thought because you expected the transaction to happen without a glitch. But if the shop is missing your preferred type of milk, the registers are down, or the barista is having a bad day and taking it out on you, these mishaps might negatively influence your thoughts or actions. Your mood may turn sour, or you might tell friends to avoid that shop. When an event happens as planned, it doesn't usually stick in our minds, but when things go wrong, we take notice and sometimes take action.

In a carefully planned and supported virtual training experience, participants will focus on the learning, rather than being distracted by what's happening behind the scenes. But when a key component is missing, the technology doesn't work, or adequate support is lacking, participants will be acutely aware of it. Their focus will shift from the learning outcomes to the program's mishaps and mistakes. Producers strive to create excellent virtual events, knowing that if they do their job well, it will enhance everything about the learning experience.

What's in a Name?

We call producers *hosts*, *moderators*, *emcees*, or *co-facilitators*, depending on the virtual platform we're using, and their titles may change to reflect their session roles. Some platforms use the term host for the session leader who has full tech control of the virtual room. In that case, it makes sense to call the producer the host. Or if multiple speakers are rotating in and out of the presenter role, the producer may naturally be called a moderator. If two facilitators take turns in the producer role when they are not leading, they would each be co-facilitators.

The Producer's Multiple Roles

As we discussed in the previous chapter, the most effective virtual learning experiences have two session leaders—a facilitator and a producer. Let's focus first on why a producer adds value and why it's good to invest time and resources into including one in your virtual training plans. Producers do many things behind the scenes including:

- **Handle the technology on which the whole experience depends.** Because virtual training relies on working technology, a producer may mean the difference between having a virtual class or nothing at all. Traditional producers start the session, help everyone connect, troubleshoot problems, give instructions, manage the tools, and allow everyone else to do their jobs. Facilitators can facilitate and participants can participate, and producers are the foundation of virtual success.

- **Support facilitators.** This support allows facilitators to stay tuned in to the participants. When a technical expert runs the software and manages technology issues, it frees up the facilitator to focus fully on the learning progress. The facilitator doesn't get distracted or bogged down in tech challenges. A solid partnership and division of responsibility between producer and facilitator makes for a better participant learning experience.

- **Help participants focus on the learning goals.** A producer assists participants with tech questions, which allows them to focus their attention on learning.

Without a producer, a participant who has trouble logging in to the session may give up and simply not attend. A participant who struggles to use annotation tools may focus more on conquering the tools than on participating in the learning activity. With a producer standing by to assist, all participants can get involved and accomplish their learning goals.

- **Enable accessibility tools.** As the technology expert, the producer checks settings like closed-captioning, focus mode, keyboard shortcuts, and more. They turn on these features and provide tech instructions for how to use them.
- **Teach participants about the technology.** The producer may assist participants silently through a private chat or by giving verbal instructions. At times, they might reach out by email or phone to someone who is struggling to remain on the platform. If the producer provides the tech instructions participants need, the facilitator can keep the rest of the class going.
- **Provide a technical safety net.** If the facilitator or one of the speakers loses connectivity, the producer can step in to continue the session, which gives facilitators a tremendous sense of security. This is much easier to do if the producer is following along with the facilitator guide (explained in chapter 4), or if they met with the facilitator in advance to plan for contingencies. For example, I was once facilitating a class when the power in my home office went out. With my internet router down, I lost all connections—visual and audio. Fortunately, I avoided disaster because I had backup systems ready to go and was able to reconnect within a couple minutes. In the meantime, my producer jumped into action and got the class into the next activity while I was getting back online.

If you're a solo facilitator without a producer, you take a risk with every virtual class.

Producers and Virtual Training Satisfaction

John Hall, former senior vice president of Oracle University, measured participant satisfaction in his organization's online classes and found that those with producers consistently scored two percentage points higher on participant satisfaction surveys the ones without producers. Simply put, having a producer on board for your training makes for a better participant experience.

Creative Ways to Fill the Producer Role

Every day around the world, virtual training classes occur with just one facilitator at the helm. Many of my clients say their companies simply won't provide funding or support to bring on a co-facilitator or producer. I have facilitated many sessions without producer support myself. But even though it can be done, training without a co-facilitator or producer is risky from a technical perspective and prevents the facilitator from focusing fully on the participants.

If, despite all the reasons for investing in a dedicated, expert producer, it is not an option in your organization, consider these creative solutions:

- Ask someone to serve as a limited or partial producer, joining your sessions for the first 10 to 15 minutes to help with initial questions and connecting learners to the platform.
- Ask a facilitator-in-training to play the role of producer for some of your classes—this helps you and it also helps them learn.
- Find someone in your organization who wants to learn more about technology and take the time to train them to become a producer.
- Ask your platform vendor if they offer technical support services, which may include in-session producer support.
- Partner with your IT department and ask them to provide someone to function as a producer during your virtual training classes.
- If you have the budget, add a producer job role in your training department; that person would be a full-time producer for every virtual training class.
- Hire an external partner to supply producers on a class-by-class contract basis.

In many organizations, you'll have to use your imagination to find a solution that works.

Types of Producers

Different types of virtual events call for different types of producers. Some will stay completely behind the scenes, never speaking to the participants; others will be heavily involved in program facilitation. The platform features, program requirements, and facilitator's preferences all help determine the best type of producer for the situation. There are three main types of producers: the tech expert, the supporter, and the co-facilitator. Table 6-1 provides a quick summary, and then we'll discuss each type in more detail.

Table 6-1. The 3 Types of Producers

Producer Type	Description
Tech expert	Behind-the-scenes tech management, rarely seen or heard by participants unless there is a visible problem to solve
Supporter	Periodic input with an occasional speaking role; may help greet participants, explain tech instructions for a class activity, or stay active in the chat conversation
Co-facilitator	Active role in facilitating the learning experience; takes turns with other co-facilitators, rotating in and out of the producer seat

The Tech Expert

A tech expert producer stays behind the scenes. They help connect participants to the class, assisting with any challenges that arise. They run the software platform, open poll questions, put participants into breakout groups, and assist with other classroom tools as needed. If tech problems arise, the producer resolves them.

For example, if a participant loses connection to the audio due to a glitch in the system, the producer will use a private chat to help them get reconnected. If the facilitator accidentally loses internet connectivity, the producer can keep the class moving along while the facilitator reconnects. Participants might never even know this producer exists—unless they speak up or chat to offer instructions when someone needs additional guidance.

I describe the tech expert producer's role as similar to the role of a radio talk show or live podcast producer. You've probably seen someone in that role in a movie or TV show. The producer sits behind a control panel to oversee the mechanics of the production. They take care of callers, help the show's host stay on time, and manage any problems that occur behind the scenes or on air. A virtual class producer does the same thing, overseeing the intricate and essential details of the training class.

The level of tech involvement varies from producer to producer and class to class. Some facilitators, including me, like to manage at least some of the platform features during the session. I like to share my documents, open my polls, use annotation tools to highlight words onscreen, and help participants when they need it. Other facilitators may want to run their own slides but will ask the producer to open polls and monitor the chat. It's always a best practice for the producer and facilitator to plan how they'll work together before starting a class. You'll find guidelines for planning in Tool 6-1 at the end of this chapter.

The Supporter

Let's continue the radio talk show or live podcast analogy. A show's host may draw the producer into the on-air conversation to pique listener interest or to help explain an important and relevant detail. A virtual class facilitator can do the same thing. Producers can help greet participants as they arrive in the virtual classroom or assist with a debrief by capturing aha moments in the chat. When you interact with participants beyond offering brief technical assistance, I would call you a *supporter*.

A supporter has more responsibilities than the tech expert. They do everything the tech expert does and then some. As a supporter, you may be on camera for part of the virtual class, talking with participants and leading sessions. You actively encourage involvement in addition to managing the technology.

The best producers stay active in the chat, joining in group conversations and providing positive feedback for participants who are engaging with the content. They become another voice helping to create an interactive and interesting learning environment. And they still stay alert for tech issues and resolve them when needed.

The Co-Facilitator

A producer who takes an active role in facilitating the class is a co-facilitator. They might be responsible for small portions of the content or share equally with the other facilitator. In addition to any training responsibilities, a co-facilitator takes the lead role in addressing any technology questions or problems.

Before the session, the facilitator and co-facilitator should plan exactly who will do what and when. They might rotate between roles frequently or have a predesignated moment, such as the halfway point, for switching responsibilities.

Co-facilitator producers have more responsibilities requiring more skills than tech experts or supporters. But all co-facilitators are also tech experts, of course. You'll have to be prepared to do it all while staying in perfect synchronization with your facilitator partner. This role demands a lot of preplanning to fulfill it successfully.

Selecting Producers

The most effective producers possess a unique blend of skills and knowledge. First and foremost, they need to be experts in the technology. Not only do they need to know the virtual training platform inside and out, but they also need to have a solid understanding of computer hardware and software in general. A good producer should also be able to:

- Troubleshoot and solve problems.
- Remain calm under pressure.
- Juggle multiple tasks at once.
- Listen carefully and actively.
- Think quickly on their feet and take action as needed.
- Convey empathy when working with participants or facilitators who are struggling.
- Keep learning all the time.

One Organization's Story
Producer Selection at Elsie

When Elizabeth Beales, chief executive officer of Elsie, a leading global provider of virtual learning support, identifies new producers, she prioritizes five specific qualities in candidates—agility, solid communication skills, technical aptitude, attentiveness, and composure. She believes these attributes ensure her team delivers higher quality training that result in effective knowledge transfer and better learning outcomes.

"In our tenure at Elsie, we've seen how these qualities empower our team of virtual event producers and facilitators to elevate training, aligning with our mission to make online learning easy, effective, and enjoyable," Beales explains. "These attributes not only contribute to better participant engagement and stronger learning outcomes but also foster a positive and collaborative work environment."

Agility

Producers who can swiftly adapt to evolving technology and new situations to ensure seamless transitions and effective problem solving during virtual training sessions are especially valuable. Elsie's producers must be comfortable managing multiple breakout rooms and interactive platform features during virtual training, often switching among tasks and introducing new requests in the moment, allowing facilitators to deliver content adapted to learners and securing their engagement.

Communication Skills

Effective communication is vital because it ensures clear and efficient collaboration among team members and with clients. Producers need to articulate ideas, instructions, and feedback concisely, fostering a cohesive and productive learning environment.

Technical Aptitude

A strong technical foundation and troubleshooting skills are crucial for producers who are managing the intricacies of a variety of virtual training platforms and swiftly addressing any technical issues that arise during sessions.

Attentiveness

For Beales, attention to detail is paramount, because producers need to oversee so many aspects of virtual training—from platform setup to content delivery. Being attentive to the finer points that others might overlook helps ensure a seamless and polished training experience.

Composure

Maintaining composure under pressure is essential for new and experienced producers alike. It enables them. Even in challenging circumstances, they're expected to manage situations calmly and deliver high-quality training.

For more information about Elsie's producer team, visit elsie.co.

Producer Preparation

After selecting producers, you should ensure they are fully prepared to support the virtual learning experience. In chapter 5, we discussed some similarities in preparing facilitators and producers. Now, we'll focus on the unique aspects of the producer role.

Producers and facilitators are like musicians who do their work in front of a live audience. To achieve their best performances, they lay the groundwork weeks, months, or years in advance. World-class musicians master the basics before moving on to their performance pieces. Leading up to showtime, the intensity of their preparation increases—and while each musician has their own routine and habits, the key elements of the process are typically the same.

Effective virtual producers begin by mastering the entire tech stack related to virtual training. They gain confidence working with a variety of computers and learn the intricacies of specific hardware and software. They master virtual platforms, set up a workspace, and familiarize themselves with the program content. They meet with the program facilitator to clarify roles and responsibilities and prepare the necessary presession details.

Producers specifically focus on three things to get ready: the platform, the program, and the workspace.

Learn the Platform

Like seasoned facilitators, the best producers are experts in the virtual classroom platform. They have mastered the software's settings and tools, which means they know every menu, button, setting, and command. They know how it works and looks from the presenter's view as well as the participant's view. They can use all the features with ease and can help participants use them too. Chapter 5 outlined several ways to learn about the platform, and those tips also apply to producers.

Some organizations offer formal producer upskilling programs, which include learning the platform and spending time with a more experienced producer to learn the ropes. In my producer certification program, I take people through a blended learning journey that covers most of the topics in this chapter.

Keep in mind that learning how to use the virtual platform is not a one-and-done step on your path to producing. Vendors frequently change or enhance platform features and may make updates monthly or even weekly. Some producers work in tandem with one another and with facilitators to keep abreast of changes; others frequently check the vendor's website for news. However you choose to do it, keeping up with platform changes should be part of your regular workflow.

Learn the Program

Producers rarely need to be content experts unless they are also co-facilitators. (And if that's the case, simply refer to chapter 5.) Producers should be familiar enough with the program content to know what activities are coming and when, as well as what's expected in each case. They need to know how the activity is supposed to work so they can respond when participants are having trouble or something in the platform is not working properly.

The easiest way for producers to become familiar with the program content is to review a detailed facilitator or producer guide. This document, created during the program design process, outlines the virtual class from start to finish, including all required preparation tasks and timing, with callouts for actions the producer should take. (Tool 6-2 at the end of this chapter contains a sample guide for reference.) Some producers also create a checklist with relevant notes or an agenda with information that tells them when and how to act. In case of tech problems, it's always a good idea for producers to have a backup copy of any slides or other materials that will be used in the virtual class.

Prepare the Workspace

Previous sections of this book explored the technology resources needed for engaging virtual training. Producers, just like facilitators, need a desktop or laptop, a reliable (and wired) internet connection, a quality audio connection, a webcam, and up-to-date software for the classroom. Producers also benefit from having additional items like an external monitor with a large screen, a backup laptop with the same specs as their primary device, and a mobile device for another layer of connectivity. The most effective producers take extra care to ensure they have the hardware and software resources necessary to provide exceptional tech support to others. To give you a visual idea of a producer's setup, Figure 6-1 is a photo of what one producer's desk looks like when they're supporting a virtual class.

Figure 6-1. Example of a Producer's Webcam Setup

Source: Michael Thatcher, Elsie producer. Used with permission.

Of course, workspace preparation also includes backup options, such as an extra headset in case the standard one unexpectedly stops working or a mobile device with the platform's app open and classroom link entered. One producer I work with sets up a physical screen behind them; it's made of special cloth that mimics a brick wall and gives them a professional appearance when on camera. This physical background doesn't require the extra bandwidth a virtual background would need.

The preparation goes beyond physical hardware—producers need to set up their workspace so it's conducive to the role. They should minimize distractions; for example, moving their to-do list out of sight so their mind won't wander to the unfinished list. And their workspace should have everything they'll need within reach, including water (with a lid), a working pen, and paper. And don't underestimate the importance of comfortable seating.

By taking just a few extra steps, producers can set themselves up for success and be prepared to handle anything that may transpire during the virtual class.

Workspace Prep Tips From a Veteran Producer

I asked Luke Chiaruttini, one of Elsie's most experienced producers, for his top tips for prepping a workspace. Here's what he said:

"Building your facilitator's and audience's trust and confidence in your technical skills is just as important as possessing those skills as a virtual producer. The most seasoned producers have a checklist of things they review just before meeting with the facilitator prior to a virtual class. Like the airplane instructions to put on your own mask before helping others, a checklist helps to ensure that your producer tech works well before you start helping participants—and you don't have to give the facilitator a sneak preview of your troubleshooting abilities. This means testing your audio and video connections, running an internet speed test before your session to determine if you have any drops in bandwidth, updating your virtual platform apps daily, and joining your sessions five to 10 minutes early just in case any settings or permissions changed since your tests.

"One more tip that producers often forget: Keep water and snacks by your desk! A five- to 10-minute break in a session can easily turn into five or 10 minutes of troubleshooting with a participant, and no time for you to step away. The participants always come first in a live session, so set yourself up with all you need ahead of time."

The Producer-Facilitator Relationship

We have already discussed the fact that a good partnership between facilitators and producers is grounded in excellent communication and a clear division of responsibilities. Have an initial meeting to talk through the program and expectations on both sides—ideally, at least a week before the virtual class. A detailed facilitator guide that includes producer notes can jump-start this conversation. See Tool 6-2 at the end of this chapter for an example.

It's standard practice for facilitators and producers to meet in the virtual classroom at least 30 minutes before the program starts. This prep time provides an opportunity for last-minute conversations to confirm details and review any new information. For instance, they can discuss adjustments to activities or chat about the breakout room assignments. Thirty minutes is enough time for a tech check and discussion before any participants join the session.

Facilitators and producers can strengthen their relationship over time while working together across multiple events. In some cases, my producers and I have become so familiar with each other's style that we can communicate quickly and efficiently with few words. For example, if I simply say, "In a moment, you will get to talk with a partner about this topic," my long-time producer knows I'm adding an unplanned breakout activity and will want two participants per room. They appreciate the warning ("In a moment . . .") and quickly start getting the rooms ready. On the flip side, if my producer adds a certain reaction as a status indicator next to their name, I know they are troubleshooting something in the background.

It's also a great idea to have a meeting between the facilitator and producer to go over lessons learned after the virtual class, especially if they are likely to team up again in future sessions. This type of meeting can be as simple as a brief discussion right after the class. Or it can be a formal debrief walking through what worked and what you would like to change next time.

"As a producer, I feel like a co-captain in the session. To best support the facilitator, I check with them in advance about specific activity requirements or anything I need to be aware of regarding the participants. For example, I might ask whether there are participants with a line manager and associate connection who we should avoid putting into the same breakout group. It is vital to have this presession time—even if it's only a few minutes—alone in the virtual space with the facilitator. The better the alignment and briefing, the more I can be of value to the facilitator."

—Marion Schilcher, Producer at Elsie

Seven Ways Producers Support Facilitators

As we've already discussed, a producer's main responsibility is to support all technical aspects of a virtual class. They do this by assisting the facilitator with the platform tools, ensuring a smooth and seamless experience for all. Seven tasks fall under the category of facilitator support, and we will examine each one in detail:

1. Check platform permissions and settings.
2. Communicate clearly throughout the session.
3. Manage the technology and keep it working for everyone.
4. Stay alert for problems or changes.
5. Be ready with backup plans.
6. Add visual instructions to verbal.
7. Use your voice.

1. Check Platform Permissions and Settings

Each virtual classroom platform is unique in its features and functionality (Figure 6-2). Something that comes standard in one may be optional in another. Participants may be able to easily draw on a built-in whiteboard in platform A, but that same ability in platform B requires you to enable whiteboards in the settings and grant participant permissions in advance. Effective producers know their platform's standard settings and when to adjust them for the activity requirements. This task alleviates pressure on the facilitator who might otherwise miss a step or get caught off guard when something doesn't work as expected.

Figure 6-2. Meeting Preferences in Adobe Connect

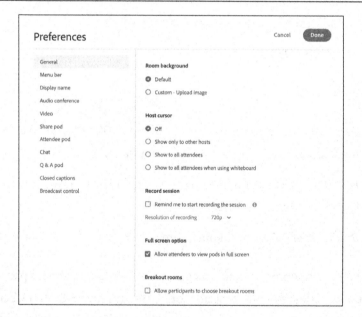

In addition, producers should confirm that everyone, including the facilitator, has the correctly assigned presenter rights. Some platforms allow for multiple hosts, while others allow for only one host with many presenters. Other platforms assume that all participants should have presenter rights by default. It's the producer's job to manage these details and ensure everyone has the appropriate privileges.

2. Communicate Clearly Throughout the Session

Producers and facilitators usually engage in a running conversation throughout the session. They talk about activity setups, participant needs, timing issues, and more—from routine chatter to emergency conversations to preventing or fixing problems. A routine conversation in a chat between a producer and facilitator might look something like this:

> *Producer:* I'm working with Samantha on her audio connection. For now, she has to stay muted but can still hear the conversation.
>
> *Facilitator:* OK, thanks!

then

> *Producer:* FYI, two participants are having trouble typing on the whiteboard. I'll invite them to type in the chat instead, and I'll transfer those words onto the screen.
>
> *Facilitator:* OK, thanks!

then

> *Producer:* We're running short on time. Would you like to make changes to the next breakout activity?
>
> *Facilitator:* Let's keep it at 10 minutes. I'll shorten the whiteboard discussion instead.
>
> *Producer:* OK. The breakout rooms are ready when you are.

Ideally, this kind of communication can occur within the virtual platform through a private chat or in a designated presenter-only area (Figure 6-3). But it's a good idea to have a backup outside communication channel in case of catastrophic tech challenges.

3. Manage Technology and Keep It Working for Everyone

This is where producers shine. They start the session, confirm that everything works as expected, and assist facilitators with their connections. They check the facilitator's audio and video to make sure it's clear and offer help when needed. They're always prepared in advance so they can execute the program plan.

At the class start time, producers help with participant greetings while supporting the facilitator's opening activities. They then assist with program interactions as planned, including polls, whiteboards, breakout rooms, and the chat. They follow

Figure 6-3. Presenter-Only Area in Adobe Connect

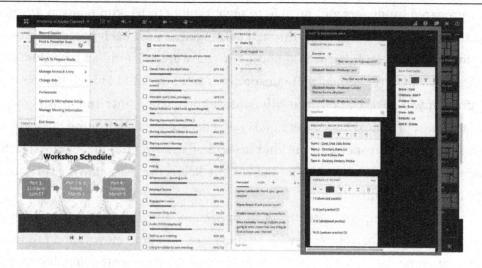

instructions in the facilitator or producer guide and take cues from the facilitator. For example, when it's time for a poll question, the producer will open the poll, watch the responses come in, close the poll, and then share the results.

Producers also set up and manage breakout rooms so the facilitator can focus on the learning objectives of the upcoming breakout activity instead of the technical components.

As a producer, the more comfortable you are with the virtual platform and the more up to date you are on the latest changes, the easier it will be to multitask and manage multiple activity streams.

4. Stay Alert for Problems or Changes

Just like a lifeguard continually scans the water for people who need assistance, producers need to stay on high alert during the virtual class. Using active listening skills, producers pay attention to the facilitator's verbal activity prompts ("Now, let's respond to the next poll question . . .") so they can leap into action when needed. They also keep their eyes on the screen as much as possible to watch for any clues that suggest someone needs assistance. For example, if the slides haven't moved in a while and no longer seem to match the current discussion, the facilitator's laptop may be glitching and causing a delay. Or if the facilitator's audio starts to sound choppy, you may need to check in with them or adjust the platform's audio settings. Later in this chapter, we will review more specific troubleshooting solutions.

5. Be Ready With Backup Plans

Well-prepared producers will be able to pivot rapidly to backup plans at any point in a session. They have thought through contingencies for each potential scenario and are ready to act. What would you do if you were working as a producer and realized that the preplanned poll question you were about to launch had outdated wording? If you post the poll, you will confuse the participants and possibly throw the facilitator off track. You think quickly and decide to verbalize the question and ask participants to respond in the chat instead of showing the inaccurate question onscreen. Your quick adaptation of the activity keeps the class moving forward toward the learning outcomes.

I've already compared producers to musicians and lifeguards; now I'll compare them to circus performers—with all due respect to both clowns and producers! Clowns often perform alone as a specialty circus act in the center ring, but they are also ready at a moment's notice to race into any situation where they're needed—especially if there's a mishap with another performer. The clowns distract the audience from the problem while making them think their appearance was right on cue. If you're a producer, you do the same thing—living by the old adage, "The show must go on!"

The best producers can switch between virtual platform tools quickly, step into speaking roles to cover for the facilitator, and pick up the slack whenever needed. If you're a producer, you probably have more than one helpful discussion question in your back pocket to keep participants engaged while waiting for a problem to be resolved. One such question might be, "Let's reflect for a moment on the program so far. What's one action you are already planning to take based on what you've learned? Type it in the chat."

6. Add Visual Instructions to Verbal

As we've discussed, virtual training participants are, by definition, scattered in various locations and surrounded by distractions. Even the most engaged participant will look away from the screen or take a brief listening break before tuning back in. Unfortunately, they might accidentally miss an important activity instruction or the current discussion question.

Producers can help facilitators communicate by using a technique that I call "adding visuals to the verbal." Like a translator who converts text from one language to another, a producer can take a facilitator's words and put them into text. This is not the same as turning on closed-captioning; instead, the producer intentionally adds keywords into the chat or uses annotation tools to highlight items on the screen (Figure 6-4). This small action helps facilitators and participants stay on track.

Figure 6-4. Example of Producer Chat Messages

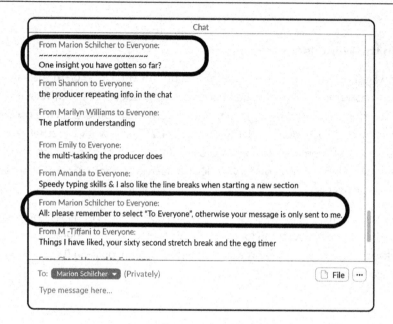

7. Use Your Voice

Producers categorized as supporters and co-facilitators often use their voices during a virtual class. But when a tech expert who planned to stay silent behind the scenes for the duration of a class needs to fill in for a facilitator unexpectedly, they should be able to do it and do it well. All types of producers need to be able to communicate in partnership with, or on behalf of, a facilitator.

Producers most often use their voices to share instructions for using the platform tools. If a facilitator explains a brainstorming activity for participants to do on a whiteboard, the producer can complete the instructions by explaining and demonstrating how to use the drawing tools. Or if the facilitator shares information about a role-play exercise, the producer can then distribute a corresponding PDF and explain how to download it.

As a producer, you may also speak up when communicating on behalf of the facilitator. For example, you might have an active speaking role when participants join, helping the facilitator greet and welcome everyone. The facilitator sets the tone, and the producer emulates it. A producer's voice should be clear, crisp, and easy to hear. All the vocal tips in the previous chapter apply to producers as well as facilitators.

I know all these tasks seem like a lot, don't they? But you've only heard only half of the story. Skilled producers simultaneously support both facilitators and participants. Let's turn to those tasks in the next section of the chapter.

Where in the World Is the Producer?

A question I get often is, "Do the facilitator and producer have to be in the same room?" The answer is no! Usually, the facilitator and producer are in different rooms, and they're often separated by long distances, operating in different cities or even different countries. They meet, facilitate, communicate, and work together on the virtual classroom platform, so seeing each other face-to-face isn't necessary. They can also connect through a secondary back channel, via text, or through a messaging program like WhatsApp.

Producers and facilitators may also want to be in separate locations for contingency planning. Should the facilitator in location A have technical or connectivity difficulties in their workspace (such as a power outage), the producer in location B can continue class until the issue is resolved.

The Producer-Participant Relationship

When virtual training was new, many participants needed help with basic functions like how to open a web browser and where to adjust their audio volume. Fortunately, the tech comfort level of most working professionals has gotten better over time. With the proliferation of video conferencing and web meetings, almost everyone has now had at least one online experience in a virtual platform. So, the work of supporting participants has shifted from teaching them how to turn on a laptop to how to navigate the features of a specific virtual platform.

For example, participants are probably familiar with using a webcam, but they might not know where to find the blur background feature. Or they may be comfortable typing in a chat but don't know how to increase the font size for easier reading. Participants may also need instructions on how to pin an interpreter's video to the top corner of their screen or where to find the list of keyboard shortcuts. As both participants and platforms get more sophisticated, the role of the producer in supporting participants will continue to evolve.

> *"A producer should have a calm demeanor and technical competence
> and be a proactive learner. They stay calm when technical challenges
> arise and handle issues with grace and ease. When they don't know
> the answer to a question, they are curious to find out and go research
> it. They should always be willing to learn more about the software,
> and to share that knowledge with facilitators and participants."*
>
> —Kassy LaBorie, author of *Producing Virtual Training, Meetings, and Webinars*

Seven Ways Producers Support Participants

Producers typically support participants in seven significant ways. Some of these duties will seem familiar now that we've discussed how producers support facilitators, but the context of the relationship is different. So, let's take a minute to examine what effective producers do for learners:

1. Help participants connect and stay connected to the platform.
2. Assist with audio and video options.
3. Explain how to use the platform tools.
4. Answer questions about technology.
5. Encourage confident engagement.
6. Defuse emotional situations.
7. Troubleshoot unexpected challenges.

1. Help Participants Connect and Stay Connected to the Platform

At the start of any virtual class, the moment is ripe for tech issues to appear. As everyone tries to join the session, connection challenges can get in the way. Participants need the virtual classroom link, a good internet connection, the ability to connect their audio, and a way to start their webcam. Producers must be available and ready to assist anyone who needs help with any of these tech touchpoints. And if the virtual platform has a lobby or waiting room, the producer is usually tasked with approving and admitting learners into the virtual classroom.

If participants can't find the classroom link, the producer may need to directly email or text it to them. It's a best practice to give producers the participants' contact information in advance of the session and for them to have their email open and ready to contact anyone outside the virtual platform. For the sake of simplicity, I recommend creating a draft email message with the virtual class connection details so that if a participant needs it at the start, the producer just has to insert the correct email address and hit send.

2. Assist With Audio and Video Options

Each virtual classroom platform has different audio and video settings. Some have a "green room" that appears on the first connection screen, which allow participants to test and change their video and connection options. Other platforms allow participants to join right away, letting them choose whether to enable their audio and video. In that scenario, producers may play a more active role in helping participants connect. Additionally, as we discussed in chapter 2, some platforms allow integrated telephony as well as VoIP computer audio, which adds another decision point for participants. Producers may need to help them make this choice based on their platform expertise.

The most common audio and video challenges happen when multiple platform systems get tangled. For example, a participant who attends a 9 a.m. online meeting on one platform and then tries to attend a 10 a.m. virtual class on another platform may have difficulty enabling their camera in the virtual classroom. The first platform is "holding onto" the camera, which makes sense in tech architecture, but creates a problem for the participant. In this situation, the producer can walk the participant through the steps to exit the first platform before rejoining the virtual classroom.

3. Explain How to Use the Platform Tools

To help participants engage in the learning activities, producers may need to explain how the platform tools work. For example, polls on some platforms require participants to hit "submit," while others immediately register a response. The drawing tools are always visible onscreen on some platforms, but participants may need to click on a button or type a command to open them in others. Producers who are intimately familiar with the tools will also need to be able to explain how to use them.

There are advantages to teaching participants how to use tools before a virtual class. However, it's also worth noting that learning the tools just in time can be beneficial. Table 6-2 breaks down the ideal times for teaching the platform tools.

My preferred method of teaching the tools is a combination of the first and third options. I want to equip participants in advance and then remind them how to use the tools in the moment.

Table 6-2. When Should You Teach the Platform Tools?

When	Description	Advantage	Disadvantage
As a prerequisite	Participants take a self-guided or facilitator-led orientation to the virtual program prior to the session.	Participants show up prepared to use the tools for learning.	If too much time has passed, participants may forget the information.
At the class start time	Participants use the first few minutes of the session to learn about the tools and how to use them.	Participants can see the platform tools in the context of the class while learning how to use them.	The lesson could be boring for anyone who is already familiar with the tools, leading them to tune out and not tune back in.
In the moment	Participants spend a moment learning how to find and use the tools when they actually need to use them.	Participants can immediately apply what they've learned about using the tool.	Requires preplanning so there's enough time allotted in the activity to quickly teach the tools.

4. Answer Questions About Technology

When technology-specific questions arise during a virtual class, it's typically the producer's responsibility to answer. These questions could be about anything—such as how to change a virtual background, disable hand gesture recognition, or erase text on the whiteboard. They could be from a participant who needs immediate help or one who is struggling with an ongoing concern. Sometimes participants simply get curious about the behind-the-scenes workings of a program and ask questions to learn more about it.

Producers may tire of answering the same question repeatedly, especially during the same session. But they need to be patient, compassionate, and empathetic, remembering that their job is to be a servant leader. In other words, a producer is a virtual classroom leader who is there to serve participant needs.

A good best practice is for producers to prepare answers to the most frequent questions in advance, ready to copy and paste from an onscreen list into the chat. This efficient method saves so much time and provides answers faster than if they had to type them out each time.

It also may be obvious, but producers should look and sound confident in their skills. They may be struggling furiously behind the scenes, but—like our duck analogy from the facilitator chapter—producers should always appear to be in control. Be authentic while also displaying confidence. If you don't know the answer to something, find out.

5. Encourage Confident Engagement

In my Virtual Producer Skills workshops, I quiz participants on the division of roles and responsibilities between facilitators and producers. Some questions are obvious—"Who helps participants with technology challenges?" But others are nuanced and require careful analysis. One interesting question is, "Who is responsible for participant engagement?" While most people initially say it's the facilitator, the correct answer is *both* the facilitator and producer.

Producers are often unsung heroes in learner engagement and the organizational impact of learning programs. I've already said multiple times that if participants aren't engaged, they aren't learning. And if they aren't learning, they won't be able to apply their new knowledge and skills back on the job. Producers help participants engage by helping them join the classroom, stay connected, and use the tools needed for learning. They also encourage learning and application when they assist a facilitator in doing their job effectively.

Producers also promote engagement by taking part in group conversations, interacting with participants in a visible but subtle way. This may include responding to their chat messages to encourage more discussion, supporting things participants say by acknowledging them in the chat, and using emoji reactions to add to the group discussion. By staying active in the conversation, producers extend the facilitator's reach so participants are more likely to feel seen and heard.

6. Defuse Emotional Situations

Tech challenges can be frustrating and sometimes exhausting. Some participants may deal with the same issues every time they attempt to connect to a virtual classroom, and they're probably tired of the struggle. Other participants may be joining the class during a stressful workday, bringing additional frustrations into the learning experience. And still others may simply have a low tolerance for technical glitches. In other words, there are many reasons that a participant's emotions can run high in a virtual class.

It may seem unusual to discuss emotions in a digital environment, but we are all human and we don't check our feelings at the door just because the classroom is a virtual one. Frustration, anger, exhaustion, and other feelings will surface in different ways. When these expressions become disruptive to the learning environment, the producer can help defuse the situation through empathy, care, and solutions.

For instance, in one of my recent classes, a participant seemed especially frustrated by a tech challenge. He wanted to switch his internal webcam to a camera with a better angle that was externally connected to his device. He adjusted his settings and logged in and out of the virtual classroom several times, but could not get the camera to work. Based on his verbal and chat comments—he was also starting to criticize other aspects of the platform—my producer and I could tell he was becoming upset. And his emotions were not only getting in the way of his learning, but they were also starting to distract other participants.

Fortunately, my producer deftly handled the situation. He acknowledged the participant's concern and reassured him they could resolve it together. He wasn't dismissive and he remained positive and encouraging. It took about 10 minutes for them to work out the problem offline, and then the participant was able to rejoin the class ready to learn.

The point to take away here is that a producer's response to a participant's struggles will make a significant difference in their ability to learn.

Responding with empathy means putting yourself in someone else's shoes, acknowledging facts, expressing confidence, and moving toward a solution. For example, a producer might say, "I know it's frustrating to experience this recurring issue. I'm sorry it's keeping you from class. Let's try two quick things. . . ."

7. Troubleshoot Unexpected Challenges

Remember, the producer typically has the task of troubleshooting any unexpected challenges that arise during class. This allows the facilitator to stay focused on the participants and their learning, while the producer works with the individual or group who needs extra care.

Producers who stay alert and continually scan the environment can stay ahead of many tech challenges. However, unexpected issues can and do occur. These challenges are an opportunity for producers to shine as they stay calm and take care of the issue or switch to a backup plan as quickly as possible.

A Producer's Biggest Challenge: Managing the Unexpected

When a problem suddenly occurs in the virtual classroom, how should a producer respond? Based on my 20-plus years of experience across dozens of different platforms, I use a five-step process for how to face unexpected challenges.

1. Stay Calm and Take a Deep Breath

Just because an emergency occurs doesn't mean it's time to panic! If you expect challenges to happen, you won't be surprised when they do. Above all, keeping your cool will allow you to take a level-headed look at the situation.

2. Scan the Environment to Gather Information

This should happen very quickly—it's an extension of the producer's ongoing task of staying alert and actively listening. When a problem surfaces, do a quick check to validate your assumptions. For example, if the facilitator's audio starts to sound choppy, first peek at your own internet connectivity to see if the problem exists on your end before taking other actions. Or, if there's an extra-long, unexpected pause at the start of a breakout activity and no one is moving into their assigned rooms, briefly glance at the breakout dialog box to ensure you hit the start breakout rooms button.

3. Find Out if It's Just One Person or Everyone

This is the golden, number one question to ask in the troubleshooting process. Is the issue only affecting one person in the virtual classroom or is it affecting everyone? You need to discover the full scope of the issue. If one participant keeps dropping from the virtual class, that could mean their internet connectivity is causing the problem. But if 10 participants drop from the virtual class every time you launch the breakout rooms, you could be facing a bigger challenge. By learning more about the extent of the issue, you'll be better able to find its root cause.

4. Let Participants Know What's Going On

When a tech issue affects the entire class and halts the learning experience, it's helpful to let everyone know what's happening. Put yourself in their shoes—do you remember the last time you showed up for an appointment but had to sit in the waiting room for much (much!) longer than expected? You probably became frustrated about the unknowns and unsure whether to keep waiting. Then, imagine if a receptionist arrived and said, "I'm so sorry. An emergency in the back is causing a delay. Thanks for your patience. We'll be with you in about 15 minutes." Your feelings would likely transform from frustration to understanding.

The same rules apply if the virtual class has to pause because of a tech issue. A quick, reassuring word from the producer will move participants from frustration to patience and understanding.

5. Start the Troubleshooting Process

This is the step that most people associate with producer support. You quickly start figuring out what is causing the tech problem and fix it. Producers are problem solvers and solution finders. They check software settings, search for anomalies, and provide answers, drawing upon their knowledge of the platform and the way technology is supposed to work to seek a resolution. They ask enough questions to determine the source of any issue and provide instructions to fix it. It could be as simple as directing a participant to click on a button or as complex as walking a group of learners through a series of steps to test multiple options. Review Table 6-3 for some common challenges and their typical solutions.

Table 6-3. Troubleshooting Tips for Common Challenges

Situation	Possible Solutions
A participant has trouble connecting their audio.	• Direct them to the audio connection button (or menu, depending on the platform). • Ask them to test their audio connection details using the platform's "check audio" feature. • Ask them to log out and then log back in so they'll see the prompt for the audio connection.
The facilitator's computer crashes in the middle of a session.	• As the producer, step in and continue running the event until the facilitator is able to reboot their computer and rejoin the session. • Have the presenter switch to a backup device (assuming it's already logged in to the event or ready to log in). • Have the presenter use a telephone connection instead of VoIP so that they won't lose audio.
A participant says they cannot hear.	• Find out if it's just one or if it's everyone. • Ask them to test their audio connection using the platform's "check audio" feature. • Ask them to log out and then log back in.
A file is not displaying correctly.	• Close the file and open it again. • Save the document as a different file type (e.g., as a .PPT instead of .PPTX) and try again. • Send the file to participants via email for viewing. • Switch to a different file.
The facilitator's audio fades in and out or has some type of interfering background noise.	• Ask the facilitator to test their audio connection using the platform's "check audio" feature. • Make sure they are using a headset. • Ask them to reposition their microphone. • Ask them to log out and then log back in. • Ask them to switch to a telephone connection instead of VoIP (or vice versa).

Table 6-3. (cont.)

Situation	Notes
Participants stay silent when the facilitator asks a question.	• Include an interactive opening activity that involves every participant. • Encourage participant interaction from the moment they log in to the event. • Teach them how to use the tools as they are introduced throughout the event. Provide instructions on how to engage. • Be active in the chat throughout the event to encourage participation.

In Summary: Key Points From Chapter 6

- Producers add value to virtual classes, allowing the facilitator to stay focused on the learning content.
- There are three types of producers: tech experts, supporters, and co-facilitators.
- Producer preparation includes learning about the platform and the content and setting up the workspace.
- Producers support facilitators and participants.
- Producers should follow a simple, five-step process to manage issues in the moment.

Take Action

✓ If your organization is not already using producers, consider how to include them in your virtual training programs. If needed, refer back to the list of creative ways to find a producer.

✓ Make a list of your virtual classroom platform's most common tech challenges and create a solution database that producers can easily access and use.

Tool 6-1. Advance Preparation Meeting Checklist for Producers

It's a best practice and common sense for session leaders to connect and communicate in advance of a virtual event. The purpose of this meeting would be to review the session outline, go over materials, determine exact responsibilities, and practice using the virtual classroom tools for all planned activities. Use this checklist to plan your meeting.

Review logistics to ensure alignment and consistency:
- ☐ Date
- ☐ Time
- ☐ Time zone
- ☐ Which platform? Which version?
- ☐ Link to event
- ☐ Host and administrative passwords and codes

Dry run (practice the class):
- ☐ Talk about the producer's role
- ☐ Discuss every activity and how it should work
- ☐ Confirm roles and responsibilities for platform features:
  - ☐ Polls
  - ☐ Whiteboards
  - ☐ Chat
  - ☐ Breakouts
  - ☐ Other:
  - ☐ Other:

Establish communication and emergency protocols:
- ☐ Decide how to communicate during class (Private chat? Presenter-only-area notes? Other?)
- ☐ Determine what type of information should be communicated during class (Timing reminders?)
- ☐ Determine a back-up communication channel (Outside the platform, such as text messaging?)
- ☐ Create back-up and contingency plans for each major activity

Tool 6-2. A Sample Facilitator Guide With Producer Notes

This facilitator guide was used at the start of a leadership training program for a global team. It was the first session in a multiweek program. The explicit purpose of this section was to create networking opportunities among the participants, setting the stage for robust collaboration in the rest of the training program. The notes here explain two breakout activities—an introductory activity lasting five minutes and a Q&A activity lasting eight minutes—with producer instructions for each exercise. Notice the detailed technical notes for the producer.

Time	Facilitator Notes and Script	Producer's Tech Notes
2 minutes	Welcome to the ABC Inc. Emerging Leaders Program! One of the best parts of getting our global team together virtually is the ability to network and learn from one another. We will be collaborating throughout the training program, so let's begin by making connections in a speed networking style of introductions. In a moment, you'll be randomly assigned to a breakout room with one or two other people. You'll first say, "hello," and then you'll share your name, location, role, how long you've been with the organization, and three words to describe your day so far. Note that you will only have 5 minutes total in your group, which will go by very quickly! If you have extra time, you can discuss the current projects that have your focus. At the end of 5 minutes, you will be rotated to a different group. We will repeat this rotation three times, so you will be in three distinct groups.	Prepare breakout rooms to automatically assign everyone to groups of two to three people. Breakout settings should include: • Yes: Allow to return to main room • Yes: Automatically move into room • Auto timer set for 5 minutes • 15-second countdown to return Type activity instructions in the chat for reference and be ready to "Broadcast Message" the instructions to all the groups.
16 minutes	Let's begin! *At the end of 5 minutes, end the breakouts, briefly return to the main room, and then scatter participants again. Repeat two more times for three rounds total.*	Start breakout rooms on facilitator cue. Send broadcast message with 1 minute remaining to wrap up. At the end of each round, recreate the groups as noted above.

Time	Facilitator Notes and Script	Producer's Tech Notes
2 minutes	Welcome back! Raise your hand if you met at least two new people. *Acknowledge raised hands!* What were some of the words you used to describe your day so far? Let's enter those in the chat. *Acknowledge several responses.* It's time for one more short breakout activity. This time, the groups will be slightly larger, and the questions will be different. If you haven't already met, start by quickly introducing yourself. Then, answer one of the following questions: • What are you most looking forward to during this training program? • What one leadership challenge do you hope to solve today? • What will it take for you to consider this training program a success? What do you need to do to make that happen? You'll have 8 minutes for this discussion.	Prepare breakout rooms to automatically assign everyone in groups of two to three people. Breakout settings should include: • Yes: Allow to return to main room • Yes: Automatically move into room • Auto timer set for 8 minutes • 15-second countdown to return Optional: If the facilitator has set up an external collaboration site to capture text responses, share the link or QR code and ask participants to record their answers there. All breakout rooms will use the same link with their responses blending on the shared screen.
8 minutes	Let's begin! *At the end of 8 minutes, end the breakouts and return to the main room.*	Start breakout rooms on the facilitator's cue. Send a broadcast message with 1 minute remaining to wrap up.
6 minutes	*Depending on the time available, ask for key conversation takeaways via chat and invite participants to summarize and call out what they have in common.*	If an optional shared collaboration site was used, share it onscreen for all to view.
1 minute	Thank you everyone for your active participation! Now it's time to start our next activity.	
35 total minutes		

CHAPTER 7

Prepare Participants

 In this chapter, you will learn how to prepare participants to learn effectively in the virtual classroom environment:

- Recognize three reasons participant preparation is key for success.
- Help participants manage their learning environments.
- Teach participants how to use the technology and make learning as accessible as possible.
- Use change management techniques to help participants learn.

The success of virtual training may hinge more on changing participants' hearts and minds about online learning than anything else you do. This is because participants often misunderstand virtual training. If they've attended a lot of passive virtual meetings and webinars, they probably assume your virtual class will be a similar experience. And, if they are entirely new to virtual training, it will be a significant change from learning in a traditional classroom. To set participants up for success with virtual training, it's helpful to provide guidance and direction. And it doesn't matter if your participants are internal employees or external customers—participants are participants, regardless of their affiliation. Whether you are a training manager who only delivers learning content to your employees or a vendor who provides virtual training to the public, the learning experience will be better if you prepare participants ahead of time.

When most organizations consider virtual training, they focus on developing content, preparing facilitators, and getting the technology they need for implementation. Unfortunately, they often forget to consider the participants. Unless you pay enough attention to this critical group, it's unlikely that any virtual training program will meet its goals for learning outcomes and on-the-job learning transfer.

If the only preparation you give your participants is to send an automated confirmation email with the virtual class connection details—just as you might for any online meeting—you are missing a prime opportunity. Participants need to do more than just show up. This chapter will help you prepare participants to learn effectively in a live online environment. We'll start by looking at the participant's typical experience and why it's so important to put time and effort into focusing on them. Then we'll explore the best ways to set up your participants—and therefore, your whole program—for success.

Why Focus on Participants?

There are three main reasons to prepare your participants before virtual training:

- Engaging in virtual training requires most participants to shift their mindset.
- Participants need to take more responsibility for their learning.
- Participant learning environments are often not conducive to uninterrupted online learning.

A Mindset Shift

Imagine the traditional classroom experience—going to school, sitting at a desk, and learning from a teacher. While this description won't capture everyone's experience, a large majority of adults have participated in formal learning in a traditional public or private schoolroom. The traditional workplace classroom has a few common features:

- The learner leaves their workspace to go to class. They might walk down the hall to a training room, or in some cases, they might have to leave home and travel overnight to the training location.
- Most of the focused learning takes place during the classroom session. While the learner might have a brief assignment to complete before class, for the most part, they only need to show up and be ready to learn when the class begins.
- The classroom feels familiar. The facility will probably have features common to most classrooms, such as the facilitator setup at the front of a room, a projector and screen for visual aids, and tables and chairs with workbooks and other necessary supplies (such as pens and sticky notes) readily available.
- The group will establish social norms, formally or informally. For example, the facilitator might lead the group in a ground rules discussion about being

on time and the proper use of mobile devices during the session. The learner typically follows all these rules during class to conform.

- The learner interacts with the facilitator and other participants through conversation, group dialogue, and structured activities.

In contrast, many of these conditions don't apply in a virtual training classroom. For example, in a virtual classroom the learner:

- Stays in their own workspace
- Is often expected to complete an assignment in advance
- May need to download software or configure their audio and video to connect to the virtual session
- May see an unfamiliar screen when logging in to the class if they haven't used that specific virtual classroom platform
- Usually gets their own supplies—anything from a printed handout to a highlighter or sticky notes—by downloading, borrowing, or purchasing them
- Is less likely to follow group social norms—even if facilitators try to discuss norms, many learners approach them as optional because they feel anonymous and believe they are invisible to others
- Will often be distracted by their environment—although they have opportunities to interact with the facilitator and other participants, learners may choose not to fully engage in the learning experience

While many of these features are the same as what happens in virtual meetings, the stakes are much higher in virtual learning. Participants are expected to leave a learning experience with new knowledge and skills they can apply on the job. The bottom line is that many participants find that virtual training can be a challenging way to learn. From staying in their own workspace to using the virtual platform, the features inherent in virtual training can be uncomfortable for learners who prefer an in-person classroom environment. Even participants who embrace the idea of engaging online training may struggle to prioritize it in the moment over other tasks with a higher perceived priority.

More Responsibility for Learning

Virtual classes rarely happen in a vacuum; they are usually part of a series or blended curriculum. Participants often need to take asynchronous learning modules, complete assignments, and get involved in the process; therefore, they now have more responsibility for their learning than ever. As facilitators, we often expect our participants to play an active role before, during, and even after a virtual training session, but the participants may perceive those expectations as extras or have other priorities that lead them to neglect assignments. When that happens, it compromises the success of your virtual training program, and you won't be able to achieve all the planned learning outcomes.

A complaint I frequently hear from virtual facilitators is that participants don't engage in their sessions. This often happens because the facilitators haven't set the right expectations. For example, participants typically need to do several things before the virtual training starts:

- Set up their computer, test their connection, and ensure appropriate software is downloaded.
- Complete an assignment intended to introduce them to the content.
- Create an appropriate environment with minimal distractions—a place where they can concentrate and focus on the learning.

While these things are not difficult, if participants neglect even one of them, it can lead to disaster. A participant who doesn't test their computer before a session might not be able to log in at the appointed time because they had to wait for the latest update to download. Someone who doesn't complete the prerequisite assignment might get lost during an activity. A distracted participant won't be able to pay attention fully, which means they won't be engaged in their learning.

Let's consider a few more essential expectations for participants in a virtual training class:

- Connect to the class on time or a few minutes early.
- Use the platform tools, including the chat, polling, and drawing.
- Collaborate with other participants during class activities.
- Actively participate in class discussions, responding to questions and contributing to the conversation.

Some learners will find these expectations easy to meet. But those who have a passive attitude toward online learning will not expect to participate actively during a virtual class. They just want to show up, put their audio on mute, and continue to go about their workday while listening to the class as background noise. It's no wonder virtual facilitators tell me over and over, "My participants are all silent. They don't engage!"

This is why I emphasize the importance of letting our participants know how valuable their contributions are to their ability to learn and the success of the group. We need to help participants to take on all the responsibilities that are keys to success.

Learning Environments Not Conducive to Learning

One of the biggest benefits of virtual training is also its greatest challenge—participants can stay in their own environment. In a traditional classroom, the facilitator creates the atmosphere: arranging the tables and chairs, choosing the lighting, putting the posters on the walls, and deciding what materials to place on each table. A participant walks into the classroom and immediately experiences that carefully crafted environment. But in a virtual classroom, because participants can join from anywhere, the environmental component depends on whatever happens to be in the participant's surroundings that day, and the facilitator has very little influence.

Many participants simply do not have a space that's appropriate for concentrating and learning. Take a moment to think about your desk and its surroundings right now. Is it an ideal learning space? My desk is often cluttered with folders, overflowing stacks of papers, beeping gadgets, and unfinished projects. I would find it hard to concentrate on an important new task without first clearing some visual space. If you work from home, you might be in a bedroom or at the kitchen table, surrounded by the distractions of daily life, from laundry to children's toys to this morning's breakfast dishes. There's benefit to a calm environment, one in which we can listen to and absorb new information. Most people, and especially neurodiverse individuals, learn better with minimal distractions. Therefore, you should encourage participants to set aside any distractions and clutter so they can focus on what's happening in the virtual classroom.

But a clean desk alone doesn't solve the problem. A typical employee is interrupted approximately every six to 12 minutes by a co-worker, a mobile device, or some other distraction (Leroy 2020). And as John Medina points out, "A person who is interrupted takes 50 percent longer to accomplish a task and makes up to 50 percent more errors" (Medina 2014). There's just no doubt that distractions and interruptions in a learner's working environment can sabotage the success of the virtual program. Let's look at some typical workspaces to understand what your participants are contending with and how you can help them overcome their obstacles.

Retail Stores

Retail organizations have distributed workforces, which seems like the ideal situation for virtual training. However, most retail store workers spend their time on the sales floor or behind a register. They're constantly interacting with customers and merchandise and are rarely in one spot for long. They may have a mobile device for looking up inventory and customer transactions, but they actively use it to serve customers, not to join facilitated learning programs. In addition, most retail stores don't have a quiet place where workers can engage in a virtual training class. They may be able to use a computer workstation used for short asynchronous learning sessions, but taking a 20- to 30-minute, self-paced class is not the same thing as actively engaging in a 90-minute live online training class.

When I worked in a retail store many years ago, we had two main private spaces—a tiny break room in the back of the store with a small lunch table and a shared manager's office with a desk and computer. Neither of these places would have been a good place to learn because of the constant traffic flow and surrounding distractions.

Construction Sites

Construction workers spend most of their time on jobsites and may not have computer access during typical working hours. When they do use computers, it's usually in a shared jobsite trailer that's being used as temporary office space. The sounds of other workers and construction site noise can make it difficult to concentrate in this environment. In addition, depending on the site's location, internet connectivity may be a challenge.

When I worked in training management for a construction company, we sent an extra training laptop to jobsites. The laptop was set up in the trailer so everyone at the site could access it, but it was mostly used by supervisors for taking required self-paced e-learning courses. While this solution worked at the time, it was often a challenge to justify sending an extra laptop to the site. Plus, it was hard for many employees to step away from the jobsite and into the trailer, even for required training.

Cubicles and Shared Office Workspaces

Many companies today have maximized their office space by installing cubicles or creating an open floor plan. The result is that employees have limited privacy, noise levels tend to be high, and distractions are abundant. Without doors or other "do not disturb" features, people face frequent interruptions, including co-workers stopping by without warning and overheard conversations.

At the last office building I worked in on a daily basis, my cube was near a busy intersection and a shared printer. Even though my co-workers tried to be courteous and mindful about noise, I was frequently distracted from my work by hallway conversations and loud equipment.

Recently, a learner in one of my virtual leadership classes could not fully participate in the activities, despite having a dedicated computer, desk, and all the other required materials. He let me know through a private chat that because his teammates were sitting in cubicle desks next to him and could hear all his conversations, he couldn't openly discuss his leadership issues and coaching challenges. His unsuitable environment prevented him from interacting with the rest of the class, so he missed out on the bulk of the learning experience.

Home Offices

In the aftermath of the COVID-19 pandemic, just over a third (35 percent) of US workers with jobs that can be done remotely are still working from home all the time (Parker 2023). For some, this arrangement creates an ideal working environment because it eliminates workplace distractions. No co-workers stopping by to chat, no office noise, and no watercooler conversations.

But while many people claim to be more productive at home, the distractions of the office are often replaced by a whole new set of challenges, including televisions, pending household chores, and other family members. Not everyone has a dedicated home office space, which means many people work at a kitchen table or from the living room couch. And even when remote workers do have dedicated home office space, they still contend with ringing doorbells, barking dogs, and children needing attention. Another frequent obstacle for people who work from home is slow internet connectivity.

Training on the Road

Salespeople, executives, and other traveling employees often find themselves in hotels, airports, and other public spaces during the workweek. They use laptops and connect via public Wi-Fi or a mobile hotspot for their internet, which can lead to connectivity problems and, as we've discussed, wreak havoc on a virtual training session. For example, I recently tried to participate in a virtual training class from a hotel room, and despite running speed tests and double-checking my connection ahead of time, I lost contact with the session twice in the first 30 minutes. The experience was frustrating, to say the least!

As a traveling speaker and trainer, I am intimately and painfully aware of how challenging it can be to find a good space in which to attend virtual training classes. I have tried using airport executive lounges, renting hotel conference room space, and reserving back tables in public coffee shops, all in a quest to find a quiet place to concentrate and learn while on the road. It takes deliberate planning and is never easy. And even when I think I've found the perfect spot, something unexpected usually happens to get in the way.

Employees who are on the road are also more likely to join a virtual training session from a mobile device. Although it will *eventually* be interchangeable with the experience you have on a laptop, the mobile version of most virtual training platforms currently has limited functionality. In other words, class participants working on a mobile device may not be able to answer a poll question, participate in a private chat, or annotate on a whiteboard. Until these platforms are fully integrated with other platform connections, mobile participation remains a limited option. If your participants don't realize this or can't figure out how to access the program from a computer, they'll be at a disadvantage.

The Bottom Line on Problematic Learning Environments

Even if you have created the best virtual learning experience in the world—something that's well designed and expertly facilitated—participants won't pay attention or learn if they can't focus due to an incompatible learning environment or poor internet connection. And if they aren't learning, they won't be able to apply their new skills on the job. The ultimate result will be wasted time and effort for everyone involved. Let's now consider how to set up participants for learning success.

Three Ways to Prepare Participants

In general, you can make it easier for participants to prepare adequately for virtual training success by helping them manage their learning environments, navigate technology and enhance accessibility, and change their mindset about virtual training.

Help Them Manage Their Learning Environment

Even though virtual learners are adults who can and should take responsibility for their learning environment, there are things you can do to help them succeed. These include creating office-based learning spaces they can use, providing tips for adapting their own spaces for better learning, or changing programs to a hybrid setup. You can also assist by adding accountability checks and offering grace when needed.

Create an Office-Based Learning Space

While it's tough to deny the convenience of staying at your own desk to attend a training class, if it's not the right place for participants to learn, then you may need to create a space dedicated to virtual training that they can use instead. This space might be temporary (a conference room) or permanent (one hotel-style office reserved for virtual training participants). You could also ask a manager to give up their office for a few hours so participants can use it when joining the virtual training classroom.

If your office building simply does not have a good space for learning, recommend participants work remotely on days they're scheduled for training. But remember, a home office may not be the ideal location for everyone, so help them find an alternative option if necessary, such as a co-working space or a public library with dedicated study rooms.

If the participants are external to your organization, such as clients or consumers, take extra care to communicate the importance of a good learning space for virtual training.

Offer Tips for Organizing a Remote Workspace

Always communicate with participants before a virtual training event about how best to set up and prepare for class. You can communicate via email, text, or even video clip. A warm welcoming message from a facilitator to participants can go a long way in establishing a good relationship, setting the stage for an interactive virtual program and offering useful information about what's expected.

If your presession communication is already automated—perhaps as a scripted registration email from an LMS—then separate your workspace preparation message from other class connection details. In other words, send two or three messages to participants before the class. One message could welcome participants to the program, a second could provide preparation information, and a third could include additional class details. See Figure 7-1 for a sample welcome message based on what I typically send to participants.

Regardless of how you convey the news, keep your instructions short and easy to follow. You don't want participants to think they have to reorganize their desks just to come to class. A simple message might say: "Clear some writing space on your desk, have the necessary materials ready to go, and close all computer programs, except for the virtual training platform." You could also provide a short checklist with technology and workspace tips. Use the sample checklist in Tool 7-1 at the end of this chapter for inspiration. If participants are connecting from home or on the road, include tips for finding a space with reliable internet connectivity and minimal distractions.

Figure 7-1. Sample Welcome Message

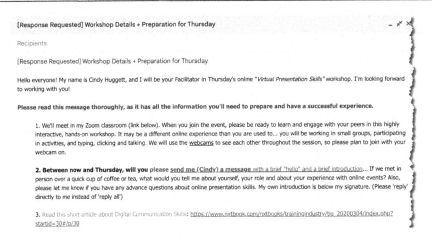

As part of the materials you send before a virtual program, include suggestions to help participants deal with interruptions. Some examples include:

- Encourage learners to silence their phones and turn on the Do Not Disturb setting before class. You could also include a downloadable do not disturb sign in the course materials that participants could print out and hang on their door or outside their cubicle.
- Suggest they block their calendars starting 10 minutes before the session and lasting five to 10 minutes after the session.
- Inform their managers (or ask participants to inform their managers) about the training times so they can plan for work coverage.

Always explain that you're recommending these steps so they will be able to fully engage in the learning. Remind them that they are participating in a training class, not just dialing into a meeting or attending a passive presentation. And be creative in sharing your tips. You may even follow the example set by a large technology company, which invites participants to watch a short four-minute orientation video before every virtual class. The video touches on essential reminders, such as how to connect to the session, which platform tools will be used, and general tips for effective learning. It's a catchy way to convey these important details to those who may not otherwise read the information.

Switch to a Hybrid Learning Setup

Hybrid learning, in which some participants are together in person and others are remote, has been around as long as virtual training. At first, it happened by accident.

When several people from the same office location registered for a virtual training class, they simply brought their laptops into a single conference room and connected to the virtual platform to participate. It is not ideal, and more than once, I've asked participants to go back to their desks simply because the program wasn't designed to be hybrid.

In the past, hybrid setups created challenging situations when everyone in the classroom tried to connect their individual audio in one space or participate in breakout activities. Today, most hybrid learning is intentionally planned and the main challenge is equalizing the experience. We want to create an environment where everyone, regardless of physical location, can actively participate in the learning experience. It doesn't happen by accident.

To effectively prepare learners in advance of a hybrid class, I recommend:

- **Ask everyone to share in advance where they will be—on-site or off-site.** Be sure you know how many people are participating in person and how many are joining remotely. This will help you plan for the experience and remind learners of the agreement they are making to participate in the hybrid class.

- **Establish expectations for webcam use.** Remote participants are at a disadvantage by not being in the room with others, so joining the discussion via video is important. Seeing the faces of remote participants, even for a short while at the start of a hybrid learning event, helps bridge the gap between in-person and virtual attendees.

- **Pair up each remote attendee with an on-site counterpart.** Let them know that they'll be partners throughout the program, with the in-person participant serving as an extra touchpoint for the remote participant. For example, if the remote attendee has trouble hearing someone in the room speaking, they can ask their partner to tell that person to move closer to the microphone. And, if you assign the pairs in advance, they can establish a separate communication channel via text or other messaging app if needed.

Calendar Options

If you send calendar invitations for virtual training classes, consider blocking additional time a few minutes before and after each session. In other words, if the session is taking place from 3 p.m. to 4 p.m., schedule the meeting to begin at 2:50 p.m. and last until 4:05 p.m. Or, be unconventional and schedule the class from 3:10 p.m. to 4:25 p.m. so that participants have built-in buffer time on their calendar.

Participants can use this extra time to get set for the class and connect to the platform. It also gives the participants a few minutes following the class to transfer notes and action items to the proper place before they have to get back to their workday.

This time also means that participants are less likely to treat the training as just another meeting they can sandwich between other meetings—it's clear that there are different expectations than an everyday appointment.

Start Each Virtual Class With an Accountability Check

As I've explained, educating participants about creating a conducive learning environment starts before each class begins, but it's also a good idea to remind them about key expectations upon login, especially if anyone missed the presession communication. I call these quick reminders "accountability checks." You can try a variety of ways to institute them, but I'll share my two favorites here:

- **Use the opening screen of your virtual training platform** (sometimes called a "waiting room" or "lobby") to display any learning tips and reminders. Even if you shared this information before the session and even if you have repeat participants, it never hurts to remind them again (Figure 7-2).
- **As class begins, ask participants to manage distractions.** Make your suggestion interactive by telling them to close their email and raise their hand after completing the task. Or give them 30 seconds to remove one distracting thing from their desk and enter a note about it in the chat window when they're done.

At Franklin Covey, every virtual class begins with a 40-second etiquette video, similar to an airplane safety spiel, says Treion Muller, former chief e-learning architect at the company. It's a fun, animated look at how to participate in an online class. The short video helps participants know what to expect and reminds them to manage their environment well so that they can participate.

I especially like virtual training expert Karen Hyder's approach. She posts a poll at the beginning of each class asking participants to rate how engaged they plan to be during the session. The question and possible answers call immediate attention to the importance of learners managing their distractions during class. And I've also watched author Michael Bungay Steiner take this approach one step further, asking his participants, "What will it take to increase your engagement level by one notch?"

The basic principle is clear: It's OK to acknowledge distractions and to ask participants to try to focus on their learning.

Figure 7-2. Sample Waiting Room Message

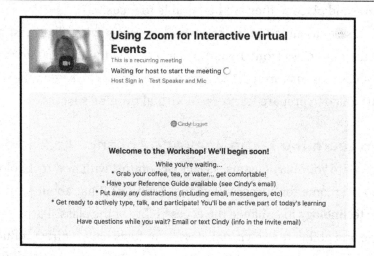

Give Learners Grace When Needed

While we know that learner engagement in any training session, including virtual classes, is a key to success, there are times when it's equally as important to give everyone a little grace. This means extending courtesy and understanding to participants, maintaining a comfortable learning environment, and expecting that participants have good intentions when joining the session. If you come from a place of acceptance and understanding, expecting that participants have followed your instructions to create a good learning space, and treating them like educated adults who are responsible for their learning, you will be much more likely to receive respect and compliance in return.

Consider this scenario: A participant follows instructions, establishing an appropriate learning environment and alerting their co-workers not to disturb them during class. However, a work emergency comes up in the middle of the session and the participant must step away from their screen for a few minutes. The interruption is not intentional, and it's not happening because the participant doesn't value the session. It's simply an emergency that needs immediate attention. The graceful response, if you're the facilitator, is to make a personal note of the participant's brief absence, but not make a big deal about it. If the participant misses a key learning point or needs a moment to catch up, the facilitator or producer can assist them with the next activity.

Most of all, it's essential to maintain a comfortable and welcoming learning environment instead of making the participant into an embarrassing example.

Sometimes, of course, you will encounter a participant who doesn't prepare, doesn't have any intention of engaging with the class, and doesn't stay connected longer than a few minutes at a time. In that case, you can ask the participant to reschedule the class to another time and place so they are better able to focus.

It's often easy to assume the worst instead of recognizing that most participants will try to connect to class from a good place. Assume the best as often as possible. Helping participants think through their preparation process is often the most important thing you can do to prepare learners for virtual training success.

Help Them Learn the Technology and Enhance Accessibility

How tech-savvy are your participants? Is lack of comfort with new technology a hurdle you'll need to overcome for successful virtual training? What about participants who need specific technology to enhance the accessibility of the class? Participants' technical knowledge and ability to use virtual classroom tools have a direct influence on the quality of their learning experiences (Falloon 2011). Most people know the basics of using a laptop, but proficiency varies in a typical workforce. Despite widespread adoption of technology, some may still be uncomfortable with it. I recently facilitated a virtual program with a group of learners who didn't use computers in their daily work. I had to walk through several basic steps simply to help them all connect to audio and video.

Even if your participants are proficient computer users, they may not be familiar with the specifics of your virtual platform. Or they may require some auxiliary hardware or software to make all the information you're sharing fully accessible. Let's examine a few specific items that can help ensure your participants have what they need to participate fully in any virtual training session.

Hardware

Find out if learners have what they need to connect to the session and if they know how to use those items. For example, if you plan to play multimedia files, do the participants' computers have sound cards? Do they know where to find the volume controls to adjust the sound? How about headsets for their audio connection? Are they able to plug them in and adjust them as needed? Do they have sufficient internet bandwidth? If they are expected to use a handout, do they know how to access it for reading on-screen or do they have access to a printer if they want a physical copy? Are participants using Macs or PCs? Will they be using their personal computers or mobile devices? Are they brand new, or are the participants experienced in using them? Will they be using assistive items like screen readers or alternative input devices? What extra setup might be required because of the learners' hardware choices?

If you partnered with your IT department when planning the virtual training program, you'll have considered many of these questions already. But participants who are external customers or not part of your organization may not have been part of your technology review, so it's valuable to ask questions and take new information into account.

Preparing VR Headsets for Immersive Activities

If your virtual class is using immersive technology such as VR headsets, you may need to take extra steps to ensure everything is set up properly. If participants supply their own headsets, communicate the tech specs they'll need, including bandwidth requirements and software downloads. And if your learners are new to VR, you may need to walk through the initial equipment setup.

You also may need to explain how to measure IPD (interpupillary distance) so they can adjust their headsets for proper fit and clear vision. If they wear glasses, you may need to show them how to add an insert. You might need to help them establish location markers for boundaries and to install the simulation software. Over time, as more and more people gain experience using VR equipment, this setup assistance won't be needed. But today it's still useful to share the information with everyone.

Participant preparation for immersive virtual activities also includes helping to create an appropriate learning environment—one that with emotional security and support. If it's someone's first time in a VR simulation, they may approach it with trepidation. They may have heard that VR can cause motion sickness, or they might be wary of interacting with others. You can help reduce participant anxiety by letting them know in advance exactly what to expect. For example, tell them what they'll see onscreen upon joining the simulation and what the first two or three actions will be. You may want to keep some aspects of the simulation hidden if discovery is part of the experience, but in general, the more you tell participants, the more comfortable they will feel.

Software

Each virtual platform has unique requirements for attendee connections. Some platforms require an app download; others allow participants to join via an internet browser. If it's necessary to download an app, find out if participants have administrative rights on their computers. If not, they'll likely need special permission or assistance from the IT department. If participants are using a mobile device to connect, are there differences between the mobile software and the desktop or web version? If the differences are significant, you'll need to educate participants about the importance of not connecting via a mobile device.

If participants don't have prior experience using your virtual training platform, consider how you'll help them learn to use it. Who should they call if they need assistance and support? The facilitator? The producer? Someone in IT? The virtual training platform vendor? There are no right or wrong answers to this question, but be sure to address it so participants will feel confident that someone is available to help them.

In addition, consider what other software programs participants may use. For example, it's increasingly common to use virtual cameras for more flexible video. These software-based cameras expand a physical webcam's capabilities. Most include special features like makeup filters, custom borders, eye contact helpers, and exciting virtual backgrounds. If your organization uses them, your participants may need help connecting them to the virtual platform.

Your design may require the use of other programs that are separate from the virtual classroom, like using Google's Jamboard or Mural to create a collaborative whiteboard. If participants need to create an account in that program to fully participate, you should tell them to do that before the program starts.

"You've got to make virtual training easy for participants
to do. You don't want them to struggle."

—Lucy Brown, Senior Training Manager, IHS

If learners are using an assistive software program to participate in the virtual class, encourage them to set it up and test it in advance. For instance, screen readers may need to be calibrated when connected to the platform. Or if you're using an external channel to collect participant questions about the learning content, ensure everyone has access to it before the program starts. Talk with participants to find out what they need and how you can help.

Five Ways to Help Participants Learn Technology

I've tested and refined five approaches over the years to help participants learn to use technology in my classes. Some of these methods have the added benefit of allowing you educate participants on other topics as well:

1. **Hold a live online orientation session to teach participants how to learn online.** Make this session a required prerequisite for attending any of your virtual classes. The program goals should be gaining experience in how to

connect to the classroom, touring the platform features and learning how to use them, setting expectations for an interactive learning experience, and learning tips for creating an appropriate learning environment. This session could be anywhere from 30- to 60-minutes long, depending on the platform, which features you cover, and how many activities you include. Many organizations hold these live events regularly, simply making them required for anyone who attends a virtual training class.

2. **Create a self-paced asynchronous program in the form of a virtual platform tour that focuses on preparation tips for participants.** This option is like the live orientation session, except that it would not replicate the connection experience for participants. You'll walk participants through the platform, setting expectations for participation by using the tools. If your organization does not have the resources to hold a live online prerequisite class or your learners can't attend, this option may be the best choice.

3. **Invite new participants to log in 30 minutes early to get an overview of the virtual platform.** Make sure to distinguish between this overview session and your actual virtual training class so both participants and the facilitator have time to transition between the two. Ask new participants to join the session 30 minutes before the normal start time, and use approximately 15 to 20 of those minutes to teach them the tools and set expectations. The remainder of the allotted time will be used to transition to class, as other participants begin joining the session.

4. **Teach the tools on an as-needed basis during the training class.** If I'm not using the first option, this what I most frequently choose. While it does not address setting up the learning environment, it gives participants the instructions they need when they need them. For example, when it's time to use the whiteboard drawing tools, I take a moment to show a screenshot or point to the toolbar and explain where and how to use them. Participants who already know how to use the tool can begin the activity, and those who need extra assistance will receive it.

5. **Share a job aid or reference card with tips for using the tech.** Create a short document to share with participants ahead of time, either along with a handout or as a separate document. You could also share it at the beginning of a class using the virtual platform's file-sharing feature. It should include screenshots of the virtual classroom platform with clear instructions on how

to use the tools that will be required during class. Keep the document simple and useful so participants can easily follow along.

Remember, your goal is to make things simple and easy, not hard and frustrating. You want participants to have a good experience preparing for and attending your virtual training class. Use the technology training method that makes the most sense for your learners and your programs. And of course, feel free to combine several options for the best results.

---

*"I spend a few minutes at the beginning of a virtual class
to educate attendees about the features and buttons that I
plan to use (such as chat, voting, and annotation)."*

—Jeff Robinson, Global Talent Management, Covance Laboratories

---

Tech Checks

One of my clients was getting ready to roll out a blended learning curriculum, which included 12 virtual training classes spread over 10 months. Most of the participants were brand new to the virtual training platform and would be joining the sessions from home.

To help prepare each participant for the technology needed and to educate them on creating an appropriate learning environment, we scheduled several "tech check" sessions before the program's start date. Participants were able to choose which session they attended, but attendance at one session was mandatory.

Each tech check lasted 30 minutes and asked participants to:

- Log in to the system with the computer they planned to use during the program so they could test their connection and learn how to join the audio connection.
- Take a tour of the virtual training platform features while using the tools to complete several introductory activities.
- Watch an overview of the blended curriculum from the facilitator, who would answer any questions they had.

By attending these mandatory tech check sessions, the first class was able to begin right away without any technology hiccups or participant issues.

Changing Hearts and Minds

As I mentioned earlier in this chapter, implementing successful virtual training is often more about changing attitudes and beliefs than about adopting new technology.

Of course, the technology is also important, but to be successful with virtual learning, recognize the critical role that change management will play.

"Think about change management that goes along with a virtual training rollout. Be mindful from the very beginning about the influence that virtual training will have on your participants."

—Erin Laughlin, former Senior Director of Global
Learning Delivery, Marriott International

While a full discussion of change management goes beyond the scope of this book, let's look at four proven techniques you can use to help participants more enthusiastically adopt virtual training as an effective and efficient way to learn:

- Start small, and then expand.
- Gain managers' support.
- Anticipate questions and concerns.
- Communicate early and often.

Start Small, and Then Expand

If this is your organization's first venture into virtual training or if your virtual training needs a reboot, start small, and then expand. Run a pilot program on a simple topic that you know will be wildly successful. Invite a small group of participants from a business unit that is struggling with a specific problem but who are eager to learn, and use the virtual training class to provide a solution to that problem. Or select a team of individuals you know will be supportive and willing to try something new. Or ask for volunteers so your first group of participants consists of those who have chosen to join in.

By focusing on a small group of eager early adopters who want to learn virtually, you will be much more likely to achieve the small initial victories that lead to larger ones later. A few quick wins will help build momentum. If people hear about a successful initiative, they will be more open to accepting it.

If your organization has already adopted virtual training, but you now realize you need to go back and make changes or revise what you have been doing, you can use the same approach. For example, many organizations that quickly pivoted to virtual classrooms at the start of the COVID-19 pandemic are now discovering they need to revise their approaches to improve quality. Start small and apply the techniques presented in this book. You might also want to consider a rebranding effort; for example, use a different name, a different logo, and a different group of participants. Once you start to see success in this small area, increase and expand your efforts.

Gain Managers' Support

If you're asking employees to prioritize virtual training, it's important to educate and involve their managers. Not only do participants need the support of their direct supervisors to fully participate in a virtual training program, but they also need support before and after the event as well. Research shows that the manager's role before and after any training event is critical to successful learning transfer (Broad and Newstrom 1992).

I experienced this truth several years ago when I delivered two leadership classes for an organization. The morning group showed up for the class on time, prepared, eager to learn, and ready to participate. We had a good discussion and participants actively planned how to apply the content to their own situations. In stark contrast, the afternoon group showed up late, most were not prepared, and participation was sparse.

After the class, I learned that the manager of the morning group had used time during a team meeting to talk about the upcoming training and its importance. He mentioned that the whole team would talk about the training again at their next meeting. The manager of the afternoon group, on the other hand, said nothing about the training. His group had only received an email notice informing them of the training date, with very little explanation and no mention of expectations.

I argue that these two managers' approaches made the difference in what each group learned and was able to apply afterward.

Your participants' managers—especially their support of the training—will have a direct influence over its success. Not only is it important for you to prepare participants for virtual training, but it's also essential for you to gain support from their managers.

You will need managers' support for both the training topic and the training modality. For example, if a manager is not aware that an employee is participating a virtual training program, they may see that employee sitting at a desk looking at a website and interrupt to ask a question, assuming they're just surfing the web.

Always educate managers about the details of your virtual training program and its expected learning outcomes. You can also include managers in your initial implementation team, as discussed in chapter 2. Additional ways to involve managers in the learning experience include:

- Inviting them to attend a kickoff session
- Creating a special communication piece that explains the learning outcomes

- Providing a dedicated manager guide for the virtual training class
- Including an assignment asking participants to talk with their managers before attending the session

---

"We get the participants' managers involved with setting up a workstation for new employees to join our virtual training classes. We send a checklist with instructions on how to set up a quiet space that is conducive to learning. This checklist also includes technical requirements, such as a wired connection, their own connection, and a headset to use for audio during training."

—Lisa Brodeth Carrick, former Executive Director, Comcast University

---

Anticipate Questions and Concerns

We all know that questions and concerns accompany any major change. By thinking through what participants might ask about virtual training, you can proactively formulate a response before the questions turn into concerns that create obstacles for a successful rollout.

For example, some participants may wonder if virtual training is the only option for learning or if the organization will continue to offer in-person programs. Some will ask about hybrid learning as an alternative. Others, who prefer attending in-person training classes with remote colleagues, might be concerned that this will limit their opportunities to visit with their colleagues in person. And still other participants will have concerns about the technology. These types of questions and concerns are normal in any change initiative. Even if participants (and future participants) stay silent, questions are probably still bubbling under the surface.

When you take the time to anticipate questions, you can quell many misunderstandings about your organization's virtual training strategy. You can also take the initiative to share correct information. The more information participants have, the more likely they will be to support the program's success.

Creating a Manager's Guide

I designed a blended learning leadership curriculum for the first-line managers of a global organization. The program included eight virtual sessions over six months, plus self-paced assignments in between. To effectively prepare participants for the full commitment and to help them maintain momentum, I decided to involve their managers.

First, I invited the participants' managers to attend an initial overview. This kickoff session explained the program's learning objectives, the training schedule, and the time commitment involved. It also reviewed participant expectations and the importance of participant interaction and engagement throughout the curriculum.

Second, I created a manager's guide that corresponded to the training curriculum and included:

- Program topics and learning outcomes
- Program schedules, including the exact times of all virtual sessions and the time commitment expected from each participant
- A topic-related discussion question or two to ask participants at set times during the curriculum
- Tips for supporting participants' success, such as allowing enough time during the workday for learning and participation

I shared the document with each manager and then invited them to refer to it often throughout the curriculum as a guide to help their participants.

When you communicate well before and after a session, participants will be more at ease and more likely to share positive feedback about their experience with others. When participants have a good experience with your virtual training, you can use their anecdotal feedback to promote future events. Collect these testimonials and success stories and share them with your stakeholders, especially future participants.

In Summary: Key Points From Chapter 7

- Successful virtual training is more about changing hearts and minds about online learning than it is about the technology.
- Participant preparation is often overlooked, but it is an essential step in successful virtual training.
- Participants have new responsibilities when learning in the virtual classroom, such as setting up their workspace and printing or accessing their own materials.
- Participants won't pay attention or learn if they are unable to focus during the session because they are in an unsuitable learning environment or are experiencing technical challenges. It's important to do everything you can to set them up for success, including making the training as accessible as possible to all participants.
- Get the participants' managers involved and educate them about virtual training.

Take Action

✓ Review each communication participants receive in advance of a virtual training program. What messages are conveyed? Is it enough information to properly prepare them for an engaging online learning experience? What needs to be updated or improved?

✓ Consider how you can involve the participants' managers or direct supervisors in the virtual learning program. Is there communication that would add value or a learning activity that could include them?

Tool 7-1. Sample Participant Preparation Checklist

Tech needs:

- ☐ Strong internet connection (wired, if possible)
- ☐ Reliable computer or laptop
- ☐ Hands-free headset or external microphone
- ☐ HD webcam with proper lighting
- ☐ Virtual classroom platform software

Other preparation:

- ☐ Find a quiet space to focus and learn.
- ☐ Set your devices to silent or do-not-disturb mode. Hang a sign on your door if necessary.
- ☐ Put away distractions, including any to-do lists.
- ☐ Close out of email and instant-messaging programs.
- ☐ Test your connection using the provided link at least 24 hours before the class starts.

Tool 7-2. Kickoff Session Sample Agenda That Involves Participants' Managers

Topic	Content
Welcome	Facilitator should briefly greet participants and their managers.
Introductions	Conduct an interactive exercise to get to know who's in attendance and begin creating community among participants.
Welcome From a Senior Leader	Share the importance of the training program and its connection to business results; express commitment to virtual training as a viable learning modality.
What to Expect: Content	Provide an overview of program learning objectives and how the program will be structured (e.g., number of sessions).
What to Expect: Participation	Set expectations about involvement and engagement; offer tips and suggestions.
What to Expect: Platform Tools	Review any platform tools not yet used during the session, along with reinforcement of ones already used.
Next Steps	Discuss logistics for the next virtual class, along with any assignments to complete between now and then.

Remember to invite the participants and their direct managers. Keep this session as interactive as possible to set expectations and help participants learn how to use the tools.

Tool 7-3. Participant Troubleshooting Guide

Challenge	Root Cause	Solution
Participants don't complete their preparation assignments.	If participants don't complete a preparation assignment, it's usually for one of two reasons: Either they didn't know they needed to do it, or they didn't think it was important enough to make time for it.	There are two solutions for this challenge: • First, don't call it prework because that sounds unimportant and uninteresting. Instead, call it something that indicates weighty importance or uses a catchy name that works in your organizational culture, such as "action assignment" or "the three-step setup." • Second, make it as easy as possible for them to complete. Let participants know exactly how long the assignment should take, give them all the necessary resources they need, and make the instructions easy to find.
Participants don't engage during a virtual class.	This is the single most common challenge I hear from online facilitators. "My participants are silent," they tell me. "I ask a question, and no one responds." Facilitators also complain that participants are multitasking (like checking email) instead of paying attention to the session.	The solution goes back to setting proper expectations before the session and having an effectively designed virtual training program with frequent interaction. The first interaction should begin within the first minute or two of the class start time. If you follow the recommendations in this book, your participants will be much more likely to engage in their own learning! For example, if the design calls for 15 minutes of lecture about how to use the platform and an overview of the class agenda, before the facilitator even asks the first question, of course, there will be silence. As we discussed in chapter 5, creating a great opening is one way to engage participants from the start. This is just one of many techniques you can use to set the stage for interaction and engagement.
Participants don't like virtual training.	Remember that many participants have only experienced lecture-style webcasts, so that's what they expect for virtual training. Very few adults like to be lectured! If participants have attended a virtual training program in the past, they may have had a bad experience. Your goal in this situation is to create a fantastic learning experience for participants.	Your goal should be to design a highly interactive session and use a skilled facilitator. Remember adult learning principles and apply them to the class. For example, most people don't like to be told what to do and prefer to make choices. Therefore, give them a choice of when to sign up for their virtual class instead of assigning them to a specific session.

CHAPTER 8

Build Success
Through Logistics

 In this chapter, you will learn how to create virtual training success through logistics:

- Recognize the importance of the administrator role.
- Plan logistics according to five key milestones.
- Create a consistent process for virtual training programs.
- Consider ongoing maintenance requirements.

Legendary basketball coach John Wooden once said, "It's the little details that are vital. Little things make big things happen" (ESPN 2010). While he was referring to success in sports, he could have been talking about virtual training. Paying attention to the details will determine the difference between success and failure in your online programs.

When organizations implement virtual learning solutions, they often underestimate the number of logistical details required for success. A common misperception is that organizing virtual training events is easy. "What is there to do? Just create a link and calendar invite, send it to participants, and you're ready to go." I have heard statements like this from many people, especially at the start of the COVID-19 pandemic when almost everyone was moving to the virtual classroom as quickly as possible.

While it may seem easy from the outside—and that's the goal—never take for granted the amount of time and effort that goes into setting up the logistics for a virtual training event. Successful virtual training requires thoughtful planning, careful preparation, and diligent execution. Like the beautiful moves of an effortlessly spinning figure skater or a gymnast who easily flips high in the air, smooth and effective virtual training comes only after significant preparation.

In this chapter, we will cover the full scope of logistics required to create success. Some of the items may seem elementary while others should get you thinking on a deeper level. We will also answer two essential questions: Who does what? And when should they do it?

> *"Virtual training needs a lot more administrative work than traditional classroom training because of what it takes to create a positive learning experience."*
>
> —Lisa Brodeth Carrick, former Executive Director, Comcast University

The Coordinator or Administrator Role

In chapter 1, we discussed roles found in typical virtual training initiatives. As a reminder, the coordinator role was defined as the administrative person who handles the logistical details of virtual training events. This person might administer the organization's LMS or LXP and communicate with participants before and after an event. Some training departments employ a learning coordinator or administrative assistant to handle coordination details, while in others, the facilitator or another training professional is responsible for these logistics. The training department structure depends on the organization's resources, budget, headcounts, and division of responsibilities.

Once upon a time, I was a one-person training department for a large global organization. I would have loved having a learning coordinator to help with all the details involved in my training programs; however, it wasn't in the budget or even a consideration. On occasion, I was able to tap into administrative help from other departments, but most of the logistics related to training were my responsibility. I had enough bandwidth during the work week to handle the details in the early days, but as my virtual training program offering grew, it became a challenge.

Whether the learning coordinator is a designated person in your organization or someone who wears multiple hats and performs these functions as part of their overall job description, the tasks associated with this administrative role are essential for virtual training success. This chapter will explore all the required logistics in detail. But first, to give you an idea of the types of tasks required, consider this partial list of hats an administrator might wear:

- Record keeper
- Communication maven

- Behind-the-scenes setup coordinator
- Knowledge manager
- Platform expert
- Technical support

To minimize any confusion between a person who holds a learning coordinator job title and others who simply perform administrative responsibilities in addition to their other duties, I will refer to both as the *administrator* from this point forward. In other words, the administrator role will include anyone who is doing logistical tasks, regardless of their actual job title.

Facilitator Role vs. Administrator Role

How do you distinguish between the facilitator's role in a virtual training program and the administrator's role, especially if your organization has one person who does everything—both logistics and facilitation?

The facilitator is usually the face and voice of the virtual training program—they're responsible for enabling the learning experience. The facilitator leads the synchronous events, coaches participants on new skills, delivers the class, and facilitates learning. They directly interact with participants before, during, and after a training program, particularly if it's a lengthy blended journey with multiple live online sessions.

The administrator usually stays behind the scenes of the program, coordinating resources and ensuring that all class details are attended to. The administrator often communicates with participants, but they have a different purpose than the facilitator. The administrator's messages are based on their program manager role. The administrator typically does not get involved in the actual learning process but instead focuses on logistics and other administrative details.

To further illustrate the difference between these roles, consider this scenario:

> In preparation for next month's virtual training class, the administrator logs in to the virtual platform (or the LMS or LXP platform). They create the event, which generates a link to share with all attendees.

> As participants register, the facilitator receives the link and registration lists from the administrator (either directly or via the LMS) and begins to connect with participants. The facilitator reaches out to welcome everyone to the training program and to see what questions they have about preparation. The facilitator begins building rapport with participants so that by the time the first live online session starts, they've established a certain comfort level.

> The facilitator delivers the program and guides participants in the learning process.
>
> After the program, the participants receive an email message from the administrator reminding them to implement their action plans and offering information about the next course in the series.

Logistics Milestones Timeline

Now that we have defined the administrator role, let's consider the specific tasks the administrator does to make virtual training successful. It's easiest to consider these tasks in terms of when they need to be completed, so we will review them according to milestones along a virtual class timeline. This logistics timeline is split into five periods: before the event, immediately before the event, during the event, at the end of the event, and after the event.

Before the Event

You may be wondering exactly what's meant by before. How long before a virtual training session should the administrative preparation begin? I hesitate to give an exact timeframe because it depends on several factors, including the complexity of the virtual training initiative and whether it's a new program rollout. However, it's is likely much earlier than you think!

For example, if you have a virtual training class that's part of a six-week blended learning journey, and it requires preparation and action assignments before each virtual session, the administrative details will be more time consuming than if you have a one-time virtual session. If you are preparing for a brand-new virtual training program that is being delivered for the first time, you'll have more logistics to work out than if it was an existing, well-established program.

For any type of virtual training program—lengthy blended journeys or one-time events—there are pre-event logistics to consider and prepare for during the period before the event, including:

- The initial project meeting
- Marketing and advertising
- Registration
- Material distribution
- Virtual classroom setup

- Communication with participants
- Practice and rehearsal

Some of these tasks may be automated, but just as it's helpful to learn basic math concepts like multiplication before using a calculator, it's worthwhile to understand each step along the way before the automation kicks in.

"Some people think that once the technology is set, you're done. But there's so much that happens behind the scenes to make virtual training look easy."

—Peggy Page, former Learning and Design Manager, TD Bank

Initial Project Meeting

A first-time virtual program rollout should begin with an initial meeting that includes anyone who will be involved with logistics. This group may include facilitators, producers, administrators, designers, IT staff, and all other program stakeholders. The purpose of this meeting is to establish roles, responsibilities, expectations, and communication methods. Once your organization gets into an operating rhythm for program logistics, you will no longer need to hold this initial meeting every time, but it's highly recommended for new programs.

The initial meeting agenda should focus on a walk-through of the administrative tasks and their timelines for completion. It should also focus on the specifics of who will do what and when. Meeting participants should agree on role clarification and strategies for dealing with any plan deviations that arise.

Marketing and Advertising

You may need to plan for a targeted marketing and advertising campaign to increase awareness of the training program and its benefits to participants and other interested stakeholders. The campaign can also motivate participants to get involved early on and actively engage in the learning process. It will communicate relevant details of interest, such as date and time commitments.

If participants are required to attend the virtual training, then the marketing will not be quite as important as if participants were choosing to attend based on open enrollment. The marketing campaign for an open enrollment learning program will need to emphasize the direct benefits for the potential participants based on expected learning outcomes and corresponding business results.

The marketing campaign will also look different if participants are nominated by their managers to attend, as in a high-potential leadership program. In that case, the main advertising would be directed to managers, emphasizing why they should send their employees to this learning experience.

Typically, there are three tasks associated with marketing a training program:

- **Write the program advertising text and graphics.** What will you say about the program?
- **Choose marketing methods.** How much will marketing focus on social media, internal websites, articles in a company newsletter, or other options?
- **Post the marketing content to chosen locations.** What locations will be best for your target audience?

While these marketing tasks are the same for all types of learning programs, a critical point to remember is that you are marketing a virtual training experience. If this is a new way of learning in your organization, it will be essential to focus on the benefits of virtual training. If it isn't a new modality but needs improvement to get better results, consider using marketing as a rebranding effort. Your campaign will increase awareness of the training program and educate participants on expectations and results.

One of my clients was implementing a blended learning journey focused on communication skills; as part of its design, I created a one-page marketing graphic to advertise the program. The graphic clearly articulated the program outcomes and reasons to attend. It also described the unique virtual approach and the benefits of learning online. My client successfully used this document to communicate the program in an internal social media campaign to their target audience.

Registration

Once you've started advertising the program, the registration and enrollment process can also begin. In the simplest approach, you'll track registrations manually in an online spreadsheet. More commonly, registration is automated through an LMS or LXP. In this case, you'll need to load everything into the database, including the learning description, program information, materials, and all other communication documents that participants should see upon registration.

An administrator will always be involved, even if the registration process is automated. They should keep an eye on enrollment numbers, ensuring the appropriate people are alerted if the program isn't meeting target expectations. If the training program has any prerequisite requirements or unusual registration qualifications, the administrator may also need to ensure each registrant meets those expectations.

"Your LMS can be a huge timesaver for managing registrations and communications for virtual events, especially if it integrates directly with your virtual classroom platform. Most LMSs can automate and track registrations, as well as send registration confirmation and reminder emails, distribute materials before and after an event, record attendance from the virtual event, and distribute and track the results of evaluations and assessments."

—Wendy Gates Corbett, author, researcher, and
former Global Training Director

Materials Distribution

Distributing materials, including all materials participants need before class, also belongs on the list of key logistical tasks that need to be completed before a virtual training program.

Recall the lengthy discussion in chapter 7 about the benefits of providing reference materials to participants. We also discussed how to choose between asking participants to download materials ahead of time and directly shipping preprinted materials. Either way, administrators will have work to do. If you ask participants to download their own class materials, the administrator will need to load those materials into a central repository (a document-sharing site or the LMS or LXP) that's accessible to everyone. In some unique cases, materials may need to be sent via email. Participants should receive explicit instructions on how to access the files and any special printing directions. The more advance notice you give to participants, the better, so they'll have time to complete this task. And of course, if you are planning to ship workbooks or other printed documents to participants, all those logistics need to be handled carefully with an eye on timing.

The World Bank Group Senior Knowledge and Learning Officer Darlene Christopher notes that it's important to plan materials distribution well in advance, especially with global participants (and thus international shipping). For some classes, Darlene's administrator sends each participant a pen and custom notepad along with the class materials. The administrator also sends an email message to confirm everyone received the materials.

LMS and LXP Administration

If your organization has an LMS or LXP, pre-event logistics can be automated. If the LMS or LXP administrator is part of the training department or even the same person as the learning coordinator, you may be able to streamline some of the responsibilities associated with these tasks. This is a big advantage of using an LMS or LXP.

However, there are pros and cons to using an LMS or LXP for complete automation of virtual training logistics. The pros are obvious: automation, economies of scale, and time saved. The drawbacks of an automated system include less personalized content and potential challenges if learners can't easily access the system. Depending upon its features, the LMS or LXP may or may not be customizable for virtual classes or a blended learning journey. But regardless of the drawbacks, if your organization uses an LMS or LXP, it's best to automate as many virtual training logistics as you can to save administrative time.

Virtual Classroom Setup

The next administrative step is setting up your virtual classroom, a task that can be broken down into two parts:

1. Create the live online event using the virtual classroom platform's administrative tools.
2. Load training content into the virtual classroom.

The person performing this task needs to be well versed in the virtual platform's administrative features so they can accurately set up the event.

Creating the Event

You should initiate each event that will occur during the class in the virtual classroom platform. It's possible to automate this step if the virtual platform is integrated behind the scenes with your LMS or LXP. The exact steps required to complete this task will depend on your platform, but most are similar in form and function. First, someone with administrative rights to the virtual platform logs in to the program and creates a new event. They enter the date, time, and estimated length of the session. They confirm program details and may be able to preset participant privileges and other particulars. They can also set access rights for facilitators, producers, and participants. Once the online event is created, the connection link can be shared with everyone who needs it.

The biggest mistake during this step of the process is assuming that just because there's a generated link, the classroom has been set up. With most platforms, you need to manually update settings for the tools to work properly. This could mean that a one-time update, such as enabling breakout rooms or changing a participant audio option, will have to be manually set each time. These simple details may not seem important, but they can make or break a learning experience. Depending on the platform, the settings may only be available by going into the back-end administrative site, and it may not be possible to change settings after the program starts.

Figure 8-1. Administrative Settings in Zoom

If your virtual platform relies on loaded content rather than screen sharing (as discussed in chapter 3), the actual program content will need to be put into the virtual classroom. Some platforms allow this to be done days or weeks in advance of the session. Other platforms require you to do it right before the session begins. If multiple people in your organization are performing administrative tasks, this is a task many facilitators take responsibility for to ensure they have access to the facilitator materials, including slides, poll questions, collaborative whiteboard activities, and any other necessary documents.

When facilitating a virtual class, I prefer to load my own training content into the classroom as part of my preprogram setup. It would save me time if someone else took on that responsibility, but there's something about the routine of setting up my own classroom that is appealing to me, and I enjoy it.

The facilitator guide should include all setup information for the class and any instructions needed for loading content online. Remember that if an administrator loads training content into the classroom, they will require access to all the materials and should follow the instructions in the facilitator guide carefully.

Virtual Classrooms: One-Time Use vs. Perpetual

On some platforms, the event room can be used only once, on the specific date and time selected during the initial setup. On other platforms, you can use the same event link over and over for multiple events, and this is considered a perpetual classroom.

The obvious advantage of a perpetual classroom is that it only needs to be set up one time. After the classroom is used for an event, it only needs to be cleaned before the next use, which involves clearing answers to poll questions, erasing annotations, and so on. Another advantage of perpetual classrooms is that you can use the same link for an entire series of events. So, in a blended learning journey with multiple facilitated events, only one link is shared with everyone.

Communicating With Participants

Administrators usually communicate connection details and other session logistics over email. Most virtual classroom platforms generate an email message when a session link is created, but this standardized message often has very little information besides connection details—typically, not enough to inspire participants to get involved in their own learning. Even if you are using an LMS or LXP, the automated communication usually lacks motivating words. Therefore, you should take the opportunity to create your own set of messages to communicate session logistics.

As we discussed in chapter 3, an interactive virtual class should be engaging from the moment your participants register. Use every session logistics communication to set and reinforce expectations that it will be an active learning experience. Of course, be sure to include links and connection details as well. For example, the first message participants receive upon class enrollment could start spurring interactivity by inviting them to do one or more of the following things:

- Engage with other participants on a discussion board or cohort channel.
- Complete a relevant preclass exercise, something they'll refer to during class.
- Respond to a topic-related question or two and bring the answers to class.
- Share questions about the topic with the facilitator.

When sending your first message, consider the participants and their likelihood of actually reading it and completing any included assignments. In his book, *To Sell Is Human*, author Daniel Pink observes that the subject line of an email message matters; it's an important factor in determining whether a message will be opened. Based on research from Carnegie Mellon University, Pink recommends that you write subject lines that readers see as useful or inspire curiosity. Pink also recommends, based on research from entrepreneur Brian Clark, that subject lines should be specific (Pink 2012). So, take time to carefully craft subject lines that are likely to catch participants' eyes and make opening your emails irresistible. For example, the email subject line of your reminder message for a time management virtual class might read, "Today's class will teach you how to gain an extra hour of time every day."

After sharing initial class connection details, the administrator should send periodic reminder messages. These reminders should include not only class logistical information and preparatory assignments, but also reinforcement that the session will be interactive. For example, remind participants that they should prepare to be hands-on during the session and that they'll be expected to collaborate with their peers. Remind them to close email and other programs at the start of the session so they can have the best internet connection and not be distracted by interruptions. Consider sending a sign that says, "Do not disturb—learning in progress" to hang on their office door. If you communicate these expectations before the session, participants will not be blindsided when asked to jump in with both feet as they log in to the virtual classroom.

The number of reminders you send depends on how far in advance participants have registered. Find a balance between overloading email inboxes and keeping the training top of mind. Send at least one reminder a few business days before the session.

Tips for Communicating With Participants

Consider both what you communicate (content) and how you communicate it (style).

Content

Make all your communications easy to read. Use clear and concise wording. Take a lesson from marketing professionals who use appealing words and catchphrases to gain attention. You can also do some simple things to make data easy to read in an email message. For example, if there are strings of numbers, such as an event passcode, separate numbers into chunks (for example, "123 45 6789" instead of "123456789"). It's easier on the eyes.

Consider carefully whether to include phone numbers along with the web link.
Even if your virtual class allows telephone options in addition to computer audio, in
most cases, it isn't necessary because the audio information will be displayed onscreen
once a participant joins the virtual classroom. Some platform audio features may not
be available if the participants dial in separately, so it's extra important that they log
in to the session first and then follow the audio prompts. By not listing the phone
connection, you can force participants to join via the web first.

Include links to class materials, event details, and tech support information in every
communication. If they search for this information, they will easily find it.

Style
**One of my favorite quotes that comes to mind when I write email messages is to
"shut down the ugly."** Virtual training experts Treion Muller and Matthew Murdoch
(2013) coined this phrase in their classic book, *The Webinar Manifesto*, to encourage
us to make sure we "write beautiful words" and "design beautiful graphics" for every
communication we send. When administrators follow this advice, they increase the
likelihood that participants will read the messages.

Practice and Rehearsal

Before your first live online virtual program, there should be at least one practice session. This allows everyone involved a chance to test connectivity and run through the
content in a dress rehearsal. It also allows the facilitator and producer to talk through
how they will partner during the event.

While it is most important for the facilitator and producer to attend the pre-event
rehearsals, an administrator sometimes attends these sessions as an observer. And
of course, if the administrator is also wearing the producer or the facilitator hat, it's a
given that they will be in attendance.

The most important role of the administrator for practice sessions is to ensure
that the virtual classroom links are created, the content is loaded, and the classroom
is ready.

Just Before (Day of the Event)

In this section, we will capture all the logistical tasks you should do on the day of the
program. In some ways, the administrator is producing a show that has a countdown
clock, with many last-minute details to handle.

Send a Reminder

It's always a good idea to send a day-of-event reminder message to participants. The administrator may even want to send a separate reminder message to the facilitators and anyone else who has a supporting role in the training. This final check-in helps everyone have the connection details at their fingertips.

Ensure Content Is Loaded

If the virtual classroom platform does not allow for content loading before the event, then you need to complete this task just before the class begins. In this case, I recommend the host log in and set up approximately 45 minutes before the session start time. While 45 minutes may seem extreme, it's only 15 minutes more than my normal recommended host login time of 30 minutes before a session. If this still seems extreme, compare it to a traditional in-person class in which the facilitator almost always shows up an hour before the start time to complete setup and other logistical tasks before the participants arrive. It's the same principle in the virtual classroom. Err on the side of caution, especially if you need to load content, enable participant features, and create polls or other activities.

What's a Host?

Virtual classroom platforms assign a role to every person who joins an online session. Each role has different privilege levels for using the platform tools. While specific names vary—one program might use *host* while another uses *presenter*—the host role has the most control over the class. They can start and end sessions, determine who has presenter rights, and grant extra privileges to attendees (such as annotation rights).

Open the Session and Greet Participants

The administrator must have host privileges so they can log in early and start (sometimes called "open") the classroom. They should then double-check all the content as well as the audio and video connections. Everything should be there as expected, but it's always a good idea to double-check.

Once the session is open, the next step is preparing to greet participants. Ideally, you have encouraged participants to join at least five to 10 minutes early. As we established in chapter 3, regardless of the official start time, the class begins the minute the first participant enters the room. The goal is immediate engagement as participants connect to the session.

Handle Last-Minute Details

The facilitator should welcome participants to class while the producer assists with any connection or technical challenges. The administrative tasks associated with this period include sending out last-minute links, connection details, or materials to participants who need them. Even if the administrator is not planning to be online, they may need to pitch in and help with the session if technical issues arise. They should know the class schedule so they can be available or on call, especially if the facilitator is flying solo without a producer. In large organizations with multiple classes running at once, keeping an accurate calendar of events will help administrators offer better support. Think of a class as a business partnership; when it's time to serve the customers (the participants), you may need an all-hands-on-deck call.

For example, recently I was about to begin a virtual training class when the platform unexpectedly stopped working. Additionally, several participants had an incorrect passcode and couldn't join the session. My producer and I needed an extra set of hands to communicate with participants, so we asked the administrator to jump in and assist. We were able to resolve the situation quickly, and class started only a few minutes late. This type of partnership requires flexibility on everyone's part to ensure a first-rate learning experience for participants. If the facilitator, producer, and administrator are working together as a team, the participants will have a seamless experience.

If there isn't a separate administrator to help with last-minute details, try this idea from virtual facilitator Kelley Eason: Set your email out-of-office message to include the connection details of the virtual training session. That way, anyone who contacts you for this information will automatically receive it.

During

By the time the session begins, much of the logistics work is done. However, you may need to complete a few key administrative tasks during the session.

Capture Attendance and Assist as Needed

Many organizations require you to capture participant attendance for recordkeeping. If the system captures login details and can produce an attendance report, this task can be automated. However, if this isn't an option, the administrator can briefly join the online session to note which participants have signed in. Alternatively, the facilitator could take a screenshot of the participant list and send it to the administrator for recordkeeping.

If other unexpected technical challenges arise during a session, the administrator might need to stay on call to assist. For example, if a remote participant needs immediate assistance, the administrator could reach out to the local IT contact in the participant's building. Or participants may need international dialing instructions, which an administrator could provide. And in an emergency, the administrator may need to find another facilitator to fill in at the last minute. While these situations are unusual, having the administrator available during a session could make the difference between success and frustration.

Ending

Near the end of a virtual training class, the administrator typically has four short but important tasks:

- Distribute additional reference materials.
- Conduct knowledge assessments.
- Manage program evaluations.
- Share what's next (especially for blended learning journeys).

These can be done in whatever order works best for the program design.

Distribute Reference Materials

If you use an LMS or LXP for material distribution, this task will be automated. If not, the virtual classroom platform's file-sharing tools can give participants access to reference materials, additional handouts, or job aids associated with the program. As a last resort, if either of those options is not available, the administrator should manually share these documents with participants. If multiple people are completing administrative tasks, ensure they know which materials to share with participants. As I advocated for in chapter 4, the slides are part of the facilitator guide and typically aren't shared with anyone. If you have the urge to share the slides, consider whether you have a presentation instead of a learning experience.

Conduct Knowledge Assessments

Another end-of-class detail is the completion of assessments or knowledge exams. While the facilitator often takes ownership of this task, it's listed here with logistics to be sure it's handled. Many virtual classroom platforms have built-in tools for these assessments, usually part of the polling or quizzing feature. The actual content for the assessment comes from the class design and should be included in the facilitator guide. The administrative task is to execute the assessment and capture participant scores.

If the virtual classroom platform does not have a quiz feature, you could use an integrated app or external third-party assessment tool. In this case, you would need to send the participants a link to the exam. In some cases, the LMS or LXP can communicate with the quiz tool (internal or external) and automatically record results. If not, the administrator may need to capture this information manually.

Provide Class Evaluations

Class evaluations are used to gather participant feedback. You might choose to combine the end-of-class evaluation and knowledge assessment into one form, using the virtual classroom tools or a third-party tool to get this feedback. A best practice is to allow time at the end of a session, before the scheduled stop time, for participants to complete these forms. This means that the evaluation should begin by at least the 55-minute mark in a 60-minute class. And if you combine the knowledge assessment with the evaluation, you may need to provide more time, which should be included in the course design.

"We end class at least three to five minutes early so participants have time to complete the evaluation form. This means we have a nearly 100 percent completion rate."

—Justin Patton, former Master Facilitator, Yum! Brands

Share What's Next

Finally, if the event has a postclass assignment or is part of a blended curriculum, tell participants about the next step in the process. They may already be aware, but it's always a good idea to provide a reminder. By communicating what's next at the end of the session, participants will be more likely to take action.

There are a few ways you can complete this administrative task:

- Post a slide in the virtual classroom showing next step details.
- Share a document with relevant details.
- Send an email reminder message to everyone's inbox.
- Provide a graphic showing the next step.
- Send a calendar reminder for the next time-based event.

After

Once a virtual session ends, there are two main administrative tasks to complete. In addition, the administrator may also need to complete any tasks from the "ending" section—sharing reference materials, assignments, assessments, evaluations, and next-step items—that didn't get finished before the class ended.

Close the Classroom

Once the program is over, the administrator will need to properly close the classroom. On some platforms, you'll need to save items such as participant annotations on the whiteboard, chat window responses, and answers to poll questions before ending the session.

A perpetual virtual classroom may require several tasks to happen before it's ready for its next use:

- Clear answers to poll questions.
- Erase whiteboards.
- Rewind video and other media files.
- Clear slide annotations.
- Refresh breakout rooms.

Hold a Follow-Up Meeting

The administrator should lead a lessons-learned meeting at some point after the session has ended. This allows the virtual training team to distill evaluation feedback, provide insight to facilitators, and share course review information with designers. The administrator takes notes on items that could be improved, changed, or updated, along with any other suggestions to improve the content or process for the next time.

One Organization's Story
Turning Synchronous Classes Into Asynchronous Learning

According to Ken Hubbell, former senior manager of learning technology at Ingersoll Rand, some of the company's virtual training classes are recorded and preserved as asynchronous lessons. Because watching a playback of a live online class is not the best way to learn, the organization repurposes the synchronous sessions in a way that makes sense for offline viewing.

Ideally, the facilitators run a virtual class at least three times, recording each one. Afterward, an administrator watches the recordings, notes the highlights, and captures commonly asked questions. They then weave together the highlight segments or modules of each class to create a shorter recording or series of modules that can be posted and viewed or incorporated into other courses.

Creating an Ongoing Administrative Process

Creating standard processes for all these administrative tasks is a wise investment and will save time and effort. The process should delineate what do to, who will do it, and when it will happen along the logistics timeline. A consistent process will guide administrators as they perform each task.

It's essential to keep your process simple! Too much complexity will only create confusion and bog down the entire process.

An organization I worked with recently had good intentions when creating their virtual training administrative process, but over time, it became so complex and confusing that no one was able to follow it. Initially, the organization simply used a short checklist detailing who would be responsible for creating the virtual event link in the LMS and ensuring the correct details were sent to participants. Exceptions to the process were allowed because some facilitators also took on administrative responsibilities. Then, the organization expanded their virtual training offerings, adding blended learning journeys and multi-event sessions. Now, there was one administrative process that applied to single-session virtual events and a separate process that applied to a series of virtual events. Additionally, they continued to allow exceptions to both processes based on factors that made sense at the time. Unfortunately, no one could figure out which process to follow for which type of program. The team eventually realized they had a problem and streamlined everything into one straightforward process. The moral of this story is to keep your processes simple so everyone can and will follow them.

Strive to create a process that allows for a rhythm you can easily replicate. Review your processes periodically and take notes on what works and what doesn't. Gather feedback from your participants and all other stakeholders to help make decisions. Then, use the lessons-learned meeting to reflect on the program's tasks, timeline, and other details.

If multiple people are involved in your typical virtual training implementations, consider using a simple RACI chart to help determine who is responsible, who needs to give authorization, who needs to contribute, and who just needs to be kept informed (Table 8-1). RACI charts are common in project management plans because they help you identify roles and responsibilities; when used and followed well, they can add tremendous value.

Table 8-1. Sample RACI Chart for Virtual Training Logistics

Task	Who Is Responsible?	Who Gives Authorization?	Who Will Contribute?	Who Should Be Informed?
Create event links.				
Send pre-event communication.				
Load content into the virtual classroom.				

If you already have a process in place for your virtual training, step back and look at it. Use the "start, stop, continue" method to evaluate your process. Make a list of logistical things you need to:

- Start doing
- Stop doing (because they are redundant or unnecessary)
- Continue doing

This simple method can revitalize and streamline your current processes to ensure they are as useful as possible.

Ongoing Maintenance

Managing general details is another category of administrative tasks associated with virtual training, but it's not tied to specific training events. These items include:

- Vendor contracts
- Technology updates
- Document controls

It's important that someone in the organization is responsible for each of these items.

Vendor Contracts

Most organizations purchase virtual training platforms on a subscription basis under contract terms that dictate the length of time for service. These contracts should be reviewed periodically to ensure vendors are meeting the service terms. When it's time to renew, someone must negotiate with the vendor and update the contract terms. This task might be delegated to your organization's purchasing group or IT department, but someone in the training group should stay involved in any discussions or negotiations, just like they were during the initial decision-making process.

Technology Updates

When the virtual classroom platform software is updated, someone needs to track what features have changed and communicate that information to everyone in the organization who uses the platform. Whether the changes are minor or major, facilitators and designers need to know so they can adjust and adapt as needed.

For example, a platform software upgrade may require users to download a new add-on the next time they launch the program. Or there may be a revision to how tools or features are used. Even a small change, such as how a participant uses the eraser tool on a whiteboard or how a facilitator can display a poll question, could have ripple effects on how a class activity works. That's why it's important to track software version changes and communicate them immediately.

Document Controls

Finally, as designers update class materials, it's important to control the different versions of all associated program materials. Many organizations establish a set period when people can make changes to materials. However, because most virtual classes use electronic documents, it's easy to make fast updates based on participant feedback. Someone must track these changes and distribute revised materials. Ideally, that person will inform the administrative person so this task can be completed efficiently.

> ### One Organization's Story
> **Setting Up the Session for Success at Yum! Brands**
>
> The virtual training programs run smoothly at Yum! Brands because of the work done by their behind-the-scenes team, says Senior Learning Technologies Analyst Trish Carr. Their goal is to "set up the session for success."
>
> When it's time to schedule a virtual training session, a facilitator completes an online form to request assistance from Trish's team. Using the form data, someone from the team sets up the virtual classroom and all associated data in the LMS. The facilitator then receives the link and participants can register for the class.
>
> Trish schedules someone from her team to join the class for at least the first 10 to 15 minutes to ensure everyone can log in and connect. They also help the facilitator and participants with any technical issues that may arise.
>
> Even though the participants rarely communicate directly with the behind-the-scenes team, the detailed work they do directly influences each participant's learning experience and contributes to the overall success of the class.

In Summary: Key Points From Chapter 8

- It's common to underestimate the number of logistical details required for virtual training success.
- The person in the administrator role performs tasks such as recordkeeping, communication, setup coordination, and platform support. Even if multiple people perform the administrator role, these logistics must all be handled.
- Begin planning for logistics as far in advance as possible.
- An LMS or LXP can automate many logistical tasks, but a personalized touch creates value.
- Carefully craft all communications with participants.
- Keep your administrative processes simple.

Take Action

✓ Review your organization's process for setting up a virtual training class. Is it consistent? Efficient? Does it have room for improvement? If so, what can you do to make it better?

✓ Identify the cadence you have established for virtual program updates. If you don't have one, create one.

Tool 8-1. Virtual Training Logistics Checklist

Before

- ☐ Initial team meeting to plan logistics
    - ○ Date and time: _____
    - ○ Invitation list: _____
- ☐ Marketing and advertising
    - ○ Where? _____
    - ○ How? _____
    - ○ When? _____
- ☐ Registration
- ☐ Materials distribution
- ☐ Virtual classroom setup
- ☐ Participant communication (include date and subject line)
    - ○ #1: _____
    - ○ #2: _____
    - ○ #3: _____
- ☐ Practice or rehearsal
    - ○ Date and time: _____
    - ○ Invitation list: _____

Just Before (Day of Event)

- ☐ Send a reminder message
- ☐ Load content into the virtual classroom (if it is part of the platform and not done in the before stage)
- ☐ Log in 30 to 45 minutes before start time
- ☐ Greet and begin to engage with participants
- ☐ Start class

During

- ☐ Capture participant attendance
- ☐ Assist as needed with technical challenges

Ending

- ☐ Distribute reference materials
- ☐ Conduct knowledge assessments
- ☐ Provide class evaluations
- ☐ Share what's next

After

- ☐ Close and clean up the virtual classroom
- ☐ Complete recordkeeping
- ☐ Hold a lessons-learned meeting to improve for next time

CHAPTER 9

Measure Results

 In this chapter, you will learn how to measure the results of virtual training and why assessment is so important:

- Recognize the importance of measuring results.
- Consider three common evaluation models.
- Create an evaluation strategy for your virtual programs.
- Collect data from remote participants.

When preparing for a journey, most people plan ahead to make the trip a success. They preview a map or use their navigation system to determine the best route to their destination. They estimate the amount of time it will take for the trip and plan accordingly. When traffic, roadblocks, or other obstacles arise, they use the tools at their disposal to expertly navigate around them. Once they've arrived, they can look back and review the highlights of the trip and assess what they did right and what they should change for the next journey.

The same thing can occur with virtual training. You begin with an end goal in mind and then create a road map to success. When roadblocks or obstacles arise, you use all your resources to avoid them. And once you complete the training program, you look at what you've achieved, and ideally, you celebrate before moving on to the next program!

This chapter addresses how to ensure your virtual learning programs successfully reach their destination—helping participants learn new skills and having a positive impact on organizational goals. If you already measure results in other types of learning modalities, you'll find that much of the advice in this chapter is familiar. We will first examine some fundamental principles of learning transfer, measurement, and evaluation; then, we'll focus on how to apply these principles in the context of virtual training.

If you followed the course design and implementation steps outlined in earlier chapters, you will already be well on your way to the business results you're looking for. Whether you have an easy road or an uphill climb ahead, you'll have a solid plan, and I hope your final destination—and the journey to get there—will exceed your expectations.

The Importance of Measuring Results

Virtual training is not inexpensive. It requires significant investments in time, technology, and resources to do it well. Showing a return on learning investments has always been important, but the emphasis on virtual learning during the COVID-19 pandemic put this delivery method in the spotlight more than ever before. Since 2020, the rapid growth of virtual learning, increased resource costs, and the rising expectations of organizational leaders have all contributed to the need for training programs to demonstrate solid business results.

In chapter 1, I encouraged you to define your organization's vision of virtual learning success. I asked you to answer questions such as:

- What's the goal for virtual learning in the organization?
- What are you trying to accomplish?
- What do you want to be different as a result of your virtual training?
- What do you need learners to be more knowledgeable about?
- What skills and capabilities do you need?
- How will the organization change or improve because of this training?
- How do these goals support organizational initiatives?
- What's the best way to achieve these goals?
- How specifically would *virtual* training (as opposed to in-person training) help achieve these outcomes?

Evaluating the success of your virtual training may be as simple as revisiting these questions to determine if you achieved the outcomes you were seeking. Simply ask yourself and your team if the training accomplished its goals. If your response indicates success, you can confidently communicate that to the stakeholders looking for results.

Of course, organizational leaders may ask for more specifics. Exactly how did the virtual training program contribute to the organization's bottom line? How has employee performance improved? Which business metrics were affected and how?

Which productivity problem did the training solve? When you can tie a virtual learning solution directly to its business impact, you are clearly making a valuable contribution. And to show a clear business impact, you must start at the beginning of the virtual training initiative.

Organizational alignment is a key part of any learning design project. You start by identifying a business need or opportunity that includes a knowledge or skills gap, which you can then fill using a learning solution. For our purposes, that solution is a virtual training program, designed to be an engaging learning experience. It's based upon the desired learning objectives, with activities that lead participants toward the targeted outcomes. If you do all these things, then evaluating results will be straight-forward. You can go back to the original need or opportunity and compare it to the current situation to see if there has been a change. This sets the stage for you to report on the learning results.

Engagement as a Step to Learning Transfer

It's easy to assume that as long as you have engaged participants who enjoyed the learning experience, you've been successful. Or to call it a victory if participants leave the program saying, "I didn't have time to check my email because I was involved in the conversation." However, while these responses are satisfying, they are not the same as showing a demonstrable impact on business results.

Much of this book has been focused on creating interactive and engaging virtual programs because engagement is a major step toward achieving the goals of applied learning and business impact. But keep in mind that there is more to successful virtual training than involved learners. You must also enable participants to apply or use what they've learned back on the job.

Learning Transfer vs. Evaluation

In any conversation about measuring the results of virtual learning, it's easy to confuse the concepts of *learning transfer* and *evaluation*. They are related and often go hand-in-hand, but they're not the same thing. A training program equips participants with new knowledge and skills, which we hope they use back on the job. An evaluation plan for that training program will examine data about the knowledge and skills learned, including whether there was effective learning transfer.

Emma Weber, one of my co-authors for *Designing Virtual Learning for Application and Impact: 50 Techniques to Ensure Results*, succinctly puts it this way: "Learning transfer helps CREATE improved outcomes, while evaluation helps MEASURE improved outcomes. Together they are perhaps learning's most dynamic duo" (Weber 2021). In other words, learning transfer leads to learning outcomes, which are measured by collecting evaluation data.

Three Evaluation Models

Evaluation is the process of determining whether a training program is effective. It involves collecting, reviewing, and analyzing the data that can point to a program's success (or lack thereof). It also looks at learning transfer among several other key indicators. By gathering and interpreting data from surveys, interviews, focus groups, observations, business reports, and other sources, you can measure the impact of your training. And by communicating these results, you can show the positive influence the program had on participants and the organization.

I recently helped an organization transition a program from a traditional classroom to a virtual one. To ensure it was still in alignment with organizational needs, we looked at the program's purpose in the context of the desired business outcomes. Its goal was to equip associates with writing skills so they could expertly craft funding proposals and other grant-related documents.

We also had to determine whether the program successfully achieved those goals. One option was to ask for the facilitator's thoughts about the value of the program. Or we could ask participants if they liked the program. We could also ask managers if they noticed a difference in their employee's writing skills after they'd completed the program. Or we could reach out to the participants a few months after completing the program and ask if they were still using the skills they learned. We could also compare the number of successfully submitted funding proposals before and after the training program. And of course, using a combination of all these options was also possible—they could all provide measurements and be used to define some stage of organizational impact.

After choosing the kinds of measurements to do, you'll need to pick the best method and process for collecting the data. An established evaluation model will help guide you in making that choice. Three models to consider are:

- Kirkpatrick's Four Levels of Evaluation
- Phillips's ROI Methodology
- Thalheimer's Learning-Transfer Evaluation Model (LTEM)

Kirkpatrick's Four Levels of Evaluation

Donald L. Kirkpatrick's four levels of evaluation is currently the best known evaluation model in the training industry. Kirkpatrick originally outlined the levels in a series of articles published in 1956, based on Raymond Katzell's four-step model. Kirkpatrick's book, *Evaluating Training Programs*, was published in 1994. Many organizations use the four levels of evaluation to determine if lessons learned in training programs are being applied on the job. The four levels are:

- Level 1—Reaction
- Level 2—Learning
- Level 3—Behavior
- Level 4—Results

Level 1—Reaction

This first level of evaluation considers participant reactions to your virtual training program, answering the simple question, "Did they like it?" Data is typically collected through an end-of-session questionnaire using the platform's polling feature or an online survey tool. A Level 1 survey usually asks for opinions about program content, facilitator effectiveness, and ease of using the platform tools, as well as comments about the class through open-ended questions.

A Level 1 evaluation can be expanded to include the reactions of all stakeholders who were involved with the virtual training initiative, which can be useful for gathering information about how they experienced and reacted to it. For example, you might check in with the IT staff who conducted any presession tech checks to gather feedback on that process. Or you could ask those involved with the administrative logistics for their reactions. In both cases, this data could contribute to your overall calculation of the training's success. You'll find a sample Level 1 evaluation survey for virtual training in Tool 9-1 at the end of this chapter.

The bottom line? Collecting Level 1 data enables you to look for trends in participant reactions, which in turn could help you improve the program. These types of postclass reaction surveys will also provide good anecdotes and participant testimonials about your training curriculum, including quotes that you can use in advertising materials for future programs.

Level 2—Learning

Level 2 evaluations measure whether participants learned anything during the training program. When you include knowledge checks or quizzes in a virtual class and track correct responses, you are measuring participant learning.

Quizzes can take place during class as an interactive activity to check intermediary learning or via end-of-program assessments to measure knowledge, or both. For hands-on skills, learning can be measured by observing participant practices or through skill demonstrations. Level 2 multiple-choice questions are often combined with Level 1 reaction surveys.

The point of a Level 2 evaluation is to find out precisely what participants learned by completing the virtual program. This data demonstrates knowledge acquisition and can be used to help measure the success of the program.

Level 3—Behavior

Level 3 evaluation occurs at least several weeks after the training program ends and measures whether participants are using their new skills and knowledge on the job. This is most closely correlated with learning transfer—you are asking if your training transferred into on-the-job behavior change.

Level 3 evaluations require deliberate effort to collect information through observing participant actions, testing for on-the-job application, or measuring qualitative data that proves the use of the new knowledge and skills.

For example, let's say your virtual training curriculum centers around coaching skills for new managers. Participants learn techniques for setting goals with employees and a process for holding performance conversations. To measure Level 3 application, you could spend time in the field with participants, shadowing them as they meet with employees to set goals. You could use a rating scale based on program-specific skills to determine if the new managers are applying what they learned about goal setting and performance conversations.

Be aware that this method of evaluation can be time consuming and potentially invasive to both manager and employee, and there are other ways to gather similar data. For example, you could survey the manager and employee, asking about the process they used to set goals and whether they used their new skills during the performance discussion. You could also request access to a sampling of anonymous employee records to see what goals managers and employees set during their meetings and evaluate if they accomplished those goals.

Because Level 3 evaluations typically take place 30 to 60 days after a training program ends, one challenge is to show that participation in the training program affected the participants' behavior, rather than some other influencing factor, such as a watercooler conversation or another on-the-job experience. Another challenge is that your virtual participants are typically dispersed, which may make it difficult to collect Level 3 observations. It's easier to gather information from remote learners using electronic surveys, but they are limited in the types of data they can collect. You may need to combine survey data with other sources.

Regardless of how you collect Level 3 evaluation data, it's a powerful measure of the success and business impact of your virtual training program. Level 3 data collection is a golden opportunity to demonstrate that participants are applying the skills they learned and that your training program is influencing performance in specific ways.

Level 4—Results

The point of a Level 4 evaluation is to measure whether your virtual training program has affected organizational results. It can be difficult to measure because there are so many other factors influencing business results. According to a 2019 ATD research report, 38 percent of organizations attempt to measure Level 4 data, compared to 83 percent that use Level 1 evaluations. And when asked to rate their proficiency at measuring the impact of their learning programs, 44 percent of respondents to a 2023 ATD research report said they considered themselves to be an expert or advanced.

Even though measuring business results can be challenging, if you can determine that your virtual training curriculum had a positive impact on the organization, by all means, take the time to complete a Level 4 evaluation. What better way to evaluate virtual training success than to show that it positively affected business results?

Phillips's ROI Methodology

In 1983, Jack Phillips wrote the first book on training evaluation, *The Handbook of Training Evaluation and Measurement Methods*, which also introduced ROI. The ROI Methodology uses different terms for some of the four levels of evaluation. At Level 3, *application* is used instead of *behavior change*, recognizing that not all actions from training are behavior changes (for example, using software is not behavior change). At Level 4, *impact* is used instead of *results*, recognizing that all levels are results. The ROI Methodology also adds a fifth level, return on investment (ROI), which provides a systematic process with credible standards for its use.

Simply stated, the ROI calculation for a virtual training program evaluates the difference between program costs and net benefits, expressed as a percentage. The ROI

Methodology goes beyond this simple measurement, however, by isolating the effects of the training program from other influences. It also converts Level 4 impact data into monetary values and captures all associated program costs. While designing learning solutions with ROI impact in mind goes beyond the scope of this book, *Designing Virtual Learning for Application and Impact* (2023)—which I wrote with Jack Phillips, Patti Phillips, and Emma Weber—provides a wealth of details and techniques.

Showing that monetary benefits exceed the cost of your learning program is often essential if the program's worth is under scrutiny. ROI is the ultimate accountability measure for learning investments. The basic calculation is:

$$\frac{\text{Benefits} - \text{Costs}}{\text{Costs}} \times 100 = \text{ROI\%}$$

According to *Effective Evaluation* (ATD 2019), only 16 percent of organizations undertook ROI measurements, mostly driven by requests from senior executives. However, this should not deter your organization from considering such a study as a way to evaluate program success. The key is to be proactive and deliver ROI for major programs, not waiting for the request.

Thalheimer's Learning-Transfer Evaluation Model

After years of research, application, and consultation with other experts, Will Thalheimer conceptualized a Learning-Transfer Evaluation Model (LTEM; pronounced "el-tem"). As its name suggests, LTEM focuses on measuring the amount of learning transferred to on-the-job behaviors. These measures, called tiers, progress from low levels of transfer (participation in learning activities) to higher levels (knowledge retention to competence). The model looks comprehensively at learning transfer and its effects (Thalheimer 2018). You can see the full model, with an explanation of its tiers, in Figure 9-1.

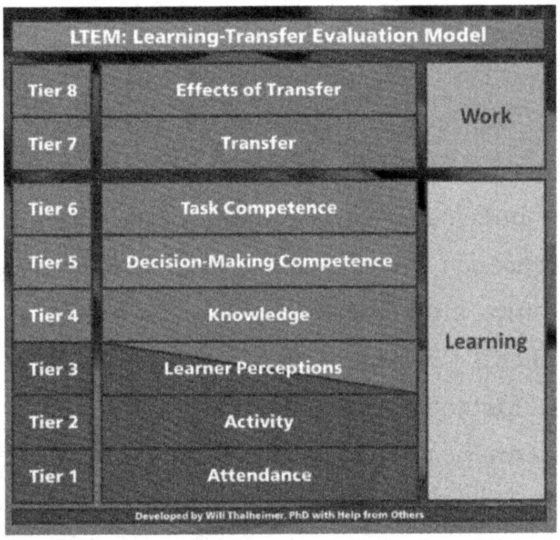

LTEM is valuable because it combines evaluation levels with the

Figure 9-1. The LTEM Model

essentials of learning transfer and the importance of organizational impact. It's a conceptual model to help you brainstorm a full range of opportunities in learning evaluation. Therefore, LTEM holds promise for organizations looking to realize specific results from their virtual training programs.

Creating an Evaluation Strategy

Regardless of which model your organization uses, creating a strategy for measuring at least some results for your virtual training programs is a worthwhile endeavor. Your evaluation strategy will dictate what data to capture, when to collect it, how to gather it, and whom to share it with. It will also guide you through the journey from an initial evaluation plan to reporting on the results.

Ideally, the evaluation process begins when the organization discovers and analyzes a business problem or opportunity and determines training is one of the recommended solutions. If the process starts this way, you can measure results by going back to see if the business problem was solved or the opportunity was realized. For example, let's say your manufacturing logs include a considerable number of data entry errors, and your team discovers that these errors stem from employees not knowing how to use the complex system properly. You design and implement a data entry training program to better equip the employees to handle the work and then point to a reduced number of data entry errors as the measure of your learning program's success.

There are many formats that evaluation plans can follow, from a simple one-page list of tasks to a full project plan with multiple lanes of stakeholder actions. At the end of this chapter, Tool 9-2 provides a sample evaluation strategy planning document that you can use.

How Much Evaluation?

When creating an evaluation strategy, organizations often struggle to determine what data to collect and whether it's worth investing resources in the evaluation. For guidance, I asked Ken Phillips, a Chicago-based expert in training evaluation, to share his wisdom. Here are his tips:

All virtual training programs should seek participant reaction data (Kirkpatrick's Level 1). Specifically, at a minimum, data should be collected on three topics:

- **The platform.** How well did it work? How easy was it to sign in and navigate? How clear was the audio? How did the tools work?

- **The facilitator.** How knowledgeable was the facilitator about the topic? How well did they keep everyone engaged? How well did they respond to participant questions?
- **The program.** How relevant was the program? How much did participants know about the topic before attending the program? How much do they know after attending?

To determine the number of additional levels of evaluation to include beyond Level 1, you should consider four factors:

- **How strategically important is the program?** The more important it is, the more reason to evaluate it at higher levels.
- **How costly is the program?** The higher the investment, the more important it will be to show ROI, or at least impact on participant performance.
- **How many participants will attend the program?** The more participants influenced by the program, the more important it could be to show results from their invested time.
- **What do business executives or other stakeholders expect or want?** Have they asked for evaluation results? If so, deliver them.

For programs in which one or more of these factors is present, additional data collection and evaluation measures should be considered. Your evaluation strategy will reflect all this information.

The Role of Stakeholders in Evaluation Success

It takes commitment from many people to measure the success of virtual learning. In chapter 1, we outlined the various stakeholders involved in most virtual training programs. Many of these roles also take part in the evaluation process. Table 9-1 clarifies who typically does what in the evaluation strategy. Review it for context before we expand on more specific details of a few of these roles.

Table 9-1. Role of Stakeholders in Evaluation

Role or Function	Role in Evaluation
Executives or leaders	They are looking for organizational impact and business results. They have the best line-of-sight into the issues and expect training programs to add value to the organization.
Designers	They are responsible for designing the learning experience in alignment with the objectives and including both practice and application activities.
Content owners or SMEs	With deep knowledge of the training topics, they can help ensure realistic practice examples and relevant content.

Table 9-1. (cont.)

Role or Function	Role in Evaluation
Facilitators	They explain objectives and expectations, encourage engagement, and enable participant learning. They also observe and provide performance feedback during practices.
Participants	They must engage in the virtual program and then apply the new knowledge and skills on the job. To do this, they need clearly defined objectives and expected outcomes.
Managers	They ensure that participants are using what they have learned and there is a corresponding impact. They must be involved in the process of creating an expectation before the program and following up afterward to make sure the expectation is met. Manager activities can help ensure that transfer of learning takes place and the material is used on the job.

The Designer's Role in Learning Transfer and Behavior Change

Design decisions may not seem like they have much to do with an evaluation strategy, but if a program isn't designed with results in mind, it will be difficult, if not impossible, to measure.

Chapters 3 and 4 explained how to design and develop engaging virtual training. The processes assumed that a needs analysis had been completed, learning objectives were effectively written, and performance results were on everyone's mind. They also presumed that the learning solutions would be designed to meet organizational needs. Another responsibility for designers is to develop the structure and sequence of a program so that it leads to learning transfer. For example, provide enough time in the program agenda for participants to practice their new skills and create action plans for applying them.

Designers should remember that practicing new skills isn't always the same as applying them, especially in a virtual classroom. Practicing is part of the learning journey to reach a new skill level, but it is equally important to focus on application. For some topics, just creating an action plan will accomplish a degree of learning transfer. For other topics, it will be important to incorporate methods to help participants follow up on their action plans. For example, a learning activity that has managers write a script for a difficult conversation with an employee and then practice it with a partner in a breakout room will set them up for this real conversation when they return to work. Their action plan will be to schedule this conversation and follow through on it.

Designers can also build in activities allowing participants to share what they plan to do, which creates more accountability. Follow-on action assignments will help participants use what they have learned. This is easy to do in a series of virtual classes or a formal blended learning journey because participants can complete the activity between sessions and then report on their success. These assignments are also important to include in stand-alone virtual classes, because they make it easier for participants to apply what they've learned. For example, in my How to Facilitate Hybrid Meetings program, participants leave with a "Hybrid Meeting Planner" worksheet to help them apply the lessons they learned. In another program for customer service agents, I give participants an assignment to meet with their direct supervisors within the week to discuss their action plans. These types of activities extend the learning beyond the formal virtual training program, helping to transfer the new skills into on-the-job behaviors.

> *"Designers can create learner-centered microlearning assets to help reinforce training content. These assets can help learners apply new knowledge and skills after a class is over. Learner-centered means you should consider how motivated your learner will be to consume your reinforcement materials, especially in the context of their other priorities. Then, use that information to create a WIIFM (What's in it for me?) and ensure the learner sees the value of the reinforcement content."*
>
> —Carla Torgerson, author of *Designing Microlearning*

Communicating Outcomes to Everyone

Everyone involved in a virtual learning experience—from the organization's leaders to the facilitators to the participants—should be aware of the expected learning outcomes and how achieving them will have a positive impact on the organization. For example, if a leadership program for high-potential employees is expected to fill the pipeline and lead to organizational growth and expansion, then all stakeholders should understand those implications. This knowledge helps increase support from all sides.

Designers should make sure they're using language that accurately describes those outcomes in the program materials. Facilitators should clearly (and creatively!) share all the program's benefits with participants, making sure to reinforce them throughout the virtual learning experience. These small but important details also contribute to the overall evaluation results.

If you want participants to understand why they are attending a virtual learning program, you'll need to communicate the objectives multiple times in varied ways. As

I've mentioned already, most virtual learning events occur in the middle of the work-day; participants may not initially see why they should stop what they're doing and shift focus to the facilitator and virtual classroom peers. By knowing the reason why, the business or organization impact, your learners will be more likely to engage and achieve the larger objectives.

Collecting Evaluation Data in Virtual Training

So far, almost everything we have covered about measurement, evaluation, and learning transfer would be true for any training program. What, then, makes evaluation different in a virtual training program? Admittedly, not much. Evaluation is evaluation regardless of the type of program, just like learning is learning regardless of the modality.

But virtual classroom platforms often provide built-in tools that can easily capture evaluation data. These programs have a dispersed audience by design; therefore, using electronic methods to collect evaluation data is prevalent and preferred.

In most evaluation strategies, data collection begins in the needs analysis phase. Then, upon program implementation, Level 1 and 2 data is collected with common collaboration tools. Follow-up data (Levels 3 and 4) is collected sometime after the virtual learning program has ended, when application of the newly acquired knowledge and skills becomes routine and enough time has passed to observe the impact on key measures.

So, if you have identified the measures that need to improve through initial analysis, you will measure the change in performance in those same measures during the evaluation. Your data collection methods during the evaluation could be the same as those used during the needs analysis.

Two of the most common methods for collecting data during a virtual program are questionnaires and observations.

Questionnaires

Ranging from short reaction queries to detailed surveys, questionnaires are used to gather information relevant to the virtual learning program, including participant reactions and knowledge gained. A questionnaire could include any of the following types of items:

- A two-way question with alternate responses, such as yes/no or agree/disagree
- A multiple-choice question that asks participants to select the most applicable or correct response

- A checklist or multianswer question that asks participants to check all items in a list of answers that apply to the question
- A ranking scale that requires participants to rank a list of items
- An open-ended question with an unlimited number of answers (this typically includes ample blank space for the participant to write their response)

Nearly all virtual classroom platforms include polling tools that can easily be used during or immediately following a training event to test for knowledge. Some platforms also have quiz tools, which add graded responses and individual response tracking. Instructional designers can build these quiz questions into the program design. While the obvious tool of choice for most questionnaires is polling, other participant input methods could be used, including capturing annotated text on a whiteboard (Figure 9-2), using reactions or other status indicators, or inviting responses in the chat. If the platform doesn't have built-in quizzing, you may be able to add an integrated third-party polling or quizzing tool.

Use the tool with the best features for your desired question type, given what's available on your platform. Sometimes you'll want to use a combination of tools, such as asking participants to answer several poll questions while also expanding upon their responses in the chat.

Figure 9-2. End of Program Survey via Annotated Whiteboard

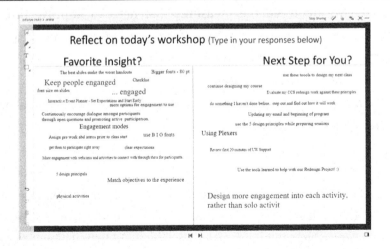

Observations

If your program develops skills that require participants to practice and demonstrate mastery, then design activities to help them practice and show off what they have learned. Virtual facilitators can observe participants in action and then provide expert feedback. In smaller-sized virtual classes, this task could be completed fishbowl-style or you may want to try other options such as using breakout rooms for smaller groups to demonstrate skills.

Breakout rooms allow multiple participants to practice at once, and some platforms allow the facilitator to peek inside each room (Figure 9-3). Alternatively, you can record breakout activities for later viewing and feedback. Participants could complete an exercise to demonstrate their new skills and report back to the large group. For example, in my virtual facilitation skills certification program, participants break into smaller groups to demonstrate their new delivery skills. The first group of five participants arrives in the virtual classroom at 9 a.m., the next group of five arrives at 11 a.m., and so on. This way I'm able to observe each participant and provide detailed feedback without the entire cohort spending much extra time waiting.

Figure 9-3. Example Breakout Pods in Adobe Connect

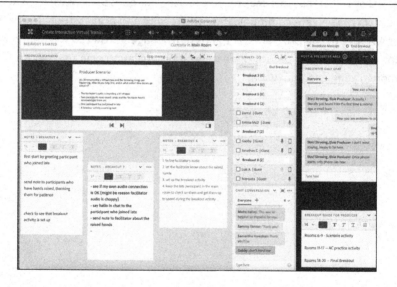

Don't Forget to Share Your Results

Your virtual training programs may have massive success, with engaged participants who love the learning activities. Participants may be able to apply their new knowledge and skills easily, and your training department may be able to quickly capture this data to prove it. But if no one knows about your success, the results may all be for naught.

Take the time to measure the results of virtual training and communicate them to stakeholders. Show the value of the virtual training program by sharing hard data and anecdotal stories.

The bottom line: Don't keep your evaluation results to yourself.

In Summary: Key Points From Chapter 9

- Virtual training investments are increasingly under scrutiny to ensure they are adding value to the organization.
- Learning transfer and evaluation are related but not the same thing.
- Several evaluation models provide good options for measuring the results of virtual learning.
- Creating an evaluation strategy begins early in the virtual training design process.
- Many stakeholders play a role in evaluation.

Take Action

✓ Review your organization's standard end-of-program surveys to see if they are sufficient for use in virtual training. If not, consider using the sample provided in Tool 9-2 at the end of this chapter to update your questions or methods.

✓ Consider how you are communicating the results and organizational impact of your virtual training programs. Is the right message getting to the right people? If not, start collecting data and create a communication plan to show how you're demonstrating program value.

Tool 9-1. Evaluation Strategy Planning Worksheet

This worksheet will help you plan a training program evaluation strategy. You may notice some similarities with the goal-setting worksheet found at the end of chapter 1 because there is an overlap between goal planning and evaluation mapping. Both exercises seek the best possible results.

Name of the Virtual Training Program:

1. What's the primary goal of this program?

2. What specifically do you hope to accomplish?

3. What do the stakeholders want to accomplish?

4. What do participants need to achieve as a result of this training program?
    - ☐ Become more knowledgeable about the topic
    - ☐ Behave differently
    - ☐ Take action on something
    - ☐ Other:

5. How will the organization or business unit change or improve as a result?

6. What are the program's measurable learning objectives?

7. Rate the following factors on a scale of 1 to 5. (The higher the total, the more important it will be to have a solid evaluation strategy.)

	1 (Low)	2	3	4	5 (High)
How strategically important is the program?	☐	☐	☐	☐	☐
How costly is the program?	☐	☐	☐	☐	☐
How many participants will ultimately attend the program?	☐	☐	☐	☐	☐
Total					

8. What type of evaluation does the organization's executive stakeholder expect or want?

9. Given all the above, what level of evaluation will you strive for?
   - ☐ Level 1
   - ☐ Level 2
   - ☐ Level 3
   - ☐ Level 4
   - ☐ Level 5 (ROI)

10. What data collection measures could you capture for each evaluation level?

Level	Description	Data to Collect
1	Reaction	
2	Learning	
3	Application	
4	Impact	
5	Return on investment (ROI)	

11. What else should you note about the program's evaluation strategy?

Tool 9-2. Sample 1: Level 1 Survey for a Virtual Class

When I'm delivering virtual train-the-trainer and train-the-designer programs, I typically share this simple Level 1 survey afterward. It's short and easy for participants to complete, and it gives me just enough feedback to make improvements.

1. Would you recommend this program to others who are interested in virtual facilitation (or virtual training design)?
   ☐ Yes
   ☐ No

2. What are the reasons for your response?

3. Rate your own level of engagement during this program:
   ☐ I was fully engaged for most of the time or the whole time!
   ☐ I experienced tech difficulties that kept me from staying engaged.
   ☐ I experienced other (nontech) challenges that kept me from staying engaged.
   ☐ I chose to remain a passive participant.
   ☐ Other:

4. What other comments or thoughts do you have about the program?

Tool 9-3. Sample 2: Level 1 Survey for a Virtual Class

Here's a more detailed version of a participant reaction survey.

1. Please provide feedback on your virtual training experience by rating your agreement with each statement below.

	Strongly Disagree	Disagree	Neither Agree nor Disagree	Agree	Strongly Agree
The program objectives were clear.					
The program met its stated objectives.					
The activities and exercises helped me learn the program material.					
The program materials (slides, handouts, and other visuals) were useful during the program.					
It was easy to use the virtual classroom tools (chat, polls, status indicators).					
The facilitator was knowledgeable about the subject matter.					
The facilitator promoted participant discussion and engagement.					
I chose to actively participate in the program (typing in chat, responding to polls, engaging in the activities).					
The program activities were accessible to me.					
This program provided information that I need to know and will use in my current role.					
I'd recommend this program to others.					

2. What was the most valuable part of the program?

3. What improvements would you suggest?

4. What other comments do you have about the program?

CHAPTER 10

Prepare for the Future

 In this chapter, you will focus on the importance of human connection while preparing for technology updates related to virtual training:

- Consider the unique issues of culturally diverse virtual training programs.
- Recognize the possibilities of immersive learning in virtual training solutions.
- Realize the challenges and opportunities of mobile devices, including wearables, in virtual training.
- Prepare for the influence of generative AI on virtual training.

In its infancy, virtual training was gradually adopted by forward-thinking organizations with dispersed workforces that invested in web conferencing technologies. It slowly increased in popularity until use surged and nearly all formal training programs moved to virtual classrooms during the COVID-19 pandemic. As virtual training reaches a saturation point, becoming the go-to learning solution for many organizations, it's critical that we not settle into complacency.

As I addressed in the introduction to this book, successful virtual training combines the best of technology with the benefits of community. It uses collaborative digital workspaces for conversation and learning. It brings together people from diverse backgrounds and varied locations. And it can break down organizational silos and geographic boundaries, as participants from around the globe meet together in an online classroom.

Yet the reliance on technology for virtual training success means that it's easy to get caught up and bogged down in the weeds of hardware challenges and software decisions. And if that's what captures your focus, you'll miss the main point of human connection. Virtual training—at its finest—is a way to bring people together in an interactive online learning experience, with a facilitator who can lead the way to performance results.

As technology continues to evolve and mature, we have to change too; however, we can't forget this foundation of synchronous social connections. The ultimate success of your virtual training programs depends on your ability to successfully combine technology and community. To help you navigate this balance, this chapter highlights several considerations to keep in mind.

Virtual Training for Diverse, Global Audiences

One of the biggest benefits of virtual training is its ability to reach across borders and draw geographically dispersed and culturally diverse people together. This means your audience may speak several different languages, have different expectations about training, or need to overcome other barriers. To manage these potential challenges, here are four essential tips for successfully designing and delivering virtual training to a diverse audience:

- Recognize different perceptions about virtual training.
- Allow extra time for communication.
- Use culturally neutral examples, graphics, and names.
- Use clear language.

Recognize Different Perceptions About and Responses to Virtual Training

Engagement isn't just a nice-to-have part of the virtual training experience, it's a key part of learning and application. However, expectations about participation and engagement may differ dramatically among your participants. Different people have different views about learning, which naturally leads to different cultural perceptions of the learning experience.

For example, many Americans consider the facilitator to be a peer or colleague, which influences how they interact. They might be more willing to engage in dialogue, interrupt to make a statement, and ask questions more freely. In contrast, participants from other cultures may view the facilitator as an expert and, out of respect, would not interrupt even if they wanted to share an important comment. They may hesitate to ask questions or wait for an invitation to participate during a virtual session.

This specific generalization comparing Americans and other cultures is not meant to stereotype; there are exceptions to generalizations in all cultures. The point here is to highlight that diversity of thought and experience are to be expected in the online classroom.

Virtual facilitators need to take extra care upfront to build rapport and establish clear participation guidelines. They should strive to make everyone feel comfortable engaging with one another despite any potential cultural barriers. One easy technique is to give participants a choice for how they'll respond during a virtual class. For example, the facilitator might ask a question and then specifically say, "You can either answer in the chat window or by raising your hand to speak verbally." This simple invitation allows participants to choose their response method based on their comfort level with speaking or typing. It also lets participants know what's expected of them.

Darlene Christopher (2012), senior global knowledge officer at the World Bank Group, recommends asking global participants to "reflect on a concept" before introducing it. This reflection time can be accomplished through a poll, a graphic, or an interesting question, and gives participants time to think about the content and respond thoughtfully, which keeps them engaged in the class.

Virtual facilitators should also be open-minded about how individuals from another culture might approach a situation. It may not be the way you would handle it, but it may be right on target for their unique situation. I recently delivered a virtual class on performance management to a mostly Korean audience. When we discussed how to assign performance ratings, several participants were more concerned about their team's collective performance than individual employee accomplishments. This approach fit their organization and their culture, and I took note of it.

When Global Training Director Wendy Gates Corbett needed to facilitate a virtual session for a global audience, she factored potential cultural differences into her scheduling decisions. She held three different sessions to accommodate multiple time zones—North America, followed by Europe and the Middle East, and finishing with an Asia-Pacific session. The Asia-Pacific audience was often the quietest group, but because that session came last, she was able to include common questions and examples from the earlier sessions as needed.

Varied backgrounds and expectations will always be a factor when bringing together a diverse audience. These can be as subtle as time zone differences or as significant as how one chooses to interact in a breakout group setting. Virtual facilitators should keep their eyes and ears open during a session to pick up on nuanced cultural differences and ensure that they don't get in the way of learning.

Allow Extra Time for Communication

A surprisingly common sentiment that I hear when working with designers and facilitators alike, is that there isn't enough time in a virtual class for interaction and engagement. They say that there's too much content to cover, or participants' busy schedules mean they don't have time to interact with others. However, because the point of coming together in an online classroom is to allow for conversation and communication, it's necessary to carve out time for this essential component of learning.

This perceived time crunch can be exacerbated when language barriers exist. For example, if a session is delivered in English to non-native English speakers, participants may need a few extra seconds to translate or mentally process an unfamiliar word or compose their chat response to a question. They might also need more time to read through a poll question and all the choices before submitting their answer. These extra seconds add up to longer activity times and longer class times. As David Smith, a global virtual training expert, notes, "With a US audience, you might be able to give two minutes for a reading activity, but a multicultural audience probably needs closer to three minutes."

Many virtual platforms now include built-in translation capabilities, including closed-captioning in different languages, live interpreter tools, and even AI-based real-time language conversion. These tools help speed up the amount of time participants need to translate and process the content, but you may still need to account for a lag when scheduling the program (Figure 10-1).

The key to having enough space for dialogue without going too slow or wasting time on frivolous activities is to find the right balance. To keep interest and engagement levels high, use techniques like keeping a running conversation in a private chat, with help from a producer, for participants who finish an activity sooner than others. The facilitator might say something like, "When you're finished typing on the whiteboard, send me a private chat with the themes you are noticing." This allows for participant interaction without adding stress to those who are still working on the exercise; because the chat is private, they won't feel like they are missing out or need to keep up with the additional conversation. You might also have extra examples, scenarios, or reflection pages in the participant handout, which participants could review if they're ready to move forward before others.

Figure 10-1. Built-In Language Translation Example

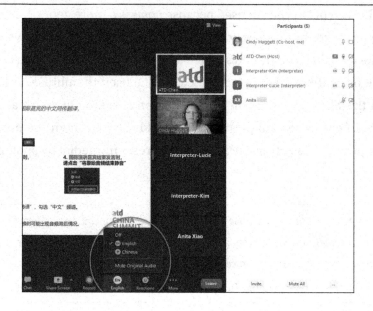

"When designing training for a global audience, I may still
plan for a one-hour session but keep the content time shorter to
allow for extra conversation and comprehension time."

—Wendy Gates Corbett, author, researcher, and
former Global Training Director

Use Culturally Neutral Examples, Graphics, and Names

To maintain an inclusive atmosphere in virtual training classes, pay extra attention to any deliberate or inadvertent cultural references. For example, an American baseball analogy may work for a US audience, but global participants might not fully understand it. Designing an activity based on a popular Australian game show could be fun—unless your audience isn't familiar with the program. And it's best to avoid pop culture references that a diverse global audience won't recognize. Television shows, games, cartoons, and the like are all potential opportunities for misunderstanding.

Even something as small as word choice can make a difference in comprehension and acceptance. I like to include an activity in my virtual train-the-trainer classes that illustrates how we give and receive instructions. I ask participants imagine they are at the office and need to write down directions telling someone how to get to their home. We then debrief their instructions: Did they draw a visual map, list step-by-step turns, or something else entirely? Whenever I do this exercise, I deliberately use the phrase "to your home" instead of "to your house," because *home* is a more generic, relatable term. The word home makes more sense to more participants, so it's a better word choice.

Also make sure that any graphics—such as photos and images—aren't unintentionally offensive or controversial. For instance, I once used the phrase "rule of thumb" along with a thumbs-up graphic on my slide when speaking to a virtual global audience. Unfortunately, as several participants quickly shared, both the phrase and the graphic were perceived as offensive in their cultures. I immediately apologized before moving on.

"I have found truth in the phrase 'a picture is worth a thousand words'—especially when it comes to global audiences, and, when it comes to subject matter experts trying to describe a new procedure or a change in process to that audience."

—Jeff Robinson, Global Talent Management, Covance Laboratories

---

In addition, when writing role-play scenarios or case studies, select character names that represent multiple cultures. Being intentional about your name choices will help more participants easily see themselves in the story. For example, if it's an interpersonal skills course that includes a manager-employee dialogue practice, select names such as Pritha or Akido, rather than traditional American names like Sally and Mike. I also like using names that are popular in more than one language, such as Adam or Maria. One of my favorite ways to find names for training scenarios is to look at lists of popular baby names on the internet. I search for "most common baby names in [*insert country name here*]."

Use Clear Language

When delivering virtual training, be aware of how you speak and the words you use. For example, your accent may make it harder for participants to understand what you're saying, so slowing down and focusing on enunciation could mean the difference between active participants and those who tune out. Many years ago, I received pointed feedback on my mispronunciation of the word "query" while teaching a course on database fundamentals. It was a key term in the class, so my frequent blundering was distracting to those who focused on my vocal errors. To fix it for future classes, I practiced saying the word correctly over and over again. It took intentional effort for me to say it clearly.

Also, virtual facilitators should learn the correct pronunciation of each participant's name and use it during class. It's OK to ask for help if you need it! When I'm facilitating and not sure how to pronounce someone's name, I'll say something like, "Andrea, am I saying your name correctly?" Once they clarify the correct pronunciation, I phonetically spell out their name on a blank sheet of paper that I keep on my desk to help myself remember how to say it.

"When facilitating a virtual class with an international audience, I speak slower and pause more. I am more strategic about checking in with participants and invite them to provide feedback on my pace. For example, I'll ask them to 'click the green check if you would like for me to slow down.'"

—Justin Patton, former Master Facilitator, Yum! Brands

Activity instructions are another place where clear language is paramount. Some people may hesitate to participate in small group discussions or do things they perceive to be difficult, like providing feedback to a practice partner when they are not completely sure of the expectations. Virtual program activities are chosen intentionally to ensure that learning objectives are met; participation isn't optional. When people don't engage or take part, they miss out on their own learning experience and may also affect someone else's ability to learn. Facilitators can mitigate these challenges by recognizing the potential issues and skillfully planning for them. For example, in a breakout activity, facilitators should:

- Create small breakout groups (just two to four people each) so everyone can have a voice in the discussion.
- Clearly explain the reason and benefits of the breakout activity so learners know its purpose and the importance of their role.
- Ensure each participant knows what to do and why they are doing it. Setting these expectations can elevate the level of participation.
- Walk through any feedback processes or guidelines for participant roles and provide written details for them to follow (like a rating sheet).

Clear language—without jargon, slang, acronyms, or assumptions—will contribute to a learning environment where everyone is more comfortable and willing to participate in the virtual learning program.

One Organization's Story
Training Around the World at IHS

IHS, a global information company, offers virtual training to its employees around the world. According to Senior Training Manager Lucy Brown, virtual training allows her team to reach managers in remote locations who might not be able to receive training otherwise. They also use virtual training to save on travel costs. The topics range from coaching to performance management to running effective meetings, and sessions are typically an hour long. The classes have been so well received that some employees who could attend in-person training classes choose to attend the virtual ones instead.

Lucy attributes the success of the global training initiative to seven factors:

- They offer sessions in the early morning and late at night (US time) to accommodate all global time zones.
- They make it easy for participants to connect by thoroughly testing all technology ahead of time and encouraging participants to join sessions 20 minutes early. Their goal is 100 percent connectivity for all participants.
- They have a producer join nearly every virtual training session to help in case of technical challenges.
- They ensure the content design is extremely interactive for participants, using the full range of tools available on their virtual classroom platform. They want to have such an effective class that participants stay engaged the entire time.
- They have three virtual trainers—each one specializes in a few topics to ensure they're well versed in both the content and the virtual training platform.
- The virtual trainers repeatedly practice their delivery skills to be fully comfortable in the online classroom. They strive to be conversational with participants so the audience can easily learn the content.
- Trainers connect with as many participants as possible prior to the session to find out their questions and challenges around the training topics. This way, the trainer can adjust the class as needed so it's as relevant as possible.

Technology Advances and Virtual Training

Virtual training's solid grasp on organizational learning means that it's here to stay. It's an established and widely recognized learning methodology that belongs in most organizations. However, just as we have watched it evolve over the past two decades, we will continue to see the technologies used for virtual training transform over the next 10 years. In closing, let's examine three specific technology trends that will be especially important to the virtual training space: immersion and spatial computing, mobile devices and wearables, and generative AI.

Immersion and Spatial Computing

Immersive learning, including AR and VR, puts participants into a realistic environment for knowledge and skill building. It's not a new training method; simulations have been around since at least the 1700s, when the French Academy of Surgeons approved a childbirth simulator created by Madame du Coudray, a midwife for King Louis XV. She traveled the countryside using experiential techniques to teach midwives about childbirth, and subsequently, infant mortality rates dropped (Walton 2017).

Simulations used as teaching tools can help participants learn better because they replicate on-the-job situations. The more realistic the practice, the better the learning outcomes. Think about the last time you participated in a role-play exercise during a training class. Was it authentic? Was your partner believable in character? Was the environment the same as you would encounter in the workplace? Simulated role plays can be valuable, but certain elements can throw them off (such as shy or reluctant participants, an unrealistic setting, or inadequate props and learning tools).

This brings us to today's immersive learning experiences. Current technology is amazing, often allowing computer-based images, graphics, settings, and scenarios to feel completely real. Instead of viewing a two-dimensional virtual learning program on a flat screen, participants can experience a three-dimensional environment. These enhancements create more realistic, and frankly more interesting, learning experiences.

Augmented reality adds digital components to the real world, such as captions appearing on a screen or something more detailed like an object springing to life in front of you. You might think of AR as a digital prop or a virtual visual aid. For example, a facilitator who needs to describe the intricacies of how something works can say, "Let's look inside to see the details" and then have participants launch an AR experience to follow along with the explanation.

Some tools we've already discussed in this book, like hand gesture recognition, video filters, and avatars, are examples of AR enhancements on the virtual training platform. These AR features can help draw participants more deeply into the learning experience, which will naturally lead to better outcomes. To see an example of augmented reality in action, focus your mobile device camera on the QR code in Figure 10-2 (and respond yes to any prompts that may appear).

Figure 10-2. A Sample AR Experience

VR transports participants into another world—an authentic, but digitally replicated environment. It's more than just an augmented, digital overlay; it's a fully immersive experience. These types of simulations are the difference between saying, "Imagine you are negotiating with a potential client on pricing" and "Let's practice negotiating with a potential client on pricing." Immersive experiences can be one activity in a virtual training program or the entire virtual learning experience.

For instance, a program can begin in a traditional virtual classroom; then, when it's time for the immersive simulation, participants can don their VR headsets and meet in the digital environment. Such simulations may only last five or 10 minutes before everyone returns to the original virtual classroom. In other cases, the group may meet exclusively in a spatial computing environment (Figure 10-3). Either way, these realistic scenarios help participants learn faster and with more confidence (Likens and Eckert 2021).

Figure 10-3. Screenshot of an Immersive Virtual Learning Scenario

Common—and valid—questions I hear often about immersive learning focus on whether the role of the facilitator is still important. For example, people will ask, "What is the facilitator's role in immersive learning?" "If designers can create realistic scenarios with artificially intelligent, preprogrammed interactions, why is a facilitator needed?" and "Shouldn't immersive scenarios be asynchronous, self-directed learning?"

As I mentioned earlier in the book, if you've ever argued with Siri or Alexa, you can imagine my answer to these questions. For the sake of clarity, however, there are several distinct circumstances in which facilitators enhance the value of an immersive, VR simulation and are necessary for its success: when the simulation is a highly emotional experience, when the scenario requires human intervention, and when participants would benefit from a debriefing discussion. Skilled facilitators make all these things happen and add value to the exercise.

This brings us to the bottom line: Virtual training will become more immersive over time, and wise organizations, designers, and facilitators will keep tabs on this trend. They will learn how to use these technologies, invest in the necessary hardware and software, and find ways to incorporate them into their organizational learning solutions.

Mobile Devices and Wearables

Several times in this book, I have cautioned against using mobile devices for facilitating (and even attending) virtual training programs. This recommendation is based on the limited functionality of current virtual classroom platform apps. Without rehashing the challenges of using mobile apps and mobile devices, let's now consider their potential.

First and foremost, mobile devices expand the reach of virtual training to those who might not otherwise be able to attend. For some participants, the choice is between using their smartphone or not joining at all. In some working environments—such as a hospital where medical professionals use digital tablets on a daily basis—tablets and smartphones may be the only option for a virtual training program.

Certainly, the functionality of mobile apps for virtual classroom platforms will continue to improve over time. As devices get more sophisticated and new apps are developed for live online training, we will see increased capability for virtual training. It will be important for you to stay abreast of changes in mobile device capability to be prepared for this change.

Remember that the category of mobile devices includes more than smartphones. It's now possible to connect to virtual classrooms from many different types of devices, including wearables like smartwatches and VR headsets. Participants can even connect to virtual classrooms from a car console's entertainment screen! While it's not necessarily prudent to use them now, as technology evolves, these devices will provide new learning methods and opportunities. For example, there may come a day when participants can use their smartwatch to connect with their peers in very short (five-or-10-minute) live virtual classes or a brief but meaningful collaboration activity to learn a just-in-time lesson.

Of course, one of the biggest limitations of mobile devices is the small display screen. It can be difficult to see all the components of a virtual classroom in a tiny square or rectangle. So, the biggest advances in this space will be the ability to combine small devices with others that have large viewing areas. As they evolve and become more commonplace, for example, wearables like smart glasses and VR and spatial computing headsets will help overcome the challenges of small mobile device screens.

The move toward mobile devices and wearables with increased functionality for learning opportunities will continue gaining momentum over time, and it's worth following this trend. Pay attention to industry and business articles on these topics, register for vendor webinars that showcase new technologies, and attend industry conferences (like the annual ATD TechKnowledge conference) to hear from organizations that are putting these things into practice.

Generative AI

Despite its futuristic-sounding name, artificial intelligence isn't new. It's been in use for decades, with scientists in the 1950s exploring and developing computer programs that could function on their own. These models solved problems and created efficiencies. Generative AI is a newer iteration of artificial intelligence, and its unique ability to *create new content* puts it in a class by itself. Generative AI uses neural networks to recognize patterns and learn from them, making decisions or predictions based on that information. A few of generative AI's benefits include rapid development and time-saving efficiencies, and its widespread adoption in the workplace is without question a trend to watch.

At the time of this writing (early 2024), generative AI is being used by learning professionals to quickly produce training program content, write scenario scripts, design eye-catching graphics, and more. Its full potential is yet to be realized. We know that generative AI is poised to make processes easier—but *which processes* and *how* still remains to be seen.

As we discussed in chapter 1, facilitated virtual training isn't the right solution for every learning experience, and it's possible to learn a lot of content without any facilitator input. Generative AI exploits this fact with its ability to analyze skills gaps and create personalized learning solutions. One fantastic application of generative AI is the design and implementation of self-directed learning experiences. In other words, your organization can use it to help people learn on their own without a formal training program. The efficiencies and savings of this choice can be profound.

That said, facilitators still belong in many learning solutions, and facilitated virtual training will never disappear completely. Even if AI-programmed bots can carry on human-like conversations, they cannot generate the human touch; they may supplement it, but they won't replace it.

Some examples of how generative AI can enhance virtual training include:

- Faster program creation by prompting AI to write case studies, polls, quizzes, role plays, and other learning activities
- Personalization and localization of training content, including fast and dynamic adaptations for diverse audiences
- Better data analysis for both needs assessments and measurement and evaluation

In a virtual class, facilitators might come to rely on generative AI to quickly summarize chat responses into themes and categories, which could then be discussed by participants in small groups. Or facilitators might ask participants to use a generative AI tool to help brainstorm answers, and then use those answers as a starting point for real-world solutions.

According to a recent study on the impact of AI in the facilitated online classroom, trust remains a significant issue for everyone involved (Sea 2021). Human touchpoints remain vitally important when learners are exploring new content, practicing new skills, receiving feedback, and debriefing the learning experience. Again, the facilitator's role still adds value.

As generative AI rapidly evolves and changes, it will be prudent for all of us to keep an eye on what's sure to be a significant disruptor in the L&D industry.

A Few Final Thoughts

When I started my virtual training journey more than 20 years ago, I needed to upskill my organization's managers without traveling, so I figured out how to use web conferencing software to train my globally dispersed audience. My goal wasn't to create engaging virtual programs or design fancy online whiteboards. I was simply trying to solve a problem and used technology-enabled learning solutions to do so. Along the way, I've refined and evolved my approach. My main goals are now solving problems, sharing resources, and adding value.

Whatever your journey, I hope it has a similar refrain. I hope your goal is to find solutions for your organization's needs, using the best possible options available. I also hope you are keeping your eyes on the horizon to get a glimpse of what's next, continuing to grow and learn.

Let's stay on this journey together. I'd love to hear from you, so I ask you to share your ideas on creating excellent virtual training that gets results. My website, cindyhuggett.com, is a good way to stay connected.

Take Action

- ✓ Create an ongoing development plan for yourself to stay abreast of trends and issues influencing virtual training. Include newsletters and other sources you'll subscribe to, webinars to register for, or conferences you will attend.
- ✓ Join a community of virtual training enthusiasts to continually learn and improve. Consider this your personal invitation to join my online community at cindyhuggett.com/community.

Acknowledgments

A book is rarely—if ever—written as a solo endeavor. It takes a tribe of supporters, reviewers, contributors, editors, and friends who walk alongside you on the journey. Some share just a few steps while others walk the entire way. I'm truly grateful for each person who took the time to share their expertise and encouragement with me as I wrote both the first and second editions of this book. Listing their names here feels like an inadequate way to say thank you; however, each one wholeheartedly deserves the recognition.

First, to the many business and training professionals who willingly shared their advice and stories: Carla Torgerson, Cheryl Scanlan, Christian Rowe, Dan Gallagher, Danielle Buscher, Darlene Christopher, David Smith, Elizabeth Beales, Erin Laughlin, Jack Phillips, Jeff Robinson, Jennifer Newton, Jill Kennedy, John Hall, Justin Patton, Kassy LaBorie, Katrina Kennedy, Ken Hubbell, Ken Phillips, Lisa Brodeth Carrick, Lorna Matty, Lucy Brown, Luke Chiaruttini, Marion Schilcher, Michael Thatcher, Patti Phillips, Peggy Page, Stephan Girard, Tracy Stanfield, Treion Muller, Trish Carr, Wendy Gates Corbett, and Will Thalheimer, along with a few who chose to remain anonymous (you know who you are!). I am grateful to each one of these individuals for their willingness to offer wisdom and their lessons learned. Their contributions have enriched this book. Thank you.

Also, to the team at ATD Press for their support along the way: Jack Harlow, Justin Brusino, and Alexandria Clapp for the initial push to update these books to a second edition; Shelley Sperry for her amazing editorial feedback; and Melissa Jones for putting all of the pieces together in a way that brought clarity to the written words.

Finally, to my son, Jonathan, and to my husband, Bobby, who endured hearing me type on the keyboard for hours on end over many nights and weekends. Without their love and support, this book would never have been finished.

Cindy Huggett
Psalm 115:1
September 2024

Trademark Attributions

Adobe and Adobe Connect are either registered trademarks or trademarks of Adobe Systems Incorporated in the United States and/or other countries.

Cisco WebEx Meeting Center, Event Center, Training Center and Support Center are trademarks of Cisco Systems, Inc. and/or one or more of its subsidiaries, and may be registered in the United States Patent and Trademark Office and in other countries.

GoToMeeting, GoToWebinar, and GoToTraining are trademarks of LogMeIn, Inc. and/or one or more of its subsidiaries, and may be registered in the United States Patent and Trademark Office and in other countries.

Microsoft, Microsoft Office, Microsoft Teams and Windows Media Player are either registered trademarks or trademarks of Microsoft Corporation in the United States and/or other countries.

Zoom and the Zoom logo are trademarks of Zoom Video Communications Inc., registered in the United States and other countries.

Glossary

Annotation. Drawing on top of shared documents or a whiteboard. Annotation tools vary from program to program, but most allow you to draw lines and other shapes, draw freehand with an electronic pencil or marker, type text on the screen, and highlight words.

Application sharing. Allows viewing of the presenter's desktop or another selected application. This is typically used when the presenter needs to demonstrate the use of a software program or show a document that can't be loaded into the virtual classroom due to file-type limitations.

Artificial intelligence (AI). Computer or machine processes that mimic human intelligence. It's helpful for completing complex tasks.

Asynchronous. Refers to learning activities that take place on the learners' own time. It's also referred to as *self-paced* or *self-directed learning*, which occurs at a time and place chosen by participants.

Audio. The ability to hear sound during a virtual class. Audio connections can be via telephone through a conference line or via computer or another device through Voice over Internet Protocol (VoIP).

Avatar. A digital replica of a person that mirrors movement and expression. It can be realistic or cartoonish.

Bandwidth. The amount of data that can be sent over an internet connection, measured in megabits per second (Mbps). The higher the bandwidth, the faster the connection.

Blended learning journey. A training curriculum that combines multiple components and uses a variety of delivery methods. A blended learning solution might include a mix of virtual classes, coaching, and participation in a discussion board. Or it could be a series of virtual classes with required self-paced assignments in between. It is a "blend" of various activities sequenced together to achieve a learning outcome.

Breakouts. Dividing attendees into smaller subgroups for discussion or an activity. Participants are temporarily moved into a separate online space where they only hear participants who have been assigned to the same group. The group can share documents and whiteboards among themselves and collaborate. These documents and whiteboards can then be displayed in the main classroom for report-outs and debrief discussions among the larger group.

Chat. The virtual classroom feature used to type text messages on screen. Usually, chat is public and visible to everyone connected to the virtual class. Most platforms also allow for private chat, which gives the ability to send private messages to individual participants or confidentially to the presenter.

Co-facilitator. A second person who shares facilitation responsibilities during a virtual class.

Debriefing. A post-event reflection process guided by a skilled facilitator.

e-learning or **eLearning.** Short for "electronic learning," and referring to any type of learning that takes place via computer or mobile device. Many years ago, this term encompassed all types of online learning, but today it specifically means self-directed or self-paced asynchronous learning.

Face-to-face. Refers to an in-person classroom experience, in which participants and the trainer meet in the same room. It's more commonly called *in-person* classes.

Facilitator. A word often used interchangeably with *trainer*. Facilitators typically focus more on discussion and dialogue instead of one-way presentations.

Facilitator guide. A document that includes detailed instructions for the virtual trainer and producer to deliver the virtual class.

File transfer. The virtual classroom feature that allows for file distribution to participants. Used when a trainer wants to send a document—such as a handout or job aid—electronically via the platform during a virtual class.

Host. One of the leaders in the virtual classroom. The host is sometimes called the *producer* or *moderator*. Some platforms designate a named *host* role as the session leader.

Hybrid learning. Typically refers to an in-person learning experience with some participants joining remotely. In other words, some participants are in the same room as the trainer, while other participants are individually connected from other remote locations. Note, however, that some training professionals in a university or educational setting may use *hybrid learning* to refer to *blended learning*.

Immersive. A digital experience that feels real, such as a virtual reality (VR) learning environment or an augmented reality (AR) element that looks like it's part of a physical environment.

Integrated app. A software program that enhances the virtual classroom platform.

Integrated telephony. A teleconference that is connected to the virtual classroom. When the teleconference is integrated, typical audio commands (such as mute and unmute) are available using the virtual classroom controls.

Learning management system (LMS). A database software program that manages training programs. It tracks participant attendance and completion of the program. Most learning management systems can also store training materials for participants to access.

Learning experience platform (LXP). A database software program that leads participants through a learning experience in a visually appealing way.

Moderator. Another name for *host* or *producer* in a virtual class.

Participants. Attendees in a virtual training class. They are sometimes referred to as *learners*. Participant names are usually visible to all in a virtual classroom, although some platforms allow them to be hidden from view.

Platform. A virtual classroom software program. The features and functions available to you in the virtual classroom depend on the software you've chosen. *See also* virtual classroom.

Polling. The virtual classroom feature that asks questions of participants. Polls allow the trainer to ask participants survey questions in real time. The questions can be multiple choice, multiple answer, or, in some programs, short answer.

Producer. One of the session leaders in a virtual classroom. Producers typically take responsibility for running the technology so the facilitator can focus on delivering the content. Producers should be experts in the virtual classroom software so they can troubleshoot any technical challenges. Producers assist participants with connecting to the virtual classroom and using the tools.

Raise hand. A participant input tool in a virtual classroom. When someone clicks on the "raise hand" button, the presenter sees a small icon next to the participant's name, which indicates the "raised hand" status.

Reactions. Participant input tools in a virtual classroom, sometimes referred to as *status indicators*. Trainers can ask participants to "change their status," which means they click on a button to indicate their response. The participant's chosen status is represented by a small icon next to their name. Status choices typically include "raise hand," "agree," "disagree," "smile/laughter," "applause," "speed up," "slow down," and "step away."

Sharing. The virtual classroom feature that allows for file or document sharing. When a document is shared, it's visible onscreen to everyone connected to the virtual classroom. It's sometimes called *share document* or *share file*.

Start-before-the-start activity. An attention-grabbing activity that's available onscreen when a participant first joins the virtual classroom. The activity is designed to get participants involved right away and—if needed—teach them how to use the platform tools.

Software platform. *See* platform.

Synchronous. In a synchronous training event, the participants and trainer meet on a set day and time.

Telephony. A broad term referring to the overall audio connection and telephone equipment used for verbal communication during a virtual class. *See also* audio.

Video conferencing. Participants are separated by distance but can see one another on a video screen. Video conferencing is distinguished from virtual training because it usually has a group of people gathered around a screen, while virtual training has only one person per online connection.

vILT (or VILT). An acronym for *virtual instructor-led training*.

Virtual classroom. The online meeting room for a virtual training class. Virtual training uses a software program specifically designed for real-time collaboration on the web. This software application is called a virtual classroom and is sometimes referred to as a *platform*.

Virtual trainer. The main session leader in a virtual classroom. Sometimes called the *virtual facilitator* or *virtual presenter*, they're a skilled professional who has command of the subject matter and enables participant learning and application back on the job.

Virtual training. A highly interactive, online synchronous facilitator-led class that has defined learning objectives, with participants who are connected individually from geographically dispersed locations, using a web-based virtual classroom platform.

VoIP (Voice over Internet Protocol). A method for hearing audio via computer speakers and speaking into the computer's microphone. *See also* telephony.

Wearables. Mobile devices that are worn somewhere on the body, such as smartwatches, smart glasses, and virtual reality (VR) headsets.

Webcast. A one-way presentation held online with a presenter and participants. In a webcast, there is typically little interaction between the presenter and participants, except for possible question-and-answer opportunities during the program. A webcast usually has a large audience.

Webinar. A live online program that may or may not be interactive. Webinar is a loosely defined word that still has several meanings. Some consider it to be a highly interactive live online event, while others consider a it to be the same as a passive webcast.

Whiteboard. A common feature found in most virtual classroom platforms. It allows the trainer and participants to draw on the screen using annotation tools.

Recommended Resources

I encourage you to continue learning about designing, delivering, and implementing virtual training. If you are interested in diving deeper into the topics covered in this book, then here are a few resources from my own bookshelf that I recommend.

Elaine Biech, *The Art and Science of Training* (Alexandria, VA: ATD Press, 2016).

Elaine Biech, *ATD's Handbook for Training and Talent Development* (Alexandria, VA: ATD Press, 2022).

Robert O. Brinkerhoff, Anne M. Apking, and Edward W. Boon, *Improving Performance Through Learning: A Practical Guide for Designing High Performance Learning Journeys* (Independently published, 2019).

Brandon Carson, *L&D's Playbook for the Digital Age* (Alexandria, VA: ATD Press, 2021).

Darlene Christopher, *The Successful Virtual Classroom: How to Design and Facilitate Interactive and Engaging Live Online Learning* (New York: AMACOM, 2014).

Ruth Colvin Clark and Richard E. Mayer, *E-Learning and the Science of Instruction: Proven Guidelines for Consumers and Designers of Multimedia Learning*, 4th ed. (Hoboken, NJ: Wiley, 2016).

Ruth Colvin Clark, *Evidence-Based Training Methods*, 3rd ed. (Alexandria, VA: ATD Press, 2019).

Cynthia Clay, *Great Webinars: How to Create Interactive Learning That Is Captivating, Informative and Fun* (Punchy Publishing, 2019).

Julie Dirksen, *Design for How People Learn*, 2nd ed. (Berkeley, CA: New Riders, 2015).

Tamar Elkeles, Jack J. Phillips, and Patricia P. Phillips, *Measuring the Success of Learning Through Technology: A Guide for Measuring Impact and Calculating ROI on E-Learning, Blended Learning, and Mobile Learning* (Alexandria, VA: ATD Press, 2014).

Jennifer Hofmann, *Blended Learning* (Alexandria, VA: ATD Press, 2018).

Diana L. Howles, *Next Level Virtual Training: Advance Your Facilitation* (Alexandria, VA: ATD Press, 2022).

Cindy Huggett, *The Facilitator's Guide to Immersive, Blended, and Hybrid Learning* (Alexandria, VA: ATD Press, 2022).

Cindy Huggett, Patricia Pulliam Phillips, Jack J. Phillips, and Emma Weber, *Designing Virtual Learning for Application and Impact: 50 Techniques to Ensure Results* (Alexandria: ATD Press, 2023).

Kassy LaBorie, *Producing Virtual Training, Meetings, and Webinars: Master the Technology to Engage Participants* (Alexandria, VA: ATD Press, 2022).

Kassy LaBorie and Tom Stone, *Interact and Engage!: 75+ Activities for Virtual Training, Meetings, and Webinars*, 2nd ed. (Alexandria, VA: ATD Press, 2022).

Kristopher Newbauer, *Aligning Instructional Design With Business Goals* (Alexandria VA: ATD Press, 2023).

Patricia P. Phillips, ed., *ASTD Handbook of Measuring and Evaluating Training* (Alexandria, VA: ASTD Press, 2010).

Robert W. Pike, *Master Trainer Handbook: Tips, Tactics, and How-Tos for Delivering Effective Instructor-Led, Participant-Centered Training*, 4th ed. (Amherst, MA: HRD Press, 2015).

Becky Pike Pluth, *Creative Training: A Train-the-Trainer Field Guide* (Minneapolis, MN: Creative Training Productions, 2016).

Clark N. Quinn, *Learning Science for Instructional Designers* (Alexandria, VA: ATD Press, 2021).

Karin M. Reed and Joseph A. Allen, *Suddenly Hybrid: Managing the Modern Meeting* (Hoboken, NJ: John Wiley & Sons, 2022).

Brian Washburn, *What's Your Formula? Combine Learning Elements for Impactful Training* (Alexandria, VA: ATD Press, 2021).

References

ATD. 2014. *State of the Industry*. Alexandria, VA: ATD Press.

ATD. 2019. *Effective Evaluation: Measuring Learning Programs for Success*. Alexandria, VA: ATD Press.

BBC News. 2008. "Formula 'Secret of Perfect Voice.'" *BBC News*, May 30. news.bbc.co.uk/2/hi/uk/7426923.stm.

Brady, S., N. Rao, P. Gibbons, L. Williams, M. Hakel, and T. Pape. 2018. "Face-to-Face Versus Online Training for the Interpretation of Findings in the Fiberoptic Endoscopic Exam of the Swallow Procedure." *Advances in Medical Education and Practice* 9:433–441. doi.org/10.2147/amep.s142947.

Broad, M.L., and J.W. Newstrom. 1992. *Transfer of Training: Action-Packed Strategies to Ensure High Payoff From Training Investments*. Reading, MA: Addison-Wesley.

Chernikova, O., N. Heitzmann, M. Stadler, D. Holzberger, T. Seidel, and F. Fischer. 2020. "Simulation-Based Learning in Higher Education: A Meta-Analysis." *Review of Educational Research* 90(4): 499–541. doi.org/10.3102/0034654320 933544.

Christopher, D. 2012. "Keeping Participants' Attention in Global Virtual Classrooms," Learning Circuits Newsletter, February 1.

Clark, R.C., and A. Kwinn. 2007. *The New Virtual Classroom*. San Francisco: Pfeiffer.

Corbo, G. 2023. "Council Post: Leading in the Age of Remote Work: Key Factors for Corporate Success." *Forbes*, September 15. forbes.com/sites/forbestechcouncil/2023/09/14/leading-in-the-age-of-remote-work-key-factors-for-corporate-success/?sh=29e17bd114a5.

Courville, R. 2012. Survey conducted via website, thevirtualpresenter.com.

Covey, S. 1983. *The 7 Habits of Highly Effective People: Powerful Lessons in Personal Change*. New York: Free Press.

Dirksen, J. 2015. *Design for How People Learn*, 2nd ed. San Francisco: New Riders.

Driscoll, J., and B. Teh. 2001. "The Potential of Reflective Practice to Develop Individual Orthopaedic Nurse Practitioners and Their Practice." *Journal of Orthopaedic Nursing* 5(2): 95–103. doi.org/10.1054/joon.2001.0150.

ESPN.com Staff. 2010. "John Wooden's Greatest Quotes." ESPN, June 4. sports.espn.go .com/ncb/news/story?id=5249709.

Falloon, G. 2011. "Exploring the Virtual Classroom: What Students Need to Know (and Teachers Should Consider)." *Journal of Online Learning and Teaching* 7(4) 439-451.

Gallup. "Gallup's Q12 Employee Engagement Survey - Gallup." gallup.com/q12.

Huggett, C. 2018. *Virtual Training Basics*, 2nd ed. Alexandria, VA: ATD Press.

Huggett, C. 2024. "The State of Virtual Training 2024." Cindy Huggett, April 16. cindyhuggett.com/blog/2024sovt.

Huggett, C., P.P. Phillips, J.J. Phillips, and E. Weber. 2023. *Designing Virtual Learning for Application and Impact: 50 Techniques to Ensure Results*. Alexandria, VA: ATD Press.

Jacobs School of Engineering. 2013. "Working Alone Won't Get You Good Grades." UCSD Jacobs School of Engineering, January 30. jacobsschool.ucsd.edu/news /news_releases/release.sfe?id=1308.

Kirkpatrick, D.L., and J.D. Kirkpatrick. 2006. *Evaluating Training Programs: The Four Levels,* 3rd ed. San Francisco: Berrett-Koehler.

Kolb, D.A. 1984. *Experimental Learning: Experience as the Source of Learning and Development*. Englewood Cliffs, NJ: Prentice-Hall.

Leroy, S., and T.M. Glomb. 2020. "A Plan for Managing (Constant) Interruptions at Work." *Harvard Business Review*, June 30. hbr.org/2020/06/a-plan-for-managing -constant-interruptions-at-work.

Likens, S., and D.L. Eckert. 2021. "How Virtual Reality Is Redefining Soft Skills Training." PwC, June 4. pwc.com/us/en/tech-effect/emerging-tech/virtual-reality -study.html.

Martin, F., M.A. Parker, and D.F. Deale. 2012. "Examining Interactivity in Virtual Classrooms." *The International Review of Research in Open and Distance Learning* 13(3), irrodl.org/index.php/irrodl/article/view/1174/2253.

Medina, J. 2014. *Brain Rules: 12 Principles for Surviving and Thriving at Work, Home and School*. Seattle: Pear Press.

Mervis, J. 2011. "A Better Way to Teach?" *Science*, May 12. news.sciencemag.org /sciencenow/2011/05/a-better-way-to-teach.html.

Mina, A. 2012. "Virtual Training: Tips to Reduce Budget Without Sacrificing Engagement." *GP Strategies*, October 9. blog.gpstrategies.com/learning-content /virtual-training-improve-engagement.

Murdoch, M., and T. Muller. 2013. T*he Webinar Manifesto: Never Design, Deliver, or Sell Lousy Webinars Again*. New York: RosettaBooks.

Newman, E.J., and N. Schwarz. 2018. "Good Sound, Good Research: How Audio Quality Influences Perceptions of the Research and Researcher." *Science Communication* 40(2): 246–57. doi.org/10.1177/1075547018759345.

Ozimek, A. 2021. *Future Workforce Report 2021*. upwork, September 29. upwork.com /research/future-workforce-report.

Parker, K. 2023. "About a Third of U.S. Workers Who Can Work from Home Now Do so All the Time." Pew Research Center, March 30. pewresearch.org/short -reads/2023/03/30/about-a-third-of-us-workers-who-can-work-from-home -do-so-all-the-time.

Paul, J., and F. Jefferson. 2019. "A Comparative Analysis of Student Performance in an Online vs. Face-to-Face Environmental Science Course from 2009 to 2016." *Frontiers in Computer Science* 1(November 12). doi.org/10.3389/fcomp .2019.00007.

Pike, R.W. 2002. *Creative Training Techniques Handbook,* 3rd ed. Amherst, MA: HRD Press.

Pike, R.W. 2011. "Creative Training Techniques for Webinars: Seven Ways to Add Impact and Wow—NOW!" Session presented at ASTD TechKnowledge 2011, San Jose, CA, February.

Pink, D.H. 2012. *To Sell Is Human: The Surprising Truth About Moving Others.* New York: Riverhead Books.

Phillips, J.J., and P.P. Phillips. 2007. Show Me the Money. San Francisco: Berrett-Koehler.

Rossett, A., and R.V. Frazee. 2006. AMA Special Report "Blended Learning Opportunities." American Management Association.

Seo, K., J. Tang, I. Roll, S. Fels, and D. Yoon. 2021. "The Impact of Artificial Intelligence on Learner–Instructor Interaction in Online Learning." *International Journal of Educational Technology in Higher Education* 18(1). doi.org/10.1186/s41239-021-00292-9.

Stack, S. 2015. "Learning Outcomes in an Online vs Traditional Course." *Georgia Educational Researcher* 9(1). doi.org/10.20429/ijsotl.2015.090105.

TalentLMS and Vyond. 2023. "Research: What Employees Want From L&D in 2024." TalentLMS, December 6. talentlms.com/research/learning-development-trends.

Thalheimer, W. 2018. "LTEM—Work-Learning Research." Work-Learning Research. worklearning.com/ltem.

Towards Maturity. 2019. *The Transformation Journey: 2019 Annual Research Report.* Towards Maturity, February 14. towardsmaturity.org/2019/02/14/the -transformation-journey-2019-annual-research-report.

Walton, G. 2017. "Pioneering French Midwife: Angélique du Coudray." Geri Walton, April 17. geriwalton.com/pioneering-french-midwife-angelique-du-coudray.

Weber, E. 2018. "5 Essential Elements for Effective Action Planning." LinkedIn, March 8. linkedin.com/pulse/5-essential-elements-effective-action-planning-emma -weber.

Weber, E. 2021. "Learning Transfer vs. Evaluation of Learning." LinkedIn, October 20. linkedin.com/pulse/learning-transfer-vs-evaluation-emma-weber.

Westerman, G. 2012. "IT Is From Venus, Non-IT Is From Mars." *Wall Street Journal,* April 2.

Index

Page numbers followed by *f* and *t* refer to figures and tables, respectively.

About the Author

**Cindy Huggett** is a pioneer in the field of online learning with more than 20 years of experience in providing virtual training solutions and more than 30 years in the world of talent development. She's a leading industry expert known for teaching thousands of training professionals how to design and deliver practical, engaging interactive online classes to today's global workforce through workshops, speaking, coaching, and consulting. Cindy partners with organizations to upskill facilitators, maximize online learning design, and facilitate actionable learning solutions that meet today's needs and leverage tomorrow's technologies.

Cindy has written several acclaimed books on virtual training, including *The Facilitator's Guide to Immersive, Blended, and Hybrid Learning* and *Virtual Training Basics*, as well as the first editions of *Virtual Training Tools and Templates* and *The Virtual Training Guidebook*. She's a co-author of *Designing Virtual Learning for Application and Impact* and two *Infoline* issues, and she has contributed to many other industry publications, including *TD* magazine, *ATD's Handbook for Consultants*, and the third edition of *ATD's Handbook for Training and Talent Development*.

A sought-after conference speaker, Cindy has presented at the ATD International Conference & EXPO, ATD TechKnowledge, Training, DevLearn, TechLearn, Learning, and the annual SHRM Conference. She also delivers ATD's Master Trainer and Master Instructional Designer Programs.

Cindy holds a master's degree in public and international affairs from the University of Pittsburgh and a bachelor's degree from James Madison University. She also has a Certified Professional in Talent Development (CPTD) designation. Cindy is a past member of the global ATD board of directors, was recognized by the *Triangle*

Business Journal as a 40-Under-40 Award recipient, and co-founded a nonprofit organization to promote volunteering and community service in her local area. She's also a yoga teacher with a special focus on mobility for aging seniors. You can reach Cindy at cindy@cindyhuggett.com.

About ATD

atd The Association for Talent Development (ATD) is the world's largest association dedicated to those who develop talent in organizations. Serving a global community of members, customers, and international business partners in more than 100 countries, ATD champions the importance of learning and training by setting standards for the talent development profession.

Our customers and members work in public and private organizations in every industry sector. Since ATD was founded in 1943, the talent development field has expanded significantly to meet the needs of global businesses and emerging industries. Through the Talent Development Capability Model, education courses, certifications and credentials, memberships, industry-leading events, research, and publications, we help talent development professionals build their personal, professional, and organizational capabilities to meet new business demands with maximum impact and effectiveness.

One of the cornerstones of ATD's intellectual foundation, ATD Press offers insightful and practical information on talent development, training, and professional growth. ATD Press publications are written by industry thought leaders and offer anyone who works with adult learners the best practices, academic theory, and guidance necessary to move the profession forward.

We invite you to join our community. Learn more at **TD.org**.